Focus on
Grammar
4B

Marjorie Fuchs
Margaret Bonner

with Jane Curtis

Focus on Grammar 4: An Integrated Skills Approach, Fifth Edition, Volume B

Pearson Education, 221 River Street, Hoboken, NJ 07030

Staff credits: The people who made up the *Focus on Grammar 4, Fifth Edition, Volume B* team, representing content creation, design, manufacturing, marketing, multimedia, project management, publishing, rights management, and testing, are Pietro Alongi, Rhea Banker, Elizabeth Barker, Stephanie Bullard, Jennifer Castro, Tracey Cataldo, Aerin Csigay, Mindy DePalma, Dave Dickey, Warren Fischbach, Pam Fishman, Nancy Flaggman, Lester Holmes, Gosia Jaros-White, Leslie Johnson, Barry Katzen, Amy McCormick, Julie Molnar, Brian Panker, Stuart Radcliffe, Jennifer Raspiller, Lindsay Richman, Robert Ruvo, Alexandra Suarez, Paula Van Ells, and Joseph Vella.

Text design and layout: Don Williams
Composition: Page Designs International
Project supervision: Bernard Seal
Contributing editors: Françoise Leffler and Bernard Seal

Cover image: Andy Roberts / Getty Images

Printed in the United States of America

ISBN 10: 0-13-413280-7
ISBN 13: 978-0-13-413280-8

2   18

Contents

WELCOME TO
FOCUS ON GRAMMAR
FIFTH EDITION

BUILDING ON THE SUCCESS of previous editions, *Focus on Grammar* continues to provide an integrated-skills approach to engage students and help them understand, practice, and use English grammar. Centered on thematic instruction, *Focus on Grammar* combines comprehensive grammar coverage with abundant practice, critical thinking skills, and ongoing assessment, helping students accomplish their goals of communicating confidently, accurately, and fluently in everyday situations.

New in the Fifth Edition

New and Updated Content
Focus on Grammar continues to offer engaging and motivating content that appeals to learners from various cultural backgrounds. Many readings and activities have been replaced or updated to include topics that are of high interest to today's learners.

Updated Charts and Redesigned Notes
Clear, corpus-informed grammar presentations reflect real and natural language usage and allow students to grasp the most important aspects of the grammar. Clear signposting draws attention to common usage, the difference between written and spoken registers, and common errors.

Additional Communicative Activities
The new edition of *Focus on Grammar* has been expanded with additional communicative activities that encourage collaboration and the application of the target grammar in a variety of settings.

Expanded Writing Practice
Each unit in *Focus on Grammar* now ends with a structured "From Grammar to Writing" section. Supported by pre-writing and editing tasks, students engage in activities that allow them to apply the target grammar in writing.

New Assessment Program
The new edition of *Focus on Grammar* features a variety of new assessment tools, including course diagnostic tests, formative and summative assessments, and a flexible gradebook. The assessments are closely aligned with unit learning outcomes to inform instruction and measure student progress.

Revised MyEnglishLab
The updated MyEnglishLab offers students engaging practice and video grammar presentations anywhere, anytime. Immediate feedback and remediation tasks offer additional opportunities for successful mastery of content and help promote accuracy. Instructors receive instant access to digital content and diagnostic tools that allow them to customize the learning environment to meet the needs of their students.

The *Focus on Grammar* Approach

At the heart of the *Focus on Grammar* series is its unique and successful four-step approach that lets learners move from comprehension to communication within a clear and consistent structure. The books provide an abundance of scaffolded exercises to bridge the gap between identifying grammatical structures and using them with confidence and accuracy. The integration of the four skills allows students to learn grammar holistically, which in turn prepares them to understand and use English more effectively.

STEP 1: Grammar in Context integrates grammar and vocabulary in natural contexts such as articles, stories, dialogues, and blog posts. Students engage with the unit reading and theme and get exposure to grammar as it is used in real life.

STEP 2: Grammar Presentation presents the structures in clear and accessible grammar charts and notes with multiple examples of form and meaning. Corpus-informed explanations and examples reflect natural usage of the target forms, differentiate between written and conversational registers whenever appropriate, and highlight common errors to help students avoid typical pitfalls in both speaking and writing.

STEP 3: Focused Practice provides numerous and varied contextualized exercises for both the form and meaning of the new structures. Controlled practice ensures students' understanding of the target grammar and leads to mastery of form, meaning, and use.

STEP 4: Communication Practice provides practice with the structures in listening exercises as well as in communicative, open-ended speaking activities. These engaging activities provide ample opportunities for personalization and build students' confidence in using English. Students also develop their critical thinking skills through problem-solving activities and discussions.

Each unit now culminates with the **From Grammar to Writing** section. Students learn about common errors in writing and how to recognize them in their own work. Engaging and motivating writing activities encourage students to apply grammar in writing through structured tasks from pre-writing to editing.

Recycling

Underpinning the scope and sequence of the *Focus on Grammar* series is practice that allows students to use target structures and vocabulary many times, in different contexts. New grammar and vocabulary are recycled throughout the book. Students have maximum exposure, leading them to become confident in using the language in speech and in writing.

Assessment

Extensive testing informs instruction and allows teachers and students to measure progress.

- **Unit Reviews** at the end of every unit assess students' understanding of the grammar and allow students to monitor their own progress.

- **Diagnostic Tests** provide teachers with a valid and reliable means to determine how well students know the material they are going to study and to target instruction based on students' needs.

- **Unit Review Tests, Mid- and End-of-Term Review Tests, and Final Exams** measure students' ability to demonstrate mastery of skills taught in the course.

- The **Placement Test** is designed to help teachers place students into one of the five levels of the *Focus on Grammar* course.

The Importance of Context

A key element of *Focus on Grammar* is presenting important grammatical structures in context. The contexts selected are most relevant to the grammatical forms being introduced. Contextualized grammar practice also plays a key role in improving fluent use of grammar in communicative contexts. It helps learners to develop consistent and correct usage of target structures during all productive practice.

The Role of Corpus

The most important goal of *Focus on Grammar* has always been to present grammar structures using natural language. To that end, *Focus on Grammar* has incorporated the findings of corpus linguistics,* while never losing sight of what is pedagogically sound and useful. By taking this approach, *Focus on Grammar* ensures that:

- the language presented reflects real, natural usage

- themes and topics provide a good fit with the grammar point and elicit the target grammar naturally

- findings of the corpus research are reflected in the syllabus, readings, charts, grammar notes, and practice activities

- examples illustrate differences between spoken and written registers, and formal and informal language

- students are exposed to common errors in usage and learn how to recognize and avoid errors in their own speech and writing

Focus on Grammar Efficacy

The fifth edition of *Focus on Grammar* reflects an important efficacy initiative for Pearson courses—to be able to demonstrate that all teaching materials have a positive impact on student learning. To support this, *Focus on Grammar* has been updated and aligned to the **Global Scale of English** and the **Common European Framework** (CEFR) to provide granular insight into the objectives of the course, the progression of learning, and the expected outcomes a learner will be able to demonstrate upon successful completion.

To learn more about the Global Scale of English, visit www.English.com.

Components

Student Books with Essential Online Resources include access codes to the course audio, video, and self-assessment.

Student Books with MyEnglishLab offer a blended approach with integration of print and online content.

Workbooks contain additional contextualized practice in print format.

Digital Teacher's Resources include printable teaching notes, GSE mapping documents, answer keys, audio scripts, and downloadable tests. Access to the digital copy of the student books allows teachers to project the pages for whole-class instruction.

FOG Go app allows users to access the student book audio on their mobile devices.

---

* A principal resource has been Douglas Biber et al, *Longman Grammar of Spoken and Written English*, Harlow: Pearson Education Ltd., 1999.

The *Focus on Grammar* Unit

Focus on Grammar introduces grammar structures in the context of unified themes. All units follow a four-step approach, taking learners from grammar in context to communicative practice. Thematic units add a layer to learning so that by the end of the unit students will be able to discuss the content using the grammar points they have just studied.

STEP 1 GRAMMAR IN CONTEXT

Before You Read activities create interest and elicit students' knowledge about the topic.

Vocabulary exercises help students improve their command of English.

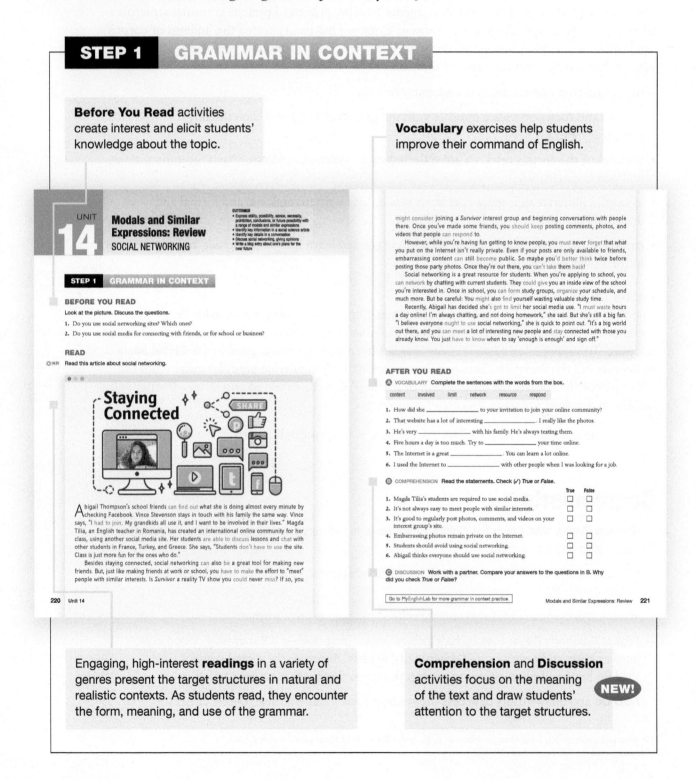

Engaging, high-interest **readings** in a variety of genres present the target structures in natural and realistic contexts. As students read, they encounter the form, meaning, and use of the grammar.

Comprehension and **Discussion** activities focus on the meaning of the text and draw students' attention to the target structures. **NEW!**

Grammar Charts present the structures in a clear, easy-to-read format.

NEW!

The newly designed **Grammar Notes** highlight the main point of each note, making navigation and review easier. Simple corpus-informed **explanations** and **examples** ensure students' understanding.

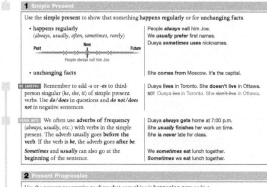

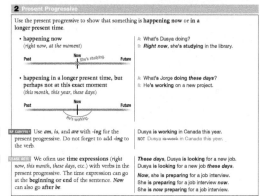

NEW!

Clear signposting provides corpus-informed notes about common usage, differences between spoken and written registers, and common errors.

PRONUNCIATION NOTE

⊙07.02 | **Intonation of Tag Questions**

In tag questions, our **voice rises** at the end when we expect another person to give us **information**.

> A: You're not moving, **are you?**
> B: Yes. I'm returning to Berlin.

Our **voice falls** at the end when we are making a comment and expect the other person to **agree**.

> A: Seoul is interesting, **isn't it?**
> B: Yes, it is.

Go to MyEnglishLab to watch the grammar presentation.

Pronunciation Notes are now included with the grammar presentation to highlight relevant pronunciation aspects of the target structures and to help students understand authentic spoken English.

NEW!

Discover the Grammar activities develop students' recognition and understanding of the target structures before they are asked to produce them.

Controlled practice activities lead students to master form, meaning, and use of the target grammar.

STEP 3   FOCUSED PRACTICE

EXERCISE 1   DISCOVER THE GRAMMAR

GRAMMAR NOTES 1–4 Read the statements. Check (✓) *Active* or *Passive*.

	Active	Passive
1. The first *National Geographic* magazine was published in October 1888.	☐	☑
2. Today, millions of people read the magazine.	☐	☐
3. The magazine is translated from English into forty other languages.	☐	☐
4. My cousin reads the Russian edition.	☐	☐
5. Some of the articles are written by famous writers.	☐	☐
6. *Young Explorer*, another publication, is written for kids.	☐	☐
7. The publication is known for its wonderful photography.	☐	☐
8. A *National Geographic* photographer took the first underwater color photos.	☐	☐
9. Photographers are sent all over the world.	☐	☐
10. The articles show a lot of respect for nature.	☐	☐
11. That picture was taken by Reza Deghati.	☐	☐
12. *National Geographic* is sold at newsstands.	☐	☐

EXERCISE 2   ACTIVE OR PASSIVE

GRAMMAR NOTES 1–4 The chart shows some of the forty language editions that *National Geographic* publishes. Use the chart to complete the sentences. Some sentences will be active; some will be passive.

Language	Number of Speakers*
Arabic	240
Chinese (all varieties)	1,200
English	340
Japanese	130
Korean	77
Russian	110
Spanish	410
Turkish	71

*first-language speakers in millions

1. Spanish *is spoken by 410 million people* ____

2. Around 110 million people *speak Russian* ____

3. Arabic ____

4. ____ Chinese.

EXERCISE 2   RELATIVE PRONOUNS AND VERBS

GRAMMAR NOTES 3–6 Complete the statements in the personality quiz. Circle the correct words. (In Exercise 9, you will take the quiz.)

Personality Quiz

Do you agree with the following statements? Check (✔) *True* or *False*.

	TRUE	FALSE
1. People who / which talk a lot tire me.	☐	☐
2. On a plane, I always talk to the stranger who take / takes the seat next to me.	☐	☐
3. I'm the kind of person that / which needs time to recover after a social event.	☐	☐
4. My best friend, that / who talks a lot, is just like me.	☐	☐
5. I prefer to have conversations which focus / focuses on feelings and ideas.	☐	☐
6. I am someone whose favorite activities include / includes reading and doing yoga.	☐	☐
7. People whose / their personalities are completely different can be close friends.	☐	☐
8. I'm someone that always see / sees the glass as half full, not half empty.	☐	☐
9. Difficult situations are often the ones that provide / provides the best opportunities.	☐	☐
10. Introverts, that / who are quiet, sensitive, and creative, are perfect friends.	☐	☐

EXERCISE 3   IDENTIFYING ADJECTIVE CLAUSES

Ⓐ GRAMMAR NOTES 1–4, 6 We often use identifying adjective clauses to define words. First, match the words on the left with the descriptions on the right.

_h_	1. difficulty	a.	This situation gives you a chance to experience something good.
____	2. extrovert	b.	This attitude shows your ideas about your future.
____	3. introvert	c.	This ability makes you able to produce new ideas.
____	4. opportunity	d.	This person usually sees the bright side of situations.
____	5. opposites	e.	This person requires a lot of time alone.
____	6. optimist	f.	This money was unexpected.
____	7. outlook	g.	This person usually sees the dark side of situations.
____	8. pessimist	h.	This problem is hard to solve.
____	9. creativity	i.	These people have completely different personalities.
____	10. windfall	j.	This person requires a lot of time with others.

A **variety of exercise types** engage students and guide them from recognition and understanding to accurate production of the grammar structures.

Editing exercises allow students to identify and correct typical mistakes.

EXERCISE 5   EDITING

GRAMMAR NOTES 1–7 Read this post to a travelers' website. There are ten mistakes in the use of embedded questions. The first mistake is already corrected. Find and correct nine more. Don't forget to check punctuation.

WORLDWIDE TRAVEL

Email this page to someone!   New Topic   Post a Poll   Post Reply

Subject: **Tipping at the Hair Salon in Italy**
Posted April 10 by Jenna Thompson

if or whether
I wonder you can help clarify some tipping situations for me. I never know what doing at the hair salon. I don't know if I should tip the person who washes my hair? What about the person who cuts it, and the person who colors it? And what happens if the person is the owner. Do you know do I still need to tip him or her? That doesn't seem logical. (And often I'm not even sure who is the owner!) Then I never know how much to tip or where should I leave the tip? Do I leave it on the counter or in the person's hands? What if somebody's hands are wet or have hair color on them? Can I just put the tip in his or her pocket? It all seems so complicated! I can't imagine how do customers figure all this out? What's the custom? I really need to find out what to do—and FAST! My hair is getting very long and dirty.

Listenings in a variety of genres allow students to hear the grammar in natural contexts.

STEP 4 COMMUNICATION PRACTICE

EXERCISE 6 LISTENING

A Claudia Leggett and her son, Pietro, are flying from Los Angeles to Hong Kong. Listen to the announcements they hear in the airport and aboard the plane. Read the statements. Then listen again and check (✓) *True* or *False*.

	True	False
Announcement 1: Claudia has two pieces of carry-on luggage, and Pietro has one. They can take them all on the plane.	☐	☑
Announcement 2: Look at their boarding passes. They can board now.	☐	☐

Announcement 3: Look at their boarding passes again. They can board now.	☐	☐
Announcement 4: Pietro is only ten years old. Claudia should put his oxygen mask on first.	☐	☐
Announcement 5: Claudia is sitting in a left-hand window seat. She can see the lights of Tokyo.	☐	☐
Announcement 6: Passengers who are taking connecting flights can get this information on the plane.	☐	☐

B Work with a partner. Listen again to the announcements. Discuss your answers.

EXAMPLE: A: OK. So, why is the answer to number 1 *False*?
B: The announcement says if you have more than one piece of carry-on luggage, you must check the extra pieces at the gate.
A: Right. And they have three pieces, so they can't take them all on the plane with them. Now, what did you choose for number 2?

Passengers on Flight 398 to Hong Kong

In the **listening activities**, students practice a range of listening skills. A **new step** has been added in which partners complete an activity that relates to the listening and uses the target grammar.

NEW!

Engaging **communicative activities** (conversations, discussions, presentations, surveys, and games) help students synthesize the grammar, develop fluency, and build their problem-solving skills.

EXERCISE 7 WHAT ABOUT YOU?

CONVERSATION Work in a group. Talk about your hobbies and interests. What did you do in the past with your hobby? What have you been doing lately? Find out about other people's hobbies.

EXAMPLE: A: Do you have any hobbies, Ben?
B: Yes. Since I was in high school, my hobby has been running. . . . Recently, I've been training for a marathon. What about you? Do you have a hobby?
C: I collect sneakers. I got my first pair of Nikes when I was ten, and I've been collecting different kinds of sneakers ever since. . . .

EXERCISE 8 DONE, DONE, NOT DONE

A INTERVIEW What did you plan to do last month to develop your hobbies and personal interests? Make a list. Include things you did and things that you still haven't done. Do not check (✓) any of the items. Exchange lists with a partner.

Buy a new pair of running shoes.
Research healthy snacks for marathon runners.

B Now ask questions about your partner's list. Check (✓) the things that your partner has already done. Answer your partner's questions about your list. When you finish, find out if the information that you recorded on your partner's list is correct.

EXAMPLE: A: Have you bought your new running shoes yet?
B: Yes, I have. I bought them last week.
A: And what about the research on healthy snacks?
B: I haven't done it yet.
A: OK. I think we've talked about everything on our lists. Let's make sure our answers are correct.

FROM GRAMMAR TO WRITING

A **From Grammar to Writing** section, now in every unit, helps students confidently apply the unit's grammar to their own writing.

NEW!

FROM GRAMMAR TO WRITING

A BEFORE YOUR WRITE Diplomats are people who officially represent their country in a foreign country. Imagine that you are going to attend a school for future diplomats. Complete the information about some of the features of your ideal school.

Courses required: _____

Language(s) spoken: _____

Living quarters provided: _____

Food offered: _____

Trips taken: _____

Electronic devices provided: _____

B WRITE Use your information to write one or two paragraphs about your ideal school for diplomacy. Use the passive with modals and similar expressions. Try to avoid some of the common mistakes in the chart.

EXAMPLE: I think the ideal school for diplomacy should teach a lot about cross-cultural understanding. Courses should be required in . . . More than one official language should be spoken. Classes could be offered in . . .

Common Mistakes in Using the Passive with Modals and Similar Expressions

Use *be* + past participle after the modal. Do not leave out *be*.	Language classes should *be* required. NOT Language classes should required.
Use the past participle after *be*. Do not use the base form of the verb after *be*.	A lot could *be* learned. NOT A lot could be learn.

C CHECK YOUR WORK Read your paragraph(s). Underline the passive with modals and similar expressions. Use the Editing Checklist to check your work.

Editing Checklist

Did you use . . . ?

☐ *be* + past participle to form the passive after modals or similar expressions
☐ *will* or *be going to* for certainty in the future
☐ *can* for present ability
☐ *could* for past ability or future possibility
☐ *may*, *might*, and *can't* for future possibility or impossibility
☐ *should*, *ought to*, and *had better* for advice
☐ *must* and *have (got) to* for necessity

D REVISE YOUR WORK Read your paragraph(s) again. Can you improve your writing? Make changes if necessary. Give your writing a title.

Go to MyEnglishLab for more writing practice.

The Passive with Modals and Similar Expressions   **299**

The **Before You Write** task helps students generate ideas for their writing assignment.

In the **Write** task, students are given a writing assignment and guided to use the target grammar and avoid common mistakes.

Check Your Work includes an Editing Checklist that allows students to proofread and edit their compositions.

In **Revise Your Work**, students are given a final opportunity to improve their writing.

UNIT **REVIEW**

Unit Reviews give students the opportunity to check their understanding of the target structures. Students can check their answers against the Answer Key at the end of the book. They can also complete the Review on MyEnglishLab.

UNIT 21 **REVIEW**

Test yourself on the grammar of the unit.

A Match each condition with its result.

Condition	Result
_____ 1. If it rains,	a. you might have good luck.
_____ 2. Unless you study,	b. I could pay you back tomorrow.
_____ 3. If you cross your fingers,	c. I may not buy it.
_____ 4. Unless they lower the price,	d. I'll take an umbrella.
_____ 5. If you lend me $10,	e. you could rent one.
_____ 6. If you don't own a car,	f. you won't pass.

B Complete the future real conditional sentences in these conversations with the correct form of the verbs in parentheses.

1. A: Are you going to take the bus?

   B: No. If I _____ the bus, I _____ late.
          a. (take)   b. (be)

2. A: What _____ you _____ if you _____ the job?
          a. (do)   b. (not get)

   B: I _____ in school unless I _____ the job.
          c. (stay)   d. (get)

3. A: If I _____ the test, I _____ .
          a. (pass)   b. (celebrate)

   B: Good luck, but I'm sure you'll pass. You've studied really hard for it.

   A: Thanks!

C Find and correct six mistakes. Remember to check punctuation.

It's been a hard week, and I'm looking forward to the weekend. If the weather will be nice tomorrow Marco and I are going to go to the beach. The ocean is usually too cold

xii   The *Focus on Grammar* Unit

MyEnglishLab

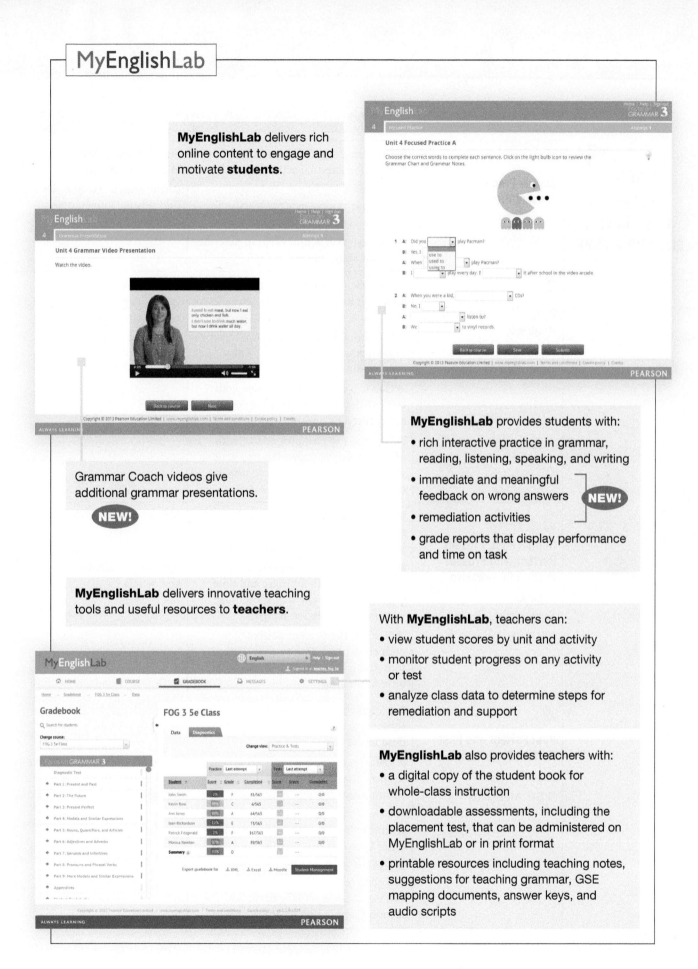

MyEnglishLab delivers rich online content to engage and motivate **students**.

Grammar Coach videos give additional grammar presentations.

NEW!

MyEnglishLab delivers innovative teaching tools and useful resources to **teachers**.

MyEnglishLab provides students with:

- rich interactive practice in grammar, reading, listening, speaking, and writing
- immediate and meaningful feedback on wrong answers
- remediation activities

NEW!

- grade reports that display performance and time on task

With **MyEnglishLab**, teachers can:

- view student scores by unit and activity
- monitor student progress on any activity or test
- analyze class data to determine steps for remediation and support

MyEnglishLab also provides teachers with:

- a digital copy of the student book for whole-class instruction
- downloadable assessments, including the placement test, that can be administered on MyEnglishLab or in print format
- printable resources including teaching notes, suggestions for teaching grammar, GSE mapping documents, answer keys, and audio scripts

Scope and Sequence

LISTENING	SPEAKING	WRITING	VOCABULARY
A conversation about people ■ Can identify people, based on descriptions in a conversation	■ Can ask people for personal details and introduce them to others ■ Can narrate a video, describing what people are doing ■ Can discuss naming customs in different countries	■ Can write a detailed paragraph about oneself	adjustment AWL consist of AWL convince AWL identity AWL in style AWL provide
A personal narrative ■ Can identify the order of events in a recorded description	■ Can describe one's first meeting with someone ■ Can ask and answer questions about important life events ■ Can create a story and present it to the class	■ Can write two paragraphs describing past events in an important relationship	accomplish cover (v) influential pursue AWL recover AWL research (n) AWL
A conversation about hobbies ■ Can recognize key ideas and details in a discussion about hobbies and personal interests	■ Can talk about hobbies and personal interests ■ Can discuss routine accomplishments ■ Can research an interesting hobby and present findings to the class	■ Can write a detailed paragraph about a recent trend	alternative (n) AWL experiment (v) motivation AWL passion survive AWL trend (n) AWL
An interview on a radio show ■ Can understand the order of events in a radio program about career and life choices	■ Can ask and answer questions about past events and personal achievements ■ Can discuss one's schedule for the previous day ■ Can research a famous child prodigy and present findings to the class ■ Can compare two similar scenes and discuss differences	■ Can write two paragraphs about a famous person's career and personal life	conduct (v) AWL contract (n) AWL ethnic AWL inspire participate AWL transform AWL

AWL = Academic Word List item

LISTENING	SPEAKING	WRITING	VOCABULARY
A discussion about a conference ■ Can follow a group discussion, identifying important details such as the speakers' schedules and plans	■ Can discuss schedules, reaching agreement on plans ■ Can offer a detailed opinion about a controversial topic relating to technology	■ Can write two paragraphs about a hypothetical scenario that is set in the future	challenge (n) AWL individual (n) AWL innovative AWL technology AWL vehicle AWL vertical (adj)
A conversation about entrepreneurship ■ Can follow a fast-paced conversation about professional aspirations, identifying key details	■ Can talk about someone's future goals and accomplishments ■ Can discuss personal long-term goals and how to achieve them	■ Can write a detailed paragraph about a classmate's future goals and what that person is doing to achieve these goals	affordable convert (v) AWL corporate (adj) AWL initiative AWL meanwhile status AWL
On-the-street conversations ■ Can identify important details from fast-paced conversations	■ Can interview a classmate, asking questions and checking information ■ Can discuss details about cities around the world, asking questions and checking information	■ Can write an interview transcript about a classmate's home city, commenting on and checking information	attracted (adj) constant (adj) AWL extremely originally structure (n) AWL supply (v)
A first-date conversation ■ Can identify key details about people in a conversation	■ Can discuss similarities and differences between two people ■ Can conduct online research about twins separated at birth and report findings ■ Can discuss the controversial topic of nature vs. nurture and give own opinion	■ Can write two paragraphs about the similarities and differences between two people	complex (adj) AWL factor (n) AWL identical AWL image AWL investigate AWL reserved (adj)

AWL = Academic Word List item

UNIT	GRAMMAR	READING
PART 4 **Gerunds, Infinitives, and Phrasal Verbs** **9** **Gerunds and Infinitives: Review and Expansion** Page 136 THEME Fast Food	■ Can use a gerund as the subject or the object of a verb ■ Can use a range of verbs followed by a gerund or an infinitive ■ Can use a gerund after a preposition or a phrasal verb, and an infinitive after certain adjectives or nouns ■ Can use infinitives to express purpose ■ Can use gerunds and infinitives to make general statements	Social Science Article: *Fast Food in a Fast World* ■ Can recognize significant points and ideas in an article about a popular trend
10 ***Make, Have, Let, Help, and Get*** Page 152 THEME Zoos and Marine Theme Parks	■ Can use *make, have, get,* or *let* to show how someone causes or allows another person/animal to do something ■ Can use *help* to show that someone makes things easier for another person/animal	Opinion Article: *That's Entertainment?* ■ Can recognize significant points and arguments in an opinion article on a controversial topic
11 **Phrasal Verbs: Review and Expansion** Page 165 THEME Telemarketing	■ Can use a range of phrasal verbs ■ Can use transitive phrasal verbs with or without separated objects ■ Can use intransitive phrasal verbs ■ Can use phrasal verbs with preposition combinations	Magazine Article: *Welcome Home!* ■ Can identify specific information in a linguistically complex article
PART 5 **Adjective Clauses** **12** **Adjective Clauses with Subject Relative Pronouns** Page 182 THEME Personality Types and Friends	■ Can use sentences with adjective clauses beginning with subject relative pronouns such as *who, that, which,* or *whose* to identify or give additional information about nouns ■ Can use identifying and nonidentifying adjective clauses PRONUNCIATION Identifying and nonidentifying adjective clauses	Psychology Article: *Extroverts and Introverts* ■ Can identify specific information in a linguistically complex article
13 **Adjective Clauses with Object Relative Pronouns** Page 199 THEME The Immigrant Experience	■ Can use adjective clauses beginning with object relative pronouns such as *who(m), that, which,* or *whose* to identify or give additional information about nouns ■ Can use adjective clauses beginning with *where* or *when* ■ Can use identifying and nonidentifying adjective clauses ■ Can use adjective clauses as objects of verbs and prepositions	Online Book Review: *Stories of a New Generation of Immigrants* ■ Can identify specific information in a book review

LISTENING	SPEAKING	WRITING	VOCABULARY
A conversation about school food services ■ Can identify key details in a conversation	■ Can complete a questionnaire and discuss results ■ Can make cross-cultural comparisons about a familiar topic ■ Can conduct online research on fast food and report findings	■ Can write two paragraphs describing plusses and minuses of a certain type of food	appealing (adj) consequence AWL convenience globe AWL objection reliability AWL
A conversation between a student and a teacher ■ Can recognize how one speaker influences the other and gets that person do something	■ Can describe how someone has influenced one's life ■ Can contribute to a group discussion about a controversial topic	■ Can write three paragraphs about a controversial topic, giving arguments for and against and stating one's personal opinion	cruel former humane physical AWL rebel (v) reinforcement AWL
A phone conversation with a telemarketer ■ Can identify key details in a conversation	■ Can justify and sustain views clearly by providing relevant explanations and arguments ■ Can analyze and discuss advertisements	■ Can write two paragraphs describing a personal experience and what one learned from the experience	authorities AWL eliminate AWL equivalent AWL feature (n) AWL firmly tactic
A conversation between friends at a high-school reunion ■ Can identify the people described in a conversation	■ Can take a personality quiz and discuss the results ■ Can give an opinion and examples in response to a literary quote or an international proverb ■ Can complete a questionnaire and discuss the answers	■ Can write two paragraphs describing the ideal friend and one's best friend	contradict AWL require AWL sensitive tendency trait unique AWL
A description of a childhood room ■ Can follow a personal narrative well enough to identify specific details	■ Can conduct online research about a successful immigrant and report findings ■ Can give an opinion and examples in response to a literary quote	■ Can write a description of a place from one's childhood and why the place was important	compelling (adj) encounter (v) AWL generation AWL issue (n) AWL poverty struggle (v)

AWL = Academic Word List item

LISTENING	SPEAKING	WRITING	VOCABULARY
A conversation about Facebook ■ Can identify key details in a conversation	■ Can discuss social networking websites, giving opinions ■ Can take a quiz and compare answers with classmates ■ Can discuss the advantages and disadvantages of social networking	■ Can write a blog entry about plans and events in the near future	content (n) involved (adj) AWL limit (v) network (v) AWL resource AWL respond AWL
A personal narrative about regrets ■ Can follow a personal narrative well enough to identify specific details	■ Can take a survey and discuss the results ■ Can discuss a situation, examining people's actions and giving opinions as to what the people should have done	■ Can write three paragraphs describing a past problem and evaluating what should or shouldn't have been done	examine exhausted (adj) paralyzed (adj) perceive AWL strategy AWL unrealistic
Conversations between archaeology students ■ Can identify key details in conversations and match each conversation with a picture	■ Can discuss ancient objects, speculating on what they are and what they might have been used for ■ Can discuss and speculate on new facts found about the Iceman	■ Can write a detailed paragraph speculating about an unsolved mystery	assume AWL decade AWL indicate AWL preserve (v) speculation victim
An academic lecture about Haiti ■ Can follow an academic lecture well enough to identify key details and complete notes	■ Can discuss and interpret an international proverb ■ Can engage in an extended conversation about geographical locations and resources found there ■ Can take a quiz and compare answers with classmates	■ Can write an essay about a country one knows well	edition AWL explorer inhabitant mission publication AWL respect (n)
Conversations from a science-fiction movie dialog ■ Can follow conversations well enough to identify key details	■ Can discuss rules for group living in close quarters ■ Can make recommendations for improvement of one's environment ■ Can discuss the pros and cons of investing money in space projects	■ Can write one or two paragraphs describing the ideal school for diplomacy	assemble AWL benefit (v) AWL concern (n) cooperate AWL perspective AWL undertaking AWL

AWL = Academic Word List item

UNIT	GRAMMAR	READING
▼ PART **7** CONTINUED		
19 **The Passive Causative** Page 301 THEME Personal Services	■ Can use the passive causative to describe services people arrange for someone to do for them ■ Can use the passive causative with *by* + agent when the agent is new or important information	Fashion Magazine Article: *Body Art* ■ Can identify specific information in an article on a familiar topic
PART **8** **Conditional Sentences** **20** **Present Real Conditional Sentences** Page 316 THEME Shopping	■ Can use present real conditional sentences with *if/when* to describe real conditions and results that are certain, such as general truths and habits ■ Can use modals or similar expressions in the result clause to express possibility, advice, or necessity ■ Can use an imperative in the result clause to express instructions, commands, or invitations	Information Article: *Pick and Click: Shopping@Home* ■ Can identify specific information in an article on a familiar topic
21 **Future Real Conditional Sentences** Page 331 THEME Cause and Effect	■ Can use future real conditional sentences with *if/unless* to describe real conditions and results that are certain ■ Can use modals or similar expressions in the result clause to express possibility, advice, or necessity	Magazine Article: *Knock on Wood!* ■ Can identify specific information in an article on a familiar topic
22 **Present and Future Unreal Conditional Sentences** Page 344 THEME Wishes	■ Can use present and future unreal conditional sentences to describe unreal conditions and results that are untrue, imagined, or impossible ■ Can use *might* or *could* in the result clause to express possibility ■ Can give advice using *If I were you* ■ Can use *wish* to express wishes related to the present or future	Fairy Tale: *The Fisherman and His Wife* ■ Can identify specific information in a story
23 **Past Unreal Conditional Sentences** Page 359 THEME Alternate Histories	■ Can use past unreal conditional sentences to describe past unreal conditions and results that are untrue, imagined, or impossible ■ Can use *might have* or *could have* in the result clause to express possibility ■ Can use *wish* + past perfect to express regret or sadness	Information Article: *What if . . . ?* ■ Can extract specific information from a linguistically complex article

LISTENING	SPEAKING	WRITING	VOCABULARY
A conversation between father and daughter ▦ Can identify key details in a conversation about tasks on a To Do list	▦ Can talk about plans and preparations for a trip to another country ▦ Can compare *Before* and *After* pictures of a person and discuss changes in appearance ▦ Can discuss steps people from different cultures take to improve their appearance	▦ Can write one or two paragraphs describing preparations for a future event	caution (n) expand AWL option AWL permanent (adj) risk (n) temporary (adj) AWL
Announcements in an airport and aboard a plane ▦ Can infer correct information from public announcements	▦ Can discuss and complete an online order form ▦ Can discuss shopping in different places ▦ Can compare the advantages and disadvantages of shopping in stores and shopping online	▦ Can write a short article describing things to do and see in one's city or town	consumer AWL dispute (v) policy AWL precaution secure (adj) AWL site (n) AWL
An interview with a candidate for student council president ▦ Can follow an animated conversation well enough to identify details	▦ Can discuss common problems and possible solutions ▦ Can discuss superstitions, giving opinions and making cross-cultural comparisons	▦ Can write a short speech about what one will do if elected class or school president	anticipate AWL attitude AWL confident insight AWL percent AWL widespread AWL
A modern fairy tale ▦ Can follow a recorded story well enough to identify key details	▦ Can discuss common problems and give advice ▦ Can discuss hypothetical questions and wishes	▦ Can write a detailed paragraph describing a wish one has for oneself or society, and what might happen if it came true	consent (v) AWL embarrassed (adj) enchanted (adj) furious grant (v) AWL regular (adj)
Conversations about past events ▦ Can follow animated conversations well enough to identify key information about past events	▦ Can speculate about past events or hypothetical situations ▦ Can analyze past situations and evaluate the decisions made ▦ Can talk about a past decision one regrets and about what one wishes had happened and why	▦ Can write one or two paragraphs speculating about what would have happened if an important event hadn't taken place	alternate (adj) AWL dominate AWL occur AWL outcome AWL parallel (adj) AWL version AWL

AWL = Academic Word List item

LISTENING	SPEAKING	WRITING	VOCABULARY
Conversations between friends and coworkers ■ Can follow animated conversations well enough to identify key details	■ Can have a discussion about lying ■ Can give an opinion and examples in response to a literary quote or international proverb ■ Can complete a questionnaire and compare answers with classmates	■ Can write one or two paragraphs about a past conversation, reporting what was said using direct and indirect speech	aware AWL justify AWL majority AWL nevertheless AWL reveal (v) AWL survey (n) AWL
A conversation about a recent weather report ■ Can identify key details in a discussion about a weather report	■ Can conduct a simple interview and report the other person's answers ■ Can do an online search about an extreme weather event and report findings	■ Can write two paragraphs about an extreme weather event, reporting another person's experience	devastation exceed AWL extreme inevitable AWL shelter (n) whereas AWL
A conversation about a visit to a headache clinic ■ Can identify key details in a conversation about medical advice	■ Can discuss health problems and possible home remedies ■ Can report on how someone followed instructions	■ Can write one or two paragraphs describing a health problem one had and reporting the advice one received	astonishing fatigue (n) interfere monitor (v) AWL persist AWL remedy (n)
A conversation about a job interview ■ Can identify key details in a conversation about a job interview	■ Can role-play a job interview and discuss with classmates ■ Can talk about a personal experience with a job interview ■ Can complete a questionnaire about work values, discuss answers, and report conversations	■ Can write a report on a job interview	appropriate (adj) AWL candidate evaluation AWL handle (v) potential (adj) AWL pressure (n)
A call-in radio show about tipping ■ Can understand a call-in radio program well enough to identify information	■ Can discuss tipping around the world, giving opinions ■ Can talk about problems encountered during first-time experiences ■ Can role-play a conversation between a hotel clerk and a guest asking for information	■ Can write a detailed paragraph about a confusing or surprising situation	clarify AWL custom depend on logical AWL ordinary ultimate AWL

AWL = Academic Word List item

About the Authors

Marjorie Fuchs has taught ESL at New York City Technical College and LaGuardia Community College of the City University of New York and EFL at Sprachstudio Lingua Nova in Munich, Germany. She has a master's degree in Applied English Linguistics and a certificate in TESOL from the University of Wisconsin-Madison. She has authored and co-authored many widely used books and multimedia materials, notably *Crossroads 4*; *Top Twenty ESL Word Games: Beginning Vocabulary Development*; *Families: Ten Card Games for Language Learners*; *Focus on Grammar 3* and *4* (editions 1–5); *Focus on Grammar 3* and *4, CD-ROM*; *Longman English Interactive 3* and *4*; *Grammar Express Basic*; *Grammar Express Basic CD-ROM*; *Grammar Express Intermediate*; *Future 1: English for Results*; *OPD Workplace Skills Builder*; workbooks for *Crossroads 1–4*; *The Oxford Picture Dictionary High Beginning* and *Low Intermediate*, (editions 1–3); *Focus on Grammar 3* and *4* (editions 1–5); and *Grammar Express Basic*.

Margaret Bonner has taught ESL at Hunter College and the Borough of Manhattan Community College of the City University of New York, at Taiwan National University in Taipei, and at Virginia Commonwealth University in Richmond. She holds a master's degree in library science from Columbia University, and she has done work toward a PhD in English literature at the Graduate Center of the City University of New York. She has authored and co-authored numerous ESL and EFL print and multimedia materials, including textbooks for the national school system of Oman; *Step into Writing: A Basic Writing Text*; *Focus on Grammar 3* and *4* (editions 1–5); *Focus on Grammar 4 Workbook* (editions 1–5); *Grammar Express Basic*; *Grammar Express Basic CD-ROM*; *Grammar Express Basic Workbook*; *Grammar Express Intermediate*; *Focus on Grammar 3* and *4, CD-ROM*; *Longman English Interactive 4*; and *The Oxford Picture Dictionary Low Intermediate Workbook* (editions 1–3).

Jane Curtis teaches in the English Language Program at Roosevelt University in Chicago. She has also taught at the Universitat de Barcelona in Barcelona, Spain, and at Wuhan University in Wuhan, China. She holds a master's degree in Spanish from the University of Illinois at Urbana-Champaign and a master's degree in Applied Linguistics from Northeastern Illinois University. She has authored materials for *Longman Academic Writing Series 3: Paragraphs to Essays*, Fourth Edition; *Future 4: English for Results*; and the workbook for *Focus on Grammar 4* (editions 3 and 4).

Acknowledgments

Before acknowledging the many people who have contributed to the fifth edition of *Focus on Grammar*, we wish to express our gratitude to the following people who worked on the previous editions and whose influence is still present in the new work: **Joanne Dresner**, who initiated the project and helped conceptualize the general approach of *Focus on Grammar*; our editors for the first four editions: **Nancy Perry**, **Penny Laporte**, **Louisa Hellegers**, **Joan Saslow**, **Laura LeDrean**, **Debbie Sistino**, and **Françoise Leffler**; and **Sharon Hilles**, our grammar consultant for the first edition.

In the fifth edition, *Focus on Grammar* has continued to evolve as we update materials and respond to valuable feedback from teachers and students who use the series. We are grateful to the following editors and colleagues:

- **Gosia Jaros-White** for overseeing with skill and sensitivity a complex series while never losing sight of the individual components or people involved in the project. She offered concrete and practical advice and was always mindful of learners' needs.

- **Bernard Seal**, of Page Designs International, who joined the *Focus on Grammar* team with a great deal of experience, expertise, energy, and enthusiasm. With his hands-on approach, he was involved in every aspect of the project. He read all manuscript, raising pertinent questions and offering sage advice.

- **Don Williams**, also of Page Designs International, for creating a fresh, new look, which is as user-friendly as it is attractive.

- **Françoise Leffler**, our editor *extraordinaire*, with whom we had the great fortune and pleasure of being able to continue our long collaboration. She provided both continuity and a fresh eye as she delved into another edition of the series, advising us on all things—from the small details to the big picture.

- **Jane Curtis** for her excellent contributions to the first half of this book. Her involvement went beyond her fine writing and choice of engaging topics. She also brought enthusiasm, dedication, and many years of invaluable classroom experience using the series.

- Series co-authors **Irene Schoenberg** and **Jay Maurer** for their suggestions and support, and Irene for sharing her experience in teaching with earlier editions of this book.

- **Julie Schmidt** for her helpful presentation of information and for her input in Part 9.

- **Sharon Goldstein** for her insightful and practical suggestions, delivered with wisdom and wit.

- **Cindy Davis** for her classroom-based recommendations at the very beginning of this edition.

Finally, as always, Marjorie thanks **Rick Smith** for his unswerving support and excellent suggestions. He was a steadfast beacon of light as we navigated our way through our fifth *FOG*.

MF and MB

To the memory of my parents, Edith and Joseph Fuchs—MF
To my parents, Marie and Joseph Maus, and to my son, Luke Frances—MB

Reviewers

We are grateful to the following reviewers for their many helpful comments:

Susanna Aramyan, Glendale Community College, Glendale, CA; **Homeretta Ayala**, Baltimore Co. Schools, Baltimore, MD; **Barbara Barrett**, University of Miami, Miami, FL; **Rebecca Beck**, Irvine Valley College, Irvine, CA; **Crystal Bock Thiessen**, University of Nebraska-PIESL, Lincoln, NE; **Janna Brink**, Mt. San Antonio College, Walnut, CA; **Erin Butler**, University of California, Riverside, CA; **Joice Cain**, Fullerton College, Fullerton, CA; **Shannonine M. Caruana**, Hudson County Community College, Jersey City, NJ; **Tonya Cobb**, Cypress College, Cypress, CA; **David Cooke**, Mt. San Antonio College, Walnut, CA; **Lindsay Donigan**, Fullerton College, Fullerton, CA; **Mila Dragushanskya**, ASA College, New York, NY; **Jill Fox**, University of Nebraska, Lincoln, NE; **Katalin Gyurindak**, Mt. San Antonio College, Walnut, CA; **Karen Hamilton**, Glendale Community College, Glendale, CA; **Electra Jablons**, International English Language Institute, Hunter College, New York, NY; **Eva Kozlenko**, Hudson County Community College, Jersey City, NJ; **Esther Lee**, American Language Program, California State University, Fullerton, CA; **Yenlan Li**, American Language Program, California State University, Fullerton, CA; **Shirley Lundblade**, Mt. San Antonio College, Walnut, CA; **Thi Thi Ma**, Los Angeles City College, Los Angeles, CA; **Marilyn Martin**, Mt. San Antonio College, Walnut, CA; **Eve Mazereeuw**, University of Guelph English Language Programs, Guelph, Ontario, Canada; **Robert Mott**, Glendale Community College, Glendale, CA; **Wanda Murtha**, Glendale Community College, Glendale, CA; **Susan Niemeyer**, Los Angeles City College, Los Angeles, CA; **Wayne Pate**, Tarrant County College, Fort Worth, TX; **Genevieve Patthey-Chavez**, Los Angeles City College, Los Angeles, CA; **Robin Persiani**, Sierra College, Rocklin, CA; **Denise Phillips**, Hudson County Community College, Jersey City, NJ; **Anna Powell**, American Language Program, California State University, Fullerton, CA; **JoAnna Prado**, Sacramento City Community College, Sacramento, CA; **Mark Rau**, American River College, Sacramento, CA; **Madeleine Schamehorn**, University of California, Riverside, CA; **Richard Skinner**, Hudson County Community College, Jersey City, NJ; **Heather Snavely**, American Language Program, California State University, Fullerton, CA; **Gordana Sokic**, Douglas College, Westminster, British Columbia, Canada; **Lee Spencer**, International English Language Institute, Hunter College, New York, NY; **Heather Stern**, Irvine Valley College, Irvine, CA; **Susan Stern**, Irvine Valley College, Irvine, CA; **Andrea Sunnaa**, Mt. San Antonio College, Walnut, CA; **Margaret Teske**, Mt. San Antonio College, Walnut, CA; **Johanna Van Gendt**, Hudson County Community College, Jersey City, NJ; **Daniela C. Wagner-Loera**, University of Maryland, College Park, MD; **Tamara Williams**, University of Guelph, English Language Programs, Guelph, Ontario, Canada; **Saliha Yagoubi**, Hudson County Community College, Jersey City, NJ; **Pat Zayas**, Glendale Community College, Glendale, CA

Credits

Modals: Review and Expansion

PART 6

OUTCOMES

- Express ability, possibility, advice, necessity, prohibition, conclusions, or future possibility with a range of modals and similar expressions
- Identify key information in a social science article
- Identify key details in a conversation
- Discuss social networking, giving opinions
- Write a blog entry about one's plans for the near future

OUTCOMES

- Express past advisability, regret, or criticism with past modals
- Identify people's opinions in a psychology article
- Identify key details in a recorded personal narrative
- Discuss past situations and decide what people should or should not have done
- Complete a survey and discuss the results
- Write about a past problem and what one should or should not have done

OUTCOMES

- Speculate about past events, expressing possible or probable conclusions
- Draw conclusions based on the information in an article about archaeology
- Identify key details in a conversation and draw conclusions
- Discuss ancient objects and historical facts, and speculate about them
- Write about an unsolved mystery

Modals and Similar Expressions: Review

SOCIAL NETWORKING

OUTCOMES
- Express ability, possibility, advice, necessity, prohibition, conclusions, or future possibility with a range of modals and similar expressions
- Identify key information in a social science article
- Identify key details in a conversation
- Discuss social networking, giving opinions
- Write a blog entry about one's plans for the near future

STEP 1   GRAMMAR IN CONTEXT

BEFORE YOU READ

Look at the picture. Discuss the questions.

1. Do you use social networking sites? Which ones?
2. Do you use social media for connecting with friends, or for school or business?

READ

▶14|01   Read this article about social networking.

Abigail Thompson's school friends can find out what she is doing almost every minute by checking Facebook. Vince Stevenson stays in touch with his family the same way. Vince says, "I had to join. My grandkids all use it, and I want to be involved in their lives." Magda Tilia, an English teacher in Romania, has created an international online community for her class, using another social media site. Her students are able to discuss lessons and chat with other students in France, Turkey, and Greece. She says, "Students don't have to use the site. Class is just more fun for the ones who do."

Besides staying connected, social networking can also be a great tool for making new friends. But, just like making friends at work or school, you have to make the effort to "meet" people with similar interests. Is *Survivor* a reality TV show you could never miss? If so, you might consider joining a *Survivor* interest group and beginning conversations with people there. Once you've made some friends, you should keep posting comments, photos, and videos that people can respond to.

However, while you're having fun getting to know people, you must never forget that what you put on the Internet isn't really private. Even if your posts are only available to friends, embarrassing content can still become public. So maybe you'd better think twice before posting those party photos. Once they're out there, you can't take them back!

Social networking is a great resource for students. When you're applying to school, you can network by chatting with current students. They could give you an inside view of the school you're interested in. Once in school, you can form study groups, organize your schedule, and much more. But be careful: You might also find yourself wasting valuable study time.

Recently, Abigail has decided she's got to limit her social media use. "I must waste hours a day online! I'm always chatting, and not doing homework," she said. But she's still a big fan. "I believe everyone ought to use social networking," she is quick to point out. "It's a big world out there, and you can meet a lot of interesting new people and stay connected with those you already know. You just have to know when to say 'enough is enough' and sign off."

AFTER YOU READ

(A) VOCABULARY **Complete the sentences with the words from the box.**

| content | involved | limit | network | resource | respond |

1. How did she _____ to your invitation to join your online community?

2. That website has a lot of interesting _____. I really like the photos.

3. He's very _____ with his family. He's always texting them.

4. Five hours a day is too much. Try to _____ your time online.

5. The Internet is a great _____. You can learn a lot online.

6. I used the Internet to _____ with other people when I was looking for a job.

(B) COMPREHENSION **Read the statements. Check (✓) *True* or *False*.**

	True	False
1. Magda Tilia's students are required to use social media.	☐	☐
2. It's not always easy to meet people with similar interests.	☐	☐
3. It's good to regularly post photos, comments, and videos on your interest group's site.	☐	☐
4. Embarrassing photos remain private on the Internet.	☐	☐
5. Students should avoid using social networking.	☐	☐
6. Abigail thinks everyone should use social networking.	☐	☐

(C) DISCUSSION **Work with a partner. Compare your answers to the questions in B. Why did you check *True* or *False*?**

MODALS AND SIMILAR EXPRESSIONS: REVIEW

Ability or Possibility: *Can* and *Could*

Subject	Modal	Base Form of Verb	
She	can (not)	join	now.
	could (not)		last year.

Ability or Possibility: *Be able to*

Subject	*Be able to*		Base Form of Verb	
She	is (not)	able to	join	now.
	was (not)			last year.

Advice: *Should, Ought to, Had better*

Subject	Modal	Base Form of Verb	
You	should (not) ought to had better (not)	post	photos.

Necessity or Prohibition: *Must* and *Can't*

Subject	Modal	Base Form of Verb	
You	must (not) can't	post	photos.

Necessity: *Have (got) to*

Subject	*Have to* *Have (got) to*	Base Form of Verb	
They	(don't) have to have got to	post	photos.
He	has to has got to		

Conclusions: *May, Might, Could, Must, Can't*

Subject	Modal	Base Form of Verb	
They	may (not) might (not) could (not) must (not) can't	know	him.

Conclusions: *Have (got) to*

Subject	*Have to* *Have got to*	Base Form of Verb	
They	have to have got to	know	him.
He	has to has got to		

Future Possibility: *May, Might, Could*

Subject	Modal	Base Form of Verb	
It	may (not) might (not) could	happen	soon.

GRAMMAR NOTES

1 Modals and Similar Expressions: Functions and Forms

Modals are auxiliary verbs. We use modals (such as *can*, *should*, and *might*) and similar expressions (such as *be able to*, *have to*, and *had better*) to express **social functions** and **logical possibilities**.

Social functions include:

- **ability** or **possibility**
  (*can, could, be able to*)

  He **can learn** to use it.
  He**'s able to learn** quickly.

- **advice**
  (*should, ought to, had better*)

  She **should join** Facebook.
  You**'d better not give** your home address.

- **necessity**
  (*have to, have got to, must*)

  You **have to register** to use this site.
  You **must create** a strong password.

- **prohibition**
  (*must not, can't*)

  You **must not give** anyone your password.
  Children under thirteen **can't join**.

Logical possibilities include:

- **conclusions**
  (*may, might, could, must, have to, can't*)

  It **could be** the best site.
  There **must be** other good sites.

- **future possibility**
  (*may, might, could*)

  I **may join**.
  Sean **might join**, too.

BE CAREFUL! Modals have **only one form**. They do not have -*s* in the third person singular. Always use **modal + base form** of the verb.

She **might post** photos.
NOT She ~~mights~~ post photos.
NOT She might ~~to post~~ photos.

However, with the expressions *have to* and *be able to*, the form of the verb changes.

She **has to register** in order to use the site.
He **had to change** his password yesterday.
They **weren't** able to sign on.

2 Ability or Possibility

Use *can*, *could*, or *be able to* to express **ability** or **possibility**.

- **present** ability or possibility

  She **can speak** French.
  We **aren't able to view** his site.

- **past** ability or possibility

  Before she took lessons, she **could speak** French, but she **wasn't able to speak** English.

- **future** ability or possibility

  She **can register** for class soon.
  She**'ll be able to register** tomorrow.
  She**'s going to be able to attend** next semester.

USAGE NOTE *Can* is much more common than *be able to* for ability or possibility.

She **can speak** French. *(more common)*
She **is able to speak** French. *(less common)*

3 Advice

Use *should*, *ought to*, and *had better* to express **advice**.

• *should*	You **should watch** *Survivor* tonight.
• *ought to*	Terri **ought to watch** it, too.
• *had better* for **urgent advice** (when you believe something bad will happen if the person does not follow the advice)	You**'d better spend** less time online or your grades will go down.

USAGE NOTE *Should* is much more common than *ought to*.

They **should join**. *(more common)*
They **ought to join**. *(less common)*

Use *should* to **ask for advice**.

Should I **join** Facebook?

Use *shouldn't* and *had better not* for **negative advice**.

You **shouldn't spend** so much time online.
You**'d better not stay up** too late.

4 Necessity

Use *have to*, *have got to*, and *must* to express **necessity**.

• *have to*	I **have to get** a new email address.
• *have got to*	You**'ve got to see** this cartoon! It's really funny!
• *must*	People **must register** to use this site.

USAGE NOTE We use *have got to* in **conversation** and in **informal writing**. It often expresses strong feeling.

You**'ve got to keep** your password private. It's very important for Internet safety.

USAGE NOTE When we use *must* in **conversation**, the speaker is usually in a position of power or expressing urgent necessity.

You **must go** to bed right now, Tommy!
  (mother talking to her young son)

You **must see** a doctor about that terrible cough!
  (friend talking to a friend)

IN WRITING *Must* is common in **writing**, such as forms, signs, and manuals.

You **must be** at least 13 years old to join.
  (instructions for joining a networking site)

Students **must post** their homework today.
  (teacher to students on an online course site)

Use *must not* or *can't* to express **prohibition** (things that are against the rules or law).

• *must not*	Students **must not leave** before the test ends. *(written instructions on a test form)*
• *can't*	You **can't leave** yet. The test isn't over. *(teacher speaking to a student)*

USAGE NOTE *Can't* is much more common than *must not* in conversation.	We **can't do** that. *(more common)* We **must not do** that. *(less common)*
BE CAREFUL! *Must* and *have to* have very similar meanings. However, *must not* and *don't have to* have very different meanings. Use *must not* for **prohibition**. Use *don't have to* when something is **not necessary**.	They **must not stay up** past 10:00. *(They are not allowed to stay up past 10:00.)* They **don't have to stay up** past 10:00. *(It isn't necessary for them to stay up past 10:00.)*

Use *must*, *have to*, *have got to*, *may*, *might*, and *could* to express **conclusions** ("best guesses") about situations using the facts you have.

We use modals and similar expressions to show how **certain or uncertain** we are about our conclusions.

Affirmative		Negative
must	**VERY CERTAIN**	*can't, couldn't*
have (got) to		*must not*
may		*may not*
might, could	**LESS CERTAIN**	*might not*

FACT	AFFIRMATIVE CONCLUSION
That photo looks just like Abigail.	It **must be** Abigail. *(very certain)*
Abigail knows Al.	They **may be** friends. *(less certain)*

FACT	NEGATIVE CONCLUSION
Al doesn't watch TV.	He **can't be** a member of the *Survivor* fan group. *(very certain)*
I couldn't find Al's name on Facebook.	He **may not** use his real name. *(less certain)*

For **questions** about conclusions, use *can, could,* or expressions such as *Do you think...?* or *Is it possible that...?* However, in **answers**, you can use *must (not), have (got) to, may (not), might (not), could(n't),* and *can't.*

A: **Could** Magda's students **be** online now?
B: No, they **can't be**. The lab is closed.
A: **Do you think she knows** how to set up an online study group?
B: She **must**. She set up a group for her class.

Use *may*, *might*, and *could* to express the **possibility** that something **will happen** in the future.

May, *might*, and *could* have very similar meanings. You can use any one to express **future possibility**.	
• *may*	Ted **may get** online later.
• *might*	Ted **might get** online later.
• *could*	Ted **could get** online later.
	(It's possible Ted will get online later, but I'm not sure.)
To express the possibility that something will not happen in the future, you can use *may not* or *might not*. You cannot use *could not*.	
• *may not*	I **may not join** Facebook.
• *might not*	I **might not join** Facebook.
	(It's possible I won't join Facebook, but I'm not sure.)
USAGE NOTE We usually do not begin questions about possibility with *may* or *might*. Instead we use *will* or *be going to* and phrases such as *Do you think . . . ?* or *Is it possible that . . . ?* However, we often use *may*, *might*, or *could* in short answers to these questions.	A: ***Will*** Josh ***join*** our Facebook study group? B: He **might not**. He's very involved with his job right now, so he doesn't have much free time. A: ***Do you think it'll help*** us pass chemistry? B: It **could**. People say study groups help.

STEP 3   FOCUSED PRACTICE

EXERCISE 1   DISCOVER THE GRAMMAR

A GRAMMAR NOTES 1–7 Read the FAQ about joining Facebook. Underline the modals and similar expressions. Also underline the verbs that follow.

● ● ●

FAQ About Facebook

How do I join Facebook?

It's easy. You just <u>have to complete</u> an online form with some basic information—your name, birthday, and gender. Oh, and you must have an email address.

Are there any age restrictions?

Yes. You must be 13 or older to join.

I'm worried about privacy. Do I really have to provide personal information such as my date of birth?

Yes, you do. But you will be able to hide personal information if you'd like.

Do I have to post a photo of myself?

It's not required, but most people do. To get the full benefit of making connections, you ought to give as much information as you feel comfortable with. Remember: Facebook is a great resource, so get involved!

Can someone post a photo of me without my permission?

Yes. As long as it doesn't break any of Facebook's rules, people don't have to ask. However, if the photo is embarrassing, a lot of users feel the poster really ought to get permission.

What if I don't like a photo that someone has posted of me?

Unfortunately, Facebook cannot remove a photo if it hasn't broken any rules. If you're unhappy with the photo, however, you can remove your name from it.

There must be some dangers in social networking. What should I do to protect myself?

The number 1 rule is this: You must not give your password to anyone. Ever. Also, you should never give out information that strangers could use to contact you in the real world.

B Write each underlined modal/expression + verb from A under the correct category.

Ability or Possibility	Advice	Necessity	Prohibition
1.	1.	1. *have to complete*	1.
2.	2.	2.	
3.	3.	3.	**Conclusions**
			1.
4.	4.	4.	
			Future Possibility
		5.	1.
		6.	

EXERCISE 2 STATEMENTS, QUESTIONS, AND SHORT ANSWERS

A GRAMMAR NOTE 2 A class is discussing an ethical[1] problem. Read the problem.
Complete the discussion with the correct form of the verbs in parentheses or with short
answers. Choose between affirmative and negative. Use contractions when possible.

> **PROBLEM:** Greg, a college student, worked successfully for a clothing store for a year. He spent
> most of his salary on books and tuition. One week, he wanted some extra money to buy a sweater
> to wear to a party. He asked for a raise, but his boss, Mr. Thompson, refused. The same week, Greg
> discovered an extra sweater in a shipment he was unpacking. It was very stylish and just his size.
> Greg "borrowed" it for the weekend and then brought it back. Mr. Thompson found out and fired him.

TEACHER: ____Should____ Mr. Thompson ____have given____ Greg a raise?
1. (should / give)

STUDENT A: Yes, he ____should've____ . After all, Greg had worked there for a
2.

whole year, and it's normal to get a raise after a year. In my opinion, Mr. Thompson

____shouldn't have refused____ at that point.
3. (should / refuse)

STUDENT B: But maybe Mr. Thompson couldn't afford to give Greg a raise. Anyway, Greg still

____should not have taken____ the sweater. It wasn't his.
4. (should / take)

TEACHER: What strategy ____should____ Greg ____should have used____ instead?
5. (should / use)

STUDENT C: He ____might have asked____ Mr. Thompson to sell him the sweater. Then
6. (might / ask)

he ____could have paid____ for it slowly, out of his salary.
7. (could / pay)

STUDENT A: He ____ought to have worn____ his old clothes to the party. His behavior was
8. (ought to / wear)

destructive. He just hurt himself by taking the sweater.

TEACHER: Well, ____should____ Mr. Thompson ____have fired____ Greg?
9. (should / fire)

STUDENT B: No, he ____could have examined____ the situation more carefully before taking
10. (could / examine)

action. Greg had been a good employee for a year, and he brought the sweater back. Now

Greg's reputation might be ruined.

TEACHER: Well, how ____should____ Mr. Thompson ____should have handled____
11. (should / handle)

the situation?

STUDENT C: I think that he ____ought to have warned____ Greg. He really
12. (ought to / warn)

____should not have fired____ Greg without any warning.
13. (should / fire)

▶15|03 **B** LISTEN AND CHECK **Listen to the discussion and check your answers in A.**

---

1 *ethical:* about what is right and wrong

EXERCISE 3 AFFIRMATIVE AND NEGATIVE STATEMENTS

GRAMMAR NOTE 2 Complete Greta's regrets or complaints about the past using the modals in parentheses. Choose between affirmative and negative.

1. I didn't go to college. Now I'm depressed about my job.

   I _should've gone to college_ .
   (should)

2. My brother quit his job. He thought he could find another job right away. *I knew right away that he was being unrealistic, but I didn't warn him. That was inconsiderate of me.*

   I _might have warned him_ .
   (might)

3. I feel sick. I ate all the chocolate.

   I _should not have eaten all chocolate_ .
   (should)

4. Christina didn't come over. She didn't even call. My entire evening was ruined.

   She _might had have called me_ .
   (might)

5. I tried to tell Christina how I felt, but it was useless. She just didn't listen to me.

   She _could could have listened to me_ .
   (could)

6. I jogged 5 miles yesterday, and now I'm exhausted.

   I _should not have ran so much_ .
   (should)

7. I didn't apply for a good job because the application process was so long. I gave up.

   I _should have completed all_ .
   (should)

8. I didn't invite Cynthia to the party. Now she's angry at me.

   I _should have invited her_ .
   (should)

9. Yesterday was my birthday, and my brother didn't call. My feelings are hurt.

   He _might have called me_ .
   (might)

10. I didn't do the laundry yesterday, so I don't have any clean socks. Everyone else gets their laundry done on time. Why can't I?

   I _ough to have done my laundry yesterday_ .
   (ought to)

EXERCISE 4 *SHOULDA, COULDA, MIGHTA, AND OUGHTA HAVE*

○15|04 PRONUNCIATION NOTE **Listen to the conversations and write the full forms of the words you hear.**

1. A: Doug _____*ought to have*_____ sent that email.

 B: I know. But you _____ told him that yesterday.

2. A: We _____ taken the train.

 B: You're right. We _____ been home by now.

3. A: I guess I _____ accepted that job.

 B: Well, maybe you _____ waited a few days before deciding.

4. A: You _____ washed that T-shirt in cold water.

 B: I guess I _____ read the label before I washed it.

5. A: I _____ asked my sister to lend me some money.

 B: She's your sister! She _____ offered to help.

EXERCISE 5 EDITING

GRAMMAR NOTES 1–2 **Read this journal entry. There are six mistakes in the use of modals. The first mistake is already corrected. Find and correct five more.**

December 15

About a week ago, Jennifer was late for work again, and Doug, our boss, told me he wanted to fire her. I was really upset. Of course, Jennifer shouldn't ~~had~~ *have* been late so often, but he might has talked to her about the problem before he decided to let her go. Then he laughed and told me to make her job difficult for her so that she would quit. He thought it was amusing! I just pretended I didn't hear him. What a mistake! It was unrealistic to think the problem would just go away. I ought confronted him right away. Or I could at least have warned Jennifer. Anyway, Jennifer is still here, but now I'm worried about my own job. Should I have telling Doug's boss? I wonder. Maybe I should handle things differently last week. The company should never has hired this guy. His behavior isn't normal! I'd better figure out some techniques for handling these situations.

Advisability in the Past **245**

EXERCISE 6 LISTENING

▶15|05 **A** Jennifer is taking Dr. David Burns's advice by recording all the things she regrets at the end of the day. Look at Jennifer's list. Then listen to her recording. Listen again and check (✓) the things she did.

TO DO

☐ Do homework

☑ Walk to work

☐ Make $100 bank deposit

☐ Buy coat

☐ Call Aunt Rose

☐ Call Ron

☐ Go to supermarket

☐ Finish David Burns's book

▶15|05 **B** Work with a partner. Listen again. Discuss Jennifer's regrets about the items on her list. Answer the questions.

1. What *didn't* she do that she should've done? Why?

   EXAMPLE: A: She didn't do her homework.
   B: Right. She should've done it.
   A: Now she has to get up early to do it.
   B: She should've done it right away. She shouldn't have waited.

2. What did she do that she shouldn't have done?

3. What could she have done differently to avoid the problem?

EXERCISE 7 YOU BE THE JUDGE!

Ⓐ SURVEY A *sense of obligation* is a feeling that you (or someone else) should have done or shouldn't have done something. How strong is your sense of obligation? Complete this survey.

Sense of Obligation Survey (S.O.S.)

INSTRUCTIONS: Read each situation. Circle the letter of your most likely response.

1. You want to lose 10 pounds, but you just ate a large dish of ice cream.
   a. I shouldn't have eaten the ice cream. I have no willpower.
   b. I deserve to enjoy things once in a while. I'll do better tomorrow.

2. Your friend quit her job. Now she's unemployed.
   a. Maybe she was really depressed at work. It's better that she left.
   b. She shouldn't have quit until she found another job.

3. You had an appointment with your doctor. You arrived on time but had to wait more than an hour.
   a. My doctor should have scheduled better. My time is valuable, too.
   b. Maybe there was an emergency. I'm sure it's not my doctor's fault.

4. You bought a coat for $140. A day later, you saw it at another store for $100.
   a. That was really bad luck.
   b. I should have looked around before I bought the coat.

5. Your brother didn't send you a birthday card.
   a. He could have at least called. He's so inconsiderate.
   b. Maybe he forgot. He's been really busy lately.

6. You just got back an English test. Your grade was 60 percent.
   a. That was a really difficult test.
   b. I should have studied harder.

7. You just found out that an electrician overcharged you.
   a. I should have known that was too much money.
   b. How could I have known? I'm not an expert.

8. You forgot to do some household chores that you had promised to do. Now the person you live with is angry.
   a. I shouldn't have forgotten. I'm irresponsible.
   b. I'm only human. I make mistakes.

9. You got a ticket for driving 5 miles per hour above the speed limit.
   a. I ought to have obeyed the speed limit.
   b. The police officer could've overlooked it and not given me the ticket. It was only 5 miles over the speed limit.

10. You went to the movies but couldn't get a ticket because it was sold out.
    a. I should've gone earlier.
    b. Wow! This movie is really popular!

B Put a check (✓) next to each of the answers below that you have. Give yourself one point for each answer that is checked. The higher your score, the stronger your sense of obligation.

☐ 1. a   ☐ 2. b   ☐ 3. a   ☐ 4. b   ☐ 5. a   ☐ 6. b   ☐ 7. a   ☐ 8. a   ☐ 9. a   ☐ 10. a

My Score _____

C Work with a partner and compare your survey results.

EXAMPLE: A: What was your answer to Question 1?
           B: I said I shouldn't have eaten the ice cream. What about you?

EXERCISE 8 WHAT A DISASTER!

GAME Work with a partner. Look at the picture of Alicia's apartment. What should she have done? What shouldn't she have done? Write as many sentences as you can in five minutes. When you are done, compare your answers with those of your classmates. Who had the most answers?

EXAMPLE: A: She should have paid the electric bill.
           B: She shouldn't have left the window open.

EXERCISE 9 DID THEY DO THE RIGHT THING?

PROBLEM SOLVING Work in a group. Read and discuss each situation. Examine the people's actions. Did they do the right thing or should they have done things differently?

Situation 1: Andrew was in his last year of college when he decided to run for student council president. During his campaign, a school newspaper reporter asked him about something she had discovered about his past. In high school, Andrew had once been caught cheating on a test. He had admitted his mistake and repeated the course. He never cheated again. Andrew felt that the incident was over, and he refused to answer the reporter's questions. The reporter wrote the story without telling Andrew's side, and Andrew lost the election.

EXAMPLE: A: Should Andrew have refused to answer questions about his past?
　　　　 B: I don't think so. It's useless to refuse to answer reporters' questions. They always report about it anyway.
　　　　 C: I agree. He should've . . .

Situation 2: Sheila is a social worker who cares deeply about her clients. Recently, there was a fire in her office building. After the fire, the fire department declared the building unsafe and wouldn't allow anyone to go back in. Sheila became worried and depressed because all her clients' records were in the building. She needed their names, telephone numbers, and other information in order to help them. She decided to take the risk, and she entered the building to get the records. She thought she was doing the right thing, but her supervisor perceived the situation differently and fired her.

Situation 3: Pierre's wife has been sick for a long time. One day, the doctor told Pierre about a new medicine that might save her life. He warned Pierre that the medicine was still experimental, so Pierre's insurance would not pay for it. At the pharmacy, Pierre discovered that the medicine was so expensive that he didn't have enough money to pay for it. The pharmacist refused to let Pierre pay for it later. At first, Pierre was paralyzed by fear and hopelessness. Then he took extra work on nights and weekends to pay for the medicine. Now he's too exhausted to take care of his wife as well as he had before.

FROM GRAMMAR TO WRITING

A BEFORE YOU WRITE Think about a problem you have had. Discuss it with a classmate. Answer these questions:

1. What was the problem? _____

2. What did you do about it? _____

3. What should you have done differently? _____

4. What did you learn from the situation? _____

B WRITE Use your answers to write three paragraphs about the problem you had. In the first paragraph, describe the problem and what you did. In the second, evaluate what you should or should not have done. In the third, write about what you learned. Try to avoid the common mistakes in the chart.

EXAMPLE: A few years ago, I needed a job. I saw an ad for an assistant in a store that was twenty miles from my home. I took the job and immediately regretted my decision. The commute was long, the pay wasn't good, the boss was terrible, and the hours were long. But, I really needed the money so I stayed on for five months.

It was a terrible decision, and I was miserable. I shouldn't have taken a job so far away. Before I took the job, I should have spoken to other people who already worked there. I also should have . . .

I learned from this mistake. In the future, I will . . .

Common Mistakes in Using Modals of Advisability in the Past

Use *should have, ought to have, could have, might have* + past participle for **affirmative** past advisability. Do not use *have* + simple past.	I **should have gone** sooner. NOT I should have went sooner.
Use *shouldn't have* or *ought not to have* for **negative** past advisability. Do not use *couldn't have* or *might not have*.	I **shouldn't have taken** that job. It was a mistake. NOT I couldn't have taken that job. NOT I might not have taken that job.

C CHECK YOUR WORK Read your paragraphs. Underline the modals of past advisability. Use the Editing Checklist to check your work.

Editing Checklist

Did you use . . . ?

☐ *should have, ought to have, could have, might have* + past participle in affirmative statements

☐ *should not have* and *ought not to have* + past participle in negative statements

☐ *to* after *ought*

D REVISE YOUR WORK Read your paragraphs again. Can you improve your writing? Make changes if necessary. Give your writing a title.

UNIT 15 REVIEW

Test yourself on the grammar of the unit.

A Circle the correct words to complete the sentences.

1. I got a C on my test. I should had / ~~have~~ studied more.

2. I ~~ought~~ / should to have asked for help.

3. Dara ~~could~~ / couldn't have offered to help me. She's very good at math.

4. The teacher might have gave / ~~given~~ me a little more time.

5. I was exhausted. I couldn't / ~~shouldn't~~ have stayed up so late the night before.

6. What ~~should I~~ / I should have done differently?

B Rewrite the sentences with the correct form of the modals in parentheses. Choose between affirmative and negative.

1. I regret that I didn't study for the math test.

   I should have studied for the math test
   (should)

2. It was wrong of you not to show me your class notes.

   You could have showed me your class notes
   (could)

3. I regret that I stayed up so late the night before the test.

   I shouldn't have stayed up late.
   (should)

4. It was wrong of John not to call you.

   he ought to call you
   (ought to)

5. I blame you for not inviting me to join the study group.

   You might have invited me group
   (might)

C Find and correct nine mistakes.

I shouldn't have stay~~ed~~ up so late. I overslept and missed my bus. I ought ~~to~~ have asked Erik
for a ride. I got to the office late, and my boss said, "You might ~~had~~ *have* called." She was right.
I ~~shouldn't~~ *should* have called. At lunch, my co-workers went out together. They really could ~~of~~ *have*
invited me to join them. Should have I said something to them? Then, after lunch, my mother
called. She said, "Yesterday was Aunt Em's birthday. You could've ~~sending~~ *send* her a card!" I really
think my mother might ~~has~~ *have* reminded me. Not a good day! I shouldn't have just stayed in bed.

Now check your answers on page 479.

16

Speculations About the Past

UNSOLVED MYSTERIES

OUTCOMES
- Speculate about past events, expressing possible or probable conclusions
- Draw conclusions based on the information in an article about archaeology
- Identify key details in a conversation and draw conclusions
- Discuss ancient objects and historical facts, and speculate about them
- Write about an unsolved mystery

STEP 1   GRAMMAR IN CONTEXT

BEFORE YOU READ

Look at the photo. Discuss the questions.

1. When and where do you think the man lived?
2. Why is he called the Iceman?
3. What was his occupation?

READ

▶ 16|01   Read this article about an ancient mystery.

The Iceman

On September 19, 1991, two German tourists were hiking in the Alps between Austria and Italy when they discovered a corpse[1] half buried in the ice. They assumed the body must have belonged to a mountain climber who had recently died as the result of an accident. They couldn't have imagined the truth. The body belonged to a man who had lived more than 5,000 years ago. Not only that, he might have been the victim of a brutal murder!

Who was he? What was he doing in that remote[2] location? How did he die? In the decades since this discovery, scientists have been trying to answer these questions. The ice preserved the body amazingly well. In fact, it is the oldest intact[3] human body ever found. As a result, scientists from all over the world have X-rayed[4] and examined him. The Iceman, as he is called, has become the subject of much speculation.

Found in the ice, alongside the Iceman, were many objects. He had weapons—a copper axe,[5] a knife, a bow and arrows. Some of his clothing also survived—snowshoes, a coat, a belt, leggings, a cap. He also had a backpack and a bag, which contained some tools and dried mushrooms. These objects provide clues to the man himself and to what might have happened to him. The axe, for example, was very valuable, and it indicates that the Iceman may have been a very important and wealthy person in his community.

---

1 *corpse:* a dead body
2 *remote:* far away
3 *intact:* not damaged
4 *have X-rayed:* have taken photographs that use radiation to go through solid objects in order to see the inside of the body
5 *axe:* a tool with a heavy metal blade on a long handle, used for cutting wood

At first, scientists believed that the Iceman must have died accidently during a winter storm. However, in 2001, X-rays told another story. There was an arrowhead[6] buried in the Iceman's left shoulder. The new theory was that he was the victim of a violent attack and must have bled to death as a result of this wound. Later examination discovered wounds to other parts of his body, including his head. This led to the speculation that he may have died from a head injury. Someone could have followed him up the mountain and attacked him while he was trying to run away.

Then, in 2009, scientists discovered another clue to the mystery of the Iceman's death. A more powerful X-ray (a CT scan) showed a very full stomach. The Iceman had eaten a big meal just before his death—not the behavior of someone trying to run for his life. This led investigators to believe that the killer couldn't have been a stranger to the Iceman. He had to have known him.

Could the Iceman have fallen and hit his head after the shot from the arrow, or did an attacker hit him over the head with a rock? Why were many of his arrows unfinished and not ready to use? Why didn't his attacker take the valuable axe? Theories about the Iceman's life and death have changed a lot over time as a result of advances in medical technology. And although much has been learned about him, there are still more secrets to learn from this amazing man, frozen in time for more than 5,000 years.

---

6 *arrowhead:* the pointed piece at the end of an arrow, which is used as a weapon along with a bow

Age at Time of Death:
about forty-five years old
Age at Time of Discovery:
more than 5,000 years old
Height: 5'5" (1.65 meters)
Weight: 110 lbs (50 kg)
Hair Color: brown
Eye Color: brown
Cause of Death: head wound? arrow shot?

Re-creation of the Iceman

AFTER YOU READ

A VOCABULARY Complete the sentences with the words from the box.

assume	decade	indicate	preserve	speculation	victim

1. I _____ you've heard of him. He's very famous.

2. There is a lot of _____ about the cause of his death.

3. One theory about his death is that he was a murder _____.

4. What did the X-ray _____? Did he have any broken bones?

5. At first, detectives didn't discover the murder weapon. It took more than a(n) _____ before it was located.

6. How did scientists _____ the body after they discovered it?

B COMPREHENSION Which of the following statements are *Probably True* or *Possibly True*?

	Probably True	Possibly True
1. The Iceman had been an important man in his community.	☐	☐
2. He bled to death because of the arrow wound.	☐	☐
3. Someone followed him up the mountain.	☐	☐
4. The Iceman knew his killer.	☐	☐
5. The Iceman died from a head injury.	☐	☐

C DISCUSSION Work with a partner. Compare your answers in B. Why did you check *Probably True* or *Possibly True*?

SPECULATIONS ABOUT THE PAST: *MAY HAVE, MIGHT HAVE, COULD HAVE, MUST HAVE, HAD TO HAVE*

Statements

Subject	Modal/*Had to*	Have	Past Participle	
He	**may (not)** **might (not)** **could (not)** **must (not)** **had to**	**have**	**been**	a very important man.

Contractions

may have	=	**may've**
might have	=	**might've**
could have	=	**could've**
must have	=	**must've**
could not	=	**couldn't**

Note: We usually do not contract *may not have*, *might not have*, or *must not have*.

Questions

Do/Be	Subject	Verb	
Did	he	**know**	his killer?
Was			alone?

Short Answers

Subject	Modal/*Had to*	Have	Been
He	**may (not)** **might (not)** **could (not)**	**have.**	
	must (not) **had to**	**have**	**been.**

Yes/No Questions: *Could*

Could	Subject	Have	Past Participle	
Could	he	**have**	**known**	his killer?
			been	alone?

Short Answers

Subject	Modal/*Had to*	Have	Been
He	**may (not)** **might (not)** **could (not)**	**have.**	
	must (not) **had to**	**have**	**been.**

Wh- Questions: *Could*

Wh- Word	Could	Have	Past Participle	
Who	**could**	**have**	**killed**	him?
What			**happened**	to him?

GRAMMAR NOTES

1 Speculations About the Past with Possible Conclusions

Use *may have*, *might have*, and *could have* + **past participle** to speculate about a fact in the past when you are **unsure** about your conclusions. Your conclusions are **possible**, not certain.

	The Iceman had a knife with him. *(fact)*
• *may (not) have*	He **may have been** a hunter.
• *might (not) have*	He **might not have felt** safe in the mountains.
• *could have*	He **could have expected** trouble.

2 Speculations About the Past with Probable Conclusions

Use *must have*, *had to have*, and *couldn't have* + **past participle** to speculate about a fact in the past when you are **almost certain** about your conclusions. Your conclusions are **probable**.

	The arrow wasn't in the Iceman's back. *(fact)*
• *must have*	Someone **must have removed** it.
• *must not have*	He **must not have wanted** to leave evidence.
• *had to have*	Someone **had to have taken** it out.
Use *couldn't have* to express **impossibility**.	He **couldn't have survived** the injury.
USAGE NOTE We often use *couldn't have* to express a feeling of disbelief.	He **couldn't have been** a farmer. His hands were much too soft.

3 Questions

Questions about past possibility almost always use *could have* + **past participle**.	**Could** the killer **have followed** him up the mountain?
USAGE NOTE *May have* and *might have* + **past participle** are not very common in questions, and they sound very formal and academic.	**Could** he **have known** his killer? *(common)* **Might** he **have known** his killer? *(not common)*

4 Short Answers

There are two ways to give short answers to questions about past possibility.

In **short answers** to questions about past possibility, use:	
• **modal** + *have been* when the questions include a form of *be*	A: *Were* the hikers surprised to discover the Iceman? B: They **must have *been***. They certainly didn't expect to find a corpse on the mountain.
• **modal** + *have* when the questions do not include a form of *be*	A: **Did** they **notify** the police? B: They **must have**. The police came the next day.

PRONUNCIATION NOTE

Pronunciation of *Could(n't) have*, *May have*, and *Might have*

In **informal conversation**, we often pronounce *could have*, *may have*, and *might have* as "could of," "may of," and "might of." We often pronounce *couldn't have* as "couldn't of."	A: This **could have** been a tool.
	    (could of)
	
	 B: Or, it **may have** been a weapon.
	    (may of)
	
	 A: That's true. It **might have** been a knife.
	    (might of)
	
	 B: It **couldn't have** been a weapon. It's not sharp.
	    (couldn't of)

Remember that you can also pronounce *could have* "coulda" and *might have* "mighta."	A: It **could have** been a tool.
	    (coulda)
	
	 B: It **might have** been a knife.
	    (mighta)

REFERENCE NOTE

Could have and *might have* are also used for **past advisability**, see Unit 15 on page 240.

STEP 3   FOCUSED PRACTICE

EXERCISE 1   DISCOVER THE GRAMMAR

GRAMMAR NOTES 1–2   Match the facts with the speculations.

Facts about the Iceman	Speculations
_h_ **1.** The Iceman had a knife with him.	**a.** He must have expected cold weather.
_e_ **2.** His hands were very soft.	**b.** He might have fallen.
_a_ **3.** He had warm clothes with him.	**c.** He may have been rich.
_d_ **4.** His legs were strong and powerful.	**d.** He had to have walked a lot.
_c_ **5.** His axe was very valuable.	**e.** He couldn't have been a farmer.
_g_ **6.** His stomach was full.	**f.** It could have come from an animal.
_b_ **7.** Some of his bones were broken.	**g.** He must have eaten right before he died.
_f_ **8.** There was blood on his coat.	**h.** He could have been a hunter.

EXERCISE 2 AFFIRMATIVE AND NEGATIVE STATEMENTS

GRAMMAR NOTES 1–2 Read more about the Iceman. Complete the sentences with the correct form of the words in parentheses. Choose between affirmative and negative.

The Iceman and His Possessions

Just like the Iceman's body tells us a lot about his life and death, his clothing and other possessions reveal a lot about him.

The Axe: This copper axe is very valuable. From it, we learn that the Iceman

_____ *must have been* _____ a very important member of his
      1. (must / be)

community. It is even possible that he __ might have been __
      2. (might / be)

a community leader. If so, his death __ could have happened __
      3. (could / happen)

for political reasons. Someone __ might have wanted __ to take
      4. (might / want)

his place as a leader. One of the most interesting facts about the axe, of

course, is that the killer didn't remove it from the scene of the murder. There

has been much speculation about the reason for this. The most believable

answer is that the killer __ must not have wanted __ people to see
      5. (must / want)

him with it. People __ could have identified __ the axe as
      6. (could / identify)

belonging to the Iceman and that __ might have resulted __ in
      7. (might / result)

some kind of punishment.

Re-creation of the Iceman's axe

The Bow and Arrows: The bow and some of the arrows were unfinished. The reason for this is still

not clear, and we may never know the answer. But, like the axe, they tell us a lot. The killer didn't

take them with him. He __ must have worried __ that these items could identify him.
      8. (must / worry)

The Shoes: The construction of the shoes is very complicated. They use three kinds of material—

grass, animal skins, and some kind of cord. They were also waterproof. Because of their complicated

and detailed design, some people think the Iceman __ could not have maked __ them
      9. (could / make)

himself. They believe that there __ must have been __ professional shoemakers in
      10. (must / be)

his community that made shoes for the community members.

The Mushrooms: These were in the bag that the Iceman __ may have worn __
      11. (may / wear)

around his waist. People probably used them as medicine. The fact that the Iceman had dried

mushrooms with him indicates that he __ might have been __ sick.
      12. (might / be)

EXERCISE 3 QUESTIONS AND SHORT ANSWERS

GRAMMAR NOTES 3–4 **A reporter is interviewing an archaeologist for a magazine article. Complete the interview questions and short answers.**

Q: The food in his stomach, from different locations, shows that before his death high in the Alps,

the Iceman went up the mountain, then walked down to the valley below, and then climbed up

the mountain again. This had to have been a very long and difficult walk. What

_____*could have been*_____ the reason for this strange behavior? ___*Could*___ he
       1. (could be)

_____*have thought*_____ that someone was following him?
     2. (could / think)

A: He _____*might have*_____. Some people think that he probably felt that his life was in
     3. (might)

danger, and he was trying to escape.

Q: What did the Iceman do? At that time in history, people were just beginning to farm.

_____ he _____ a farmer?
           4. (could / be)

A: No, he _____. His hands were much too soft. They were definitely not
      5. (could)

the hands of a farmer working the land.

Q: Well, then. _____ he _____ a hunter?
          6. (could / be)

A: He _____. That's a real possibility. Or he might've been a shepherd.
     7. (could)

Climbing up and down the mountains with his sheep could explain why his legs were so strong.

Q: The Iceman's body is covered with markings that look like tattoos. What _____ they

_____?
     8. (could / mean)

A: No one knows for sure, but they might have been part of a medical procedure—something like

the ancient Chinese art of acupuncture, which uses needles to relieve pain.

Q: There has been a lot of speculation about why the killer left the valuable axe at the scene of the

crime. But what about the arrow shaft? Why didn't he take that, too? _____ it

_____ the killer?
     9. (could / identify)

A: Yes, it _____. Unlike the axe, the arrow belonged to the killer, so that
     10. (could)

might have identified him.

Q: On his last day, _____ the Iceman _____ that someone had
          11. (could / know)

followed him up the mountain?

A: No, he _____. A person running for his life doesn't stop and eat a big
     12. (must)

meal. However, some people disagree with this interpretation.

EXERCISE 4   SPECULATIONS ABOUT THE PAST

GRAMMAR NOTES 1–2   Read about these other puzzling events. Then rewrite the answers to the questions about their causes. Substitute a modal phrase for the underlined words. Use the modals and similar expressions in parentheses.

Dinosaurs existed on the Earth for about 135 million years. Then, about 65 million years ago, these giant reptiles all died in a short period of time. What could have caused the dinosaurs to become extinct?

1. It's likely that the Earth became colder. (must)

   The Earth must have become colder.

2. Probably, dinosaurs didn't survive the cold. (must not)

   Dinosaurs must not survived the cold

3. It's been suggested that the dinosaurs became extinct because a huge meteor hit the Earth. (might)

   The dinosaurs might became extinct because a huge meteor hit the Earth.

In 1924, Albert Ostman went camping alone in Canada. Later, he reported that he had an encounter with a Bigfoot (a large, hairy creature that looks human). He said the Bigfoot had kidnapped him and taken him home, where the Bigfoot family treated him like a pet. Ostman escaped after several days. What do you think happened? Could a Bigfoot really have kidnapped Ostman?

4. A Bigfoot didn't kidnap Albert Ostman—that's impossible. (couldn't)

   A Bigfood couldn't have kidpped Albert Ostman.

5. Ostman probably saw a bear. (must)

   Ostman must have seen a bear

6. It's possible that Ostman dreamed about a Bigfoot. (could)

   Ostman could have dreamed about Bigfoot.

7. Some people think that he made up the story. (might)

   he might have made up the story

In 1932, a man was taking a walk around Scotland's beautiful Loch Ness. Suddenly, a couple hundred feet from shore, the water bubbled up and a huge monster appeared. The man took a photo. When it was developed, the picture showed something with a long neck and a small head. Since then, many people have reported similar sightings. What do you think? Did the man really see the Loch Ness monster?

8. Most likely the man changed the photo. (have to)

___The man had to have changed the photo___

9. Perhaps the man saw a large fish. (might)

___The man might have seen a large fish___

10. It's possible that the man saw a dead tree trunk. (may)

___The man may have seen a dead tree trunk___

11. It's impossible that a dinosaur was in the lake. (couldn't)

___A dinosaur couldn't have been in the lake___

EXERCISE 5 *COULD'VE, COULDN'T HAVE, MAY'VE, AND MIGHT'VE*

🔘 16|03 PRONUNCIATION NOTE **Listen to the short conversations. Write the contracted forms of the past modals you hear.**

1. A: What was that used for?

B: I'm not sure. It ___could've___ been a spoon.

2. A: I called Rahul yesterday afternoon, but there was no answer.

B: Oh. He ___could've___ gone to the museum.

3. A: Is Sara still on Easter Island?

B: I'm not sure. She ___might've___ left already.

4. A: I think I saw John yesterday.

B: You ___couldn't have___ seen him. He's in Peru.

5. A: Do you agree with the author's conclusion?

B: I don't know. He ___may've___ been wrong.

6. A: Alice got an A on her archaeology test.

B: She ___might've___ been happy.

7. A: Could they have sailed that far in small boats?

B: Sure they ___could've___. They were expert sailors.

EXERCISE 6 EDITING

GRAMMAR NOTES 1–3 Read this student's essay about Easter Island. There are ten mistakes in the use of modals and similar expressions. The first mistake is already corrected. Find and correct nine more.

Rapa Nui

Rapa Nui (Easter Island) is a tiny island in the middle of the Pacific. To get there, the first settlers had to ~~had~~ *have* traveled more than 1,000 miles (1,609 kilometers) in open boats. Some scientists believed only the Polynesians of the Pacific Islands could have make the journey. Others thought that Polynesians couldn't have carved the huge stone statues on Rapa Nui. They speculated that Mayans or Egyptians maybe have traveled there. (Some people even said that space aliens might helped!) Finally, a University of Oslo scientist was able to study the DNA from ancient skeletons. Professor Erika Halberg announced, "These people has to have been the descendants[1] of Polynesians."

We now know that the islanders built the statues, but we have also learned that they must had solved even more difficult problems. The first settlers came sometime between the years 400 and 700. At first, Rapa Nui must be a paradise with its fishing, forests, and good soil. Their society may have grown too fast for the small island, however. Botanical studies show that by the 1600s, they had cut down the last tree. The soil must not have washed away, so they couldn't farm. And with no wood to build boats, they couldn't have able to fish. For a period of time, people starved and fought violently, but when the Dutch discovered Rapa Nui in 1722, they found a peaceful, healthy population growing fields of vegetables. How the islanders could have learned in this short period of time to live peacefully with so few resources? For our troubled world today, this might be the most important "mystery of Easter Island."

---

1 *descendants:* people related to people who lived a long time ago

EXERCISE 7 LISTENING

🔘16|04 **A** Some archaeology students are speculating about objects they have found at various sites. Read the statements. Then listen to the conversations. Listen again and check (✓) *True* or *False* for each statement. Correct the false statements.

	True	False
1. The woman thinks that people might have used the tool for ~~building~~ *cutting* things.	☐	☑
2. The man thinks people could have worn this object around their necks.	☐	☐
3. The woman thinks this object might have been a hole for shoelaces.	☐	☐
4. The man thinks this piece came from the bottom of an object.	☐	☐
5. The woman thinks that the people who made this object were very smart.	☐	☐
6. The man thinks this object is a rock.	☐	☐

B Work with a partner. Discuss your answers in A.

EXAMPLE: A: The answer to number 1 is *False*.
   B: Right. The woman thinks people might have used the tool for cutting high grass.
   A: So, what did you put for number 2?

🔘16|04 **C** Look at the pictures. Listen again to the conversations. Then work with your partner. Together, decide which objects the people are talking about and match the pictures with the correct conversation.

EXAMPLE: A: In the first conversation, I think they are discussing the object in picture *f* because the woman says it might have been a tool.
   B: Hmm. But the item in *c* might have been a tool, too.
   A: That's true, but the woman says it looks like a knife. The object in picture *f* is the only one that looks like a knife. The item in *c* couldn't have been a knife.
   B: Good point, and then she says . . .

a. _____   b. _____   c. _____   d. _____   e. _____   f. _/_

EXERCISE 8 WHAT COULD THEY HAVE USED THEM FOR?

PICTURE DISCUSSION Work in a group. Look at the objects that archaeologists have found in different places. Speculate on what they are and how people might have used them. Share your ideas with the rest of the class. The answers are on page 265.

1. Archaeologists found this object in the sleeping area of an ancient Chinese house. It's about the size of a basketball.

    EXAMPLE: A: I think people might have used this as a footstool. It's the right size.
    B: You're right. The floor must have gotten very cold at night.
    C: People could have rested their feet on this.

2. Archaeologists found this in Turkey. People in many places have used objects like this on their clothing for thousands of years. This one is about 3,000 years old. It's the size of a small cell phone.

3. These objects were used by ancient Egyptians. The handles are each about the length of a toothbrush.

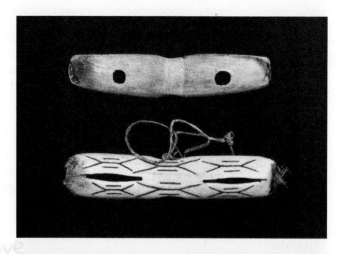

4. People in the Arctic started using these around 2,000 years ago. They used them when they were hunting or traveling. They are small enough to put in your pocket.

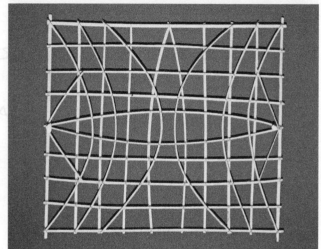

5. Polynesian people used these when they traveled. They made them with sticks, coconut fiber, and seashells. This one is about 1 foot (30 centimeters) wide and 1 foot long.

EXERCISE 9 THE ICEMAN REVISITED

DISCUSSION **Work in a group. Speculate on the reasons for these facts about the Iceman.**

1. Before he died, the Iceman climbed up the mountain, then went down, and then climbed up again. Why?

   EXAMPLE: A: He may have left something important below and needed to get it.
   B: That's possible. It might have been too heavy to carry everything up the mountain at one time.
   C: Or, he might have thought someone was following him and he was trying to escape him.

2. He was in a very remote area of the mountains. What was he doing there?

3. He had a bow and arrows, but they were unusable. Why didn't he finish them?

4. He had several broken bones. Why?

5. No one discovered his body for more than 5,000 years. Why not?

Answers to Exercise 8: 1. a pillow; **2.** a large pin used to hold clothing together; **3.** a razor and a mirror for shaving; **4.** eye protection against bright light reflected from snow and ice; **5.** a chart showing islands and wave patterns in the ocean

FROM GRAMMAR TO WRITING

A BEFORE YOU WRITE Read the paragraph about an unsolved mystery. What do you think happened? Work with a partner. Speculate and take notes.

In 2004, archaeologists discovered a jar with seven very well-made leather shoes. Someone had hidden them in a small space between two walls in the ancient Egyptian temple in Luxor. The shoes were more than 2,000 years old and in very good condition. Two pairs belonged to children. One pair belonged to an adult. The seventh shoe belonged to an adult. Who hid the shoes and why? Why were there only seven? Why didn't anyone return for them?

Very Certain: _____

Possible: _____

Impossible: _____

B WRITE Use your notes in A to write a second paragraph about the shoes. Use modals and your speculations. Try to avoid the mistakes in the chart.

EXAMPLE: The shoes present a mystery. Who were the owners and what could have happened to them? From the quality of the shoes, we can speculate that . . .

Common Mistakes in Using Modals of Speculations About the Past

Use **must have** when you are almost certain about your conclusion. Do not use *may have*, *might have*, or *could have*.	They **must have been** shocked when they learned the age of the Iceman. It's hard to believe! NOT They ~~might have been~~ shocked . . .
Use **may not have**, **might not have**, and **must not have** when you think that something is not possible. Do not use *didn't have to have*.	The police **may not have realized** the importance of the Iceman. How could they have known? NOT The police ~~didn't have to have realized~~ . . .
Use **couldn't have** when you think something is impossible. Do not use *may not have* or *might not have*.	You **couldn't have seen** her. She's away. NOT You ~~might not have seen~~ her. . . .

C CHECK YOUR WORK Read your paragraph. Underline the modals or similar expressions that speculate about the past. Use the Editing Checklist to check your work.

Editing Checklist

Did you use . . . ?

☐ *may have*, *might have*, and *could have* for things in the past you are unsure about

☐ *must have* and *had to have* for things in the past you are almost certain about

☐ *couldn't have* to show disbelief or impossibility

☐ *could have* for questions about past possibility

D REVISE YOUR WORK Read your paragraph again. Can you improve your writing? Make changes if necessary.

UNIT 16 **REVIEW**

Test yourself on the grammar of the unit.

A Circle the correct words to complete the sentences.

1. Mayans built large cities. They (must) / must not have had an advanced civilization.

2. Their civilization disappeared. It might not / (might not have rained) enough to grow crops.

3. Look at this bowl. They could of / (have) used this to serve food.

4. You must have (taken) / took a hundred photos today.

5. Trish didn't come on the tour. She (may) / couldn't have been sick. She wasn't feeling well.

6. I can't find my wallet. I could had / (have) dropped it in the hotel gift shop.

7. Carla must / (couldn't) have gotten our postcard. We just mailed it yesterday.

B Rewrite the sentences in parentheses using past modals.

1. Dan didn't call me back yesterday. He _____.
   (Maybe he didn't get my message.)

2. Selina got a C on the test. She _____.
   (It's almost certain that she didn't study.)

3. Why didn't Fahad come to dinner? He _____.
   (It's not possible that he forgot our date.)

4. Myra _____. I saw a woman there who looked like her.
   (It's possible that Myra was at the movies.)

5. The server didn't bring our dessert. She _____.
   (She probably forgot.)

6. Jan didn't say hello to me today. He _____.
   (It's almost certain that he didn't see me.)

C Find and correct seven mistakes.

Why did the Aztecs build their capital city in the middle of a lake? Could they _had_ wanted
        have

the protection of the water? They might have been. Or the location may _has_ helped them
                                                                        have

to control nearby societies. At first, it must have _being_ an awful place, full of mosquitoes
                                                      been

and fog. But it must _no_ have been a bad idea—the island city became the center of a very
                     not

powerful empire. To succeed, the Aztecs had to have _became_ fantastic engineers quite
                                                must *become*
                                                              ed

quickly. When the Spanish arrived, they couldn't have expect the amazing palaces, floating

gardens, and well-built canals. They must have been astounded.

Now check your answers on page 479.

The Passive

PART 7

OUTCOMES

- Recognize when to use the passive and when to mention the agent
- Use the passive with different tenses
- Identify specific information in a magazine article about geography
- Identify key details in an academic lecture
- Discuss and interpret international proverbs
- Discuss products found in geographical locations
- Write an essay about a familiar country

OUTCOMES

- Express certainty, ability, possibility, impossibility, advice, or necessity with passive modals and similar expressions
- Identify key information in a social science article
- Identify details in a science-fiction movie dialog
- Discuss rules for group living in close quarters
- Discuss pros and cons of investing money in space projects
- Write about the ideal school for diplomacy

OUTCOMES

- Describe services that people have done for them by others, using the passive causative
- Identify key information in an article about beauty
- Identify details in a conversation about tasks needing to be done
- Discuss preparations for a trip to another country
- Discuss steps people from different cultures take to improve their appearance
- Write about preparations for an upcoming event

UNIT 17

The Passive: Overview
GEOGRAPHY

OUTCOMES
- Recognize when to use the passive and when to mention the agent
- Use the passive with different tenses
- Identify specific information in a magazine article about geography
- Identify key details in an academic lecture
- Discuss and interpret international proverbs
- Discuss products found in geographical locations
- Write an essay about a familiar country

STEP 1   GRAMMAR IN CONTEXT

BEFORE YOU READ

Look at the title of the article and at the photo. Discuss the questions.

1. What is geography?

2. Have you ever studied geography in school? If yes, did you enjoy it?

3. Is geography an important subject? Why or why not?

READ

17|01   Read this article about *National Geographic*, a famous magazine.

Geography: The Best Subject on Earth

Geography is the study of the Earth and its people. It sounds exciting, doesn't it? Yet for decades, students yawned just hearing the word. They were forced to memorize the names of capital cities, important rivers and mountains, and natural resources. They were taught where places were and what was produced there. But they weren't shown how our world looks and feels.

And then came *National Geographic*. From the Amazon rain forest to the Sahara Desert, and from Baalbek to Great Zimbabwe, the natural

and human-made wonders[1] of our world have now been brought to life by its fascinating reporting and beautiful photographs, such as the one on page 270, which was taken by photojournalist[2] Reza Deghati, of a man planting a palm tree in Saudi Arabia.

The National Geographic Society was formed in Washington, D.C., in 1888 by a group of professionals including geographers, explorers, teachers, and mapmakers. Nine months later, the first *National Geographic* magazine was published so that the Society could fulfill its mission: to spread knowledge of and respect for the world, its resources, and its inhabitants.

In 1995, the first foreign-language edition of *National Geographic* was published in Japan. Today, the magazine is printed in English and more than forty local languages and sold all over the world. *National Geographic* also puts out a number of special publications. *National Geographic Explorer*, for example, has been created for classrooms. Other publications feature travel and adventure. *National Geographic* TV programs are watched in over 440 million homes in more than 170 countries, and digital editions are read by hundreds of thousands of people a month.

The study of geography has come a very long way since 1888. The Society's mission has been fulfilled. In fact, it has even been extended to include worlds beyond Earth. From the deep seas to deep space, geography has never been more exciting.

---

1 *wonders:* things that make you feel surprise and admiration
2 *photojournalist:* someone who takes photos and writes reports for newspapers and magazines

AFTER YOU READ

Ⓐ VOCABULARY **Match the words with their definitions.**

_____ **1. mission**

_____ **2. respect**

_____ **3. publication**

_____ **4. inhabitant**

_____ **5. explorer**

_____ **6. edition**

a. a book or magazine sold to the public

b. someone who travels for the purpose of discovery

c. an important purpose

d. the total number of copies of a magazine or book printed at the same time

e. one of the people living in a particular place

f. an attitude that shows you think someone or something is valuable or important

Ⓑ COMPREHENSION **Answer the questions.**

1. Who memorized names of capital cities? _____

2. What brought the wonders of our world to life? _____

3. Who took the photo of the Saudi man planting a palm tree? _____

4. Who formed the National Geographic Society? _____

5. Who reads digital editions of *National Geographic*? _____

6. How has the Society's mission changed? _____

Ⓒ DISCUSSION **Work with a partner. Compare your answers in B. Do you agree?**

THE PASSIVE

Active	Passive
Millions of people **buy** it.	It **is bought** by millions of people.
Someone **published** it in 1888.	It **was published** in 1888.
They **have reached** their goal.	Their goal **has been reached**.

Passive Statements

Subject	Be (not)	Past Participle	(By + Object)	
It	**is (not)**	**bought**	**by** millions of people.	
It	**was (not)**	**published**		in 1888.
Their goal	**has (not) been**	**reached**.		

Yes/No Questions

Be/Have	Subject	(Been +) Past Participle	
Is **Was**	it	**sold**	in Japan?
Has		**been sold**	

Short Answers

Affirmative				Negative		
Yes,	it	**is.** **was.** **has (been).**		**No,**	it	**isn't.** **wasn't.** **hasn't (been).**

Wh- Questions

Wh- Word	Be/Have	Subject	(Been +) Past Participle
Where	**is** **was**	it	**sold?**
	has		**been sold?**

GRAMMAR NOTES

1 Active and Passive Sentences

Active and **passive** sentences often have similar meanings, but a **different focus**.

Active sentences focus on the **agent** (the person or thing doing the action).	**Millions of people** *read* the magazine. *(The focus is on the people.)*
Passive sentences focus on the **object** (the person or thing receiving the action).	**The magazine** *is read* by millions of people. *(The focus is on the magazine.)*

2 Forms of the Passive

Form the passive with *be* + **past participle**.

• simple present	It *is printed* in more than forty languages.
• simple past	It *was published* for the first time in 1888.
• present perfect	They *have been* sold all over the world.
Only **transitive verbs** (verbs that have objects) have passive forms.	TRANSITIVE VERB + OBJECT Ed Bly **wrote** that article. That article **was written** by Ed Bly. *(passive form)*
BE CAREFUL! **Intransitive verbs** do not have passive forms.	INTRANSITIVE VERB It **arrived** on Monday. **NOT** It was arrived on Monday. *(no passive form)*

3 Uses of the Passive

Use the passive when the **agent** (the person or thing doing the action) is **unknown or not important**.	The magazine **was started** in 1888. *(I don't know who started it.)* The magazine **is sold** online. *(It is not important who sells it.)*
Use the passive when you want to **avoid mentioning** the agent.	Some mistakes **were made** in that article. *(I know who made the mistakes, but I don't want to blame the person.)*

4 The Passive with *By* + Agent

Use the **passive** with *by* if you mention the agent.

Only mention the agent when it is **important** information.	The photographs in this article are wonderful. They **were taken** *by a professional*. One of the first cameras **was invented** *by Alexander Wolcott*.
BE CAREFUL! In most cases, you do not need to mention an agent in passive sentences. Do not include an agent if the information is not necessary.	Ed Bly took a really great photo. It **was taken** last February. **NOT** Ed Bly took a really great photo. It was taken last February by him.

EXERCISE 1   DISCOVER THE GRAMMAR

GRAMMAR NOTES 1–4   Read the statements. Check (✓) *Active* or *Passive*.

	Active	Passive
1. The first *National Geographic* magazine was published in October 1888.	☐	✓
2. Today, millions of people read the magazine.	✓	☐
3. The magazine is translated from English into forty other languages.	☐	✓
4. My cousin reads the Russian edition.	✓	☐
5. Some of the articles are written by famous writers.	☐	✓
6. *Young Explorer*, another publication, is written for kids.	☐	✓
7. The publication is known for its wonderful photography.	☐	✓
8. A *National Geographic* photographer took the first underwater color photos.	✓	☐
9. Photographers are sent all over the world.	☐	✓
10. The articles show a lot of respect for nature.	✓	☐
11. That picture was taken by Reza Deghati.	☐	✓
12. *National Geographic* is sold at newsstands.	☐	✓

EXERCISE 2   ACTIVE OR PASSIVE

GRAMMAR NOTES 1–4   The chart shows some of the forty language editions that *National Geographic* publishes. Use the chart to complete the sentences. Some sentences will be active; some will be passive.

Language	Number of Speakers*
Arabic	240
Chinese (all varieties)	1,200
English	340
Japanese	130
Korean	77
Russian	110
Spanish	410
Turkish	71

*first-language speakers in millions

1. Spanish *is spoken by 410 million people* .

2. Around 110 million people *speak Russian* .

3. Arabic _is spoken by 240 million people_ .

4. _____1200 million people speak_____ Chinese.

5. _____Korean is spoken_____ by 77 million people.
6. _____Japanese is spoken_____ 130 million people.
7. Approximately 340 million people _____speak English_____.
8. _____Turkish is spoken by_____ 71 million people.

EXERCISE 3   *WH-* QUESTIONS AND STATEMENTS

A GRAMMAR NOTE 2   Jill Jones, a magazine journalist, is preparing for a trip to Bolivia.
Look at the online travel quiz she is going to take. Complete the questions with the correct
form of the verbs in parentheses. Then take the quiz. Guess the answers!

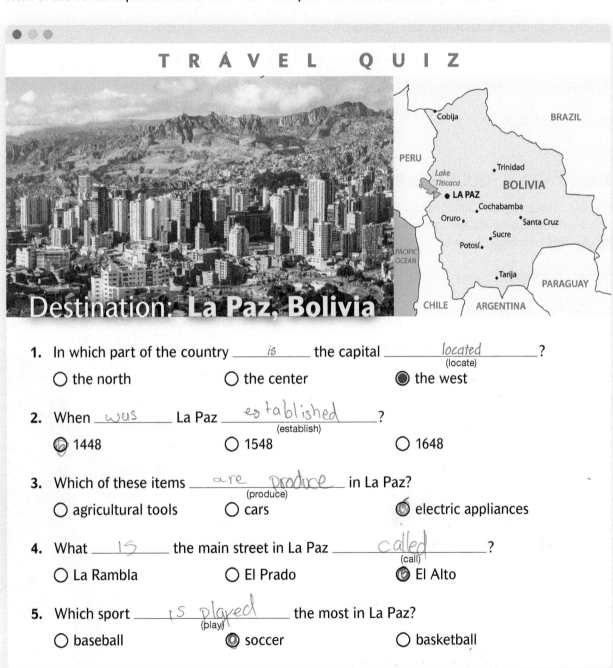

TRAVEL QUIZ

Destination: La Paz, Bolivia

1. In which part of the country ___is___ the capital ___located___?
   (locate)
   ○ the north   ○ the center   ● the west

2. When ___was___ La Paz ___established___?
   (establish)
   ◉ 1448   ○ 1548   ○ 1648

3. Which of these items ___are produce___ in La Paz?
   (produce)
   ○ agricultural tools ○ cars   ◉ electric appliances

4. What ___is___ the main street in La Paz ___called___?
   (call)
   ○ La Rambla   ○ El Prado   ◉ El Alto

5. Which sport ___is played___ the most in La Paz?
   (play)
   ○ baseball   ◉ soccer   ○ basketball

B Complete the sentences with the correct form of the verbs in parentheses. The sentences contain the answers to the questions in A. Did you guess the answers correctly?

1. The highest capital in the world, La Paz _____was built_____ in a canyon in the west of the
(build)
   country. It _'s___surround___ by mountains, such as the beautiful Illimani mountain,
   (surround)
   which ___is cover___ by snow all year.
   (cover)

2. The city _was__stablished_ in 1548 by Spanish settlers.
   (establish)

3. Agricultural tools along with food and tobacco products, clothing, and building materials
   ___are made___ in the capital.
   (make)

4. The main street's name changes in different parts of the city, but the tree-lined section in
   downtown La Paz __is___know__ as El Prado.
   (know)

5. Soccer is the most popular sport. The city has several soccer teams. The Strongest, which
   __was form___ in 1908, has won many tournaments.
   (form)

EXERCISE 4 QUESTIONS, STATEMENTS, AND SHORT ANSWERS

A GRAMMAR NOTE 2 Jill Jones is interviewing a Bolivian cultural attaché for an article she's writing. Complete her interview with the passive form of the correct verbs from the boxes and with short answers.

grow	~~inhabit~~	spell

JONES: Thanks for giving me some time today. Here's my first question: _____Was_____ the area
         first _____inhabited_____ by the Inca?
                        1.

ATTACHÉ: _____No, it wasn't_____. Long before the Inca, the Aymara
                  2.
         created a great civilization around Lake Titicaca. In fact, the
         Aymara still live in Bolivia.

JONES: Interesting. Now, let's talk about farming. I know potatoes are
         an important food crop[1] in the mountains of the Andes.
         ___is___ corn ___grown___ there as well?
                              3.

ATTACHÉ: __No__it__isn't__. The climate is too cold for corn. But
              4.
         quinoa grows well there.

JONES: Quinoa? ___is___ that ___Spelled___ with a *k*?
                                     5.

---
1 *crop:* a plant such as corn or wheat which is grown by a farmer

eat   mine[2]   use

ATTACHÉ: _No its not_ . You spell it with a *q—q-u-i-n-o-a*. Quinoa is a traditional
6.

grain, like corn and wheat in other places. It _has been eaten_ by the
7.

inhabitants of the Andes since ancient times. In fact, it's been a major source of food

for more than 5,000 years.

JONES: Now, everyone thinks of llamas when they think of Bolivia. What _are_ these

animals _used_ for?
8.

ATTACHÉ: Oh, for many things—clothing, meat, transportation. But they only do well high in

the Andes.

JONES: I see. And what about other resources? I know that tin is extremely important in

Bolivia. Where _is_ it _mined_ ?
9.

find   make   speak

ATTACHÉ: Well, the richest sources of tin _are found_ in the Andes.
10.

JONES: And how about the eastern part of the country? What resources are in that region?

ATTACHÉ: In the Oriente? Oil and natural gas.

JONES: OK. Let's talk about languages now. I know Spanish is the official language of Bolivia.

But, what other languages _are spoken_ in the country?
11.

ATTACHÉ: Actually, more people speak Native American languages than Spanish.

JONES: That's interesting. Now, I know scientists love Bolivia for its
wildlife. Are there still many jaguars there?

ATTACHÉ: Yes. In the last decades, conservation _has been made_ a
12.

top priority by our government. It's become their mission to

protect jaguars and other rare and beautiful animals. We must

show these animals respect, or we risk losing them.

JONES: Well, thank you very much for your time. I'll send you a copy of

our publication as soon as the article comes out.

▶17|02 **B** LISTEN AND CHECK **Listen to the interview and check your
answers in A.**

---

2 *mine:* to dig into the ground to get gold, coal, tin, and other natural resources

EXERCISE 5 AFFIRMATIVE AND NEGATIVE STATEMENTS

GRAMMAR NOTES 2–4 Read Jill Jones's article. Her editor has circled in red six mistakes in spelling or fact. Rewrite the correct sentences with information from Exercise 4. You will write two sentences for each item. The first sentence will show why the sentence is incorrect. The second sentence will give the correct information.

A Land of Contrasts
by Jill Jones

Visitors to Bolivia are amazed by the contrasts and charmed by the beauty of this South American country's landscapes—from the breathtaking Andes in the west to the tropical lowlands in the east.

Two-thirds of Bolivia's 10 million people are concentrated in the cool western highlands, or *altiplano*. Today, as in centuries past, corn and kuinoa are grown in the mountains. Llamas are raised only for transportation And tin, Bolivia's richest natural resource, is mined in the high Andes.

The Oriente, another name for the eastern lowlands, is mostly tropical. Rice is the major food crop there. Rubber, oil, and natural gas are also found in this region.

Bolivia is home to many fascinating forms of wildlife. The condor, for example, is still seen flying above the highest mountains. Boa constrictors, jaguars, and many other animals are found in the rain forests.

Hundreds of years before the Inca flourished, a great civilization was created on the shores of the Pacific, probably by ancestors of Bolivia's Aymara people. Their descendants still speak the Aymara language. Today, Native American languages are still widely spoken in Bolivia. Although Portuguese is spoken in the government, Quechua and Aymara are used more widely by the people. Traditional textiles are woven by hand. Music is played on reed pipes whose tone resembles the sound of the wind blowing over the high plains in the Andes.

Lake Titicaca

1. *Corn isn't grown in the mountains. Potatoes are grown there.*

2. _____

3. _____

4. _____

5. _____

6. _____

EXERCISE 6 INCLUDING OR DELETING THE AGENT

GRAMMAR NOTES 3–4 Read Ed Bly's soccer trivia column. Complete the information with the correct form of the verbs in the first set of parentheses. If the agent (in the second set of parentheses) is necessary, include it in your answer. If not, cross it out.

Soccer Trivia

- Soccer is the most popular sport in the world. It ___*is played by more than 20 million people*___.
  1. (play) (more than 20 million people)

- It ___*is called*___ football ___by people___ in 144 countries.
  2. (call)   ~~(people)~~

- Except for the goalie, players ___are not allowed___ to use their hands.
  3. (not allow) (the rules)

  Instead, the ball ___is controlled by the feet, the head, and the body___.
  4. (control) (the feet, the head, and the body)

- Soccer ___was not played___ very much in the United States until thirty years
  5. (not play) ~~(people)~~

  ago. Since then, the game _____.
  6. (make popular) (Pelé, Beckham, and other international stars)

- Forms of soccer ___have been played by different cultures___ for thousands of years.
  7. (play) (different cultures)

- A form of soccer ___it has been enjoyed___ in China 2,000 years ago.
  8. (enjoy) (Chinese people)

- It ___was banned by King Edward III of England___ in 1365—his archers spent
  9. (ban) (King Edward III of England)

  too much time playing and too little time practicing archery.

- Medieval games ___were played by players___ for entire days, over miles of territory.
  10. (play) (players)

- Every four years, the best soccer teams in the world compete in the World Cup tournament.

  This event ___it is organized by fifa___.
  11. (organize) (FIFA)

EXERCISE 7 EDITING

GRAMMAR NOTES 1–4 Read this short biography of photojournalist Reza Deghati. (He took the photo on page 270.) There are eight mistakes in the use of the passive. The first mistake is already corrected. Find and correct seven more.

Seeing the World

REZA DEGHATI ~~is~~ was born in Tabriz, Iran, in 1952. When he was only fourteen years old, he began teaching himself photography. At first, he took pictures of his own country—its people and its architecture. When he was twenty-five, he ~~was~~ decided to become a professional. During a demonstration, he was asked by a French news agency to take photos. He only shot one and a half rolls of film (instead of the usual twenty to forty), but his photos ~~was~~ were published in *Paris Match* (France), *Stern* (Germany), and *Newsweek* (U.S.A.).

Reza, as he is ~~knew~~ known professionally, has covered several wars, and he has be~~been~~ wounded on assignment.[1] Among all his assignments, the project dearest to his heart is photographing children, who he calls "the real victims of war." He has donated these photos to humanitarian organizations. Always concerned with the welfare of children, Reza has made it his life's mission to help them receive an education. His organization AINA ~~was~~ created, in part, to achieve this goal.

When he was interviewed ~~by an interviewer~~, Reza was asked to give advice to wannabe[2] photojournalists. He replied, "There is a curtain between the photographer and the subject unless the photographer is able to break through it. . . . Open your heart to people, so they know you care."

Today, Reza Deghati lives in Paris. His photos ~~is~~ are widely distributed in more than fifty countries around the world, and his work is published in *National Geographic* as well as many other internationally famous publications.

---

1 *wounded on assignment:* injured on the job
2 *wannabe:* (informal for want-to-be) a person who wants to become a member of a specific profession

EXERCISE 8 LISTENING

▶17|03 **A** Listen to a teacher talk about the country of Haiti. Then listen again and complete the student's notes.

Haiti

1. Officially, Haiti _____is called_____ the Republic of Haiti.

2. It ___is located___ on the island of Hispaniola, which it shares with the Dominican Republic.

3. Haiti ___is inhabited___ by more than 10.6 million people.

4. Both French and Haitian Creole ___are spoken___ in Haiti.

5. Haiti ___was___ really ___not discovered___ by Christopher Columbus.

6. In 1492, Haiti ___was havitated___ by the Taino people.

7. Haiti ___was ruled___ by Spain for more than 100 years, and then by France.

8. Vetiver, a plant, ___is used___ to make perfume, body creams, and soap.

9. Coffee, mangoes, nuts, corn, rice, and other crops ___are grown___ in Haiti.

10. Many of these crops ___are exported___ to other countries.

11. Haiti ___is visited___ by more than a million tourists each year.

12. Since 2012, several new hotels ___have been build___ in Haiti.

Present Perfect if you see the word since

Hispaniola

DOMINICAN REPUBLIC

HAITI

PORT-AU-PRINCE

SANTO DOMINGO

▶17|03 **B** Work with a partner. Listen again. What did you learn about Haiti? What, if anything, surprised you?

EXAMPLE: A: I didn't know that two languages are spoken in Haiti.

B: Me neither. I knew that French is spoken there, but I didn't know about Haitian Creole.

A: I was also surprised to find out that . . .

EXERCISE 9 QUOTABLE QUOTES

DISCUSSION   Work in a group. Read the proverbs from around the world. Choose three proverbs and discuss them. What do you think they mean? Are there proverbs from other cultures that mean the same thing?

1. Rome wasn't built in a day. (*English*)

    EXAMPLE: A: I think this means that big projects aren't finished quickly.
                B: Yes. They take a lot of time and you have to be patient.
                C: There's a proverb in French that means the same thing: "Paris wasn't built in a day."

2. He who was bitten by a snake avoids tall grass. (*Chinese*)

3. He ran away from the rain and was caught in a hailstorm. (*Turkish*)

4. Never promise a fish until it's caught. (*Irish*)

5. Write the bad things that are done to you in sand, but write the good things that happen to you on a piece of marble. (*Arab*)

6. Skillful sailors weren't made by smooth seas. (*Ethiopian*)

7. From one thing, ten things are known. (*Korean*)

8. What is brought by the wind will be carried away by the wind. (*Iranian*)

Rome, Italy

EXERCISE 10 THE PHILIPPINES

Ⓐ INFORMATION GAP Work with a partner. Student A will follow the instructions below. Student B will follow the instructions on page 487.

STUDENT A

- The Philippines consists of many islands and has many natural resources. Look at the map of Luzon and complete the chart. Write *Y* for *Yes* if Luzon has a particular resource and *N* for *No* if it does not.

- Student B has the map of Mindanao. Ask Student B questions about Mindanao and complete the chart for Mindanao.

    EXAMPLE: A: Is tobacco grown in Mindanao?
              B: No, it isn't.

- Student B doesn't have the map of Luzon. Answer Student B's questions about Luzon.

    EXAMPLE: B: Is tobacco grown in Luzon?
              A: Yes, it is. It's grown in the northern and central part of the island.

		MINDANAO	LUZON
G R O W	tobacco	N	Y
	corn		
	bananas		
	coffee		
	pineapples		
	sugar		
R A I S E	cattle		
	pigs		
M I N E	gold		
	manganese		
P R O D U C E	cotton		
	rubber		
	lumber		

Ⓑ When you are finished, compare the charts. Are they the same?

EXERCISE 11 TRIVIA QUIZ

A GAME *National Geographic Explorer* often has games and puzzles. Work with a partner. Complete this quiz. Then compare answers with your classmates. The answers are at the bottom of this page.

Do you know…?

1. Urdu is spoken in _____.
   a. Ethiopia　　　　　**b.** Pakistan　　　　　**c.** Uruguay

2. Air conditioning was invented in _____.
   a. 1902　　　　　**b.** 1950　　　　　**c.** 1980

3. The X-ray was invented by _____.
   a. Thomas Edison　　　　　**b.** Wilhelm Röntgen　　　　　**c.** Marie Curie

4. The Petronas Towers in Kuala Lumpur were designed by _____.
   a. Minoru Yamasaki　　　　　**b.** César Pelli　　　　　**c.** I. M. Pei

5. The 2016 Summer Olympics were held in _____.
   a. Brazil　　　　　**b.** Canada　　　　　**c.** Japan

6. An ocean route from Portugal to the East was discovered by Portuguese explorer _____.
   a. Hernán Cortés　　　　　**b.** Louis Jolliet　　　　　**c.** Vasco da Gama

7. A baby _____ is called a *cub*.
   a. cat　　　　　**b.** dog　　　　　**c.** jaguar

B Work with your partner. Make up your own quiz questions with the words in parentheses. Ask another pair to answer your questions.

1. _____ "Guernica" was painted _____ by _b_.
   (paint)
   a. _Monet_　　　　　**b.** _Picasso_　　　　　**c.** _El Greco_

2. _____ by _____.
   (invent)
   a. _____　　　　　**b.** _____　　　　　**c.** _____

3. _____ by _____.
   (compose)
   a. _____　　　　　**b.** _____　　　　　**c.** _____

4. _____ by _____.
   (write)
   a. _____　　　　　**b.** _____　　　　　**c.** _____

Answers to Trivia Quiz: 1. b; 2. a; 3. b; 4. b; 5. a; 6. c; 7. c

FROM GRAMMAR TO WRITING

A BEFORE YOU WRITE Complete the chart with information about a country you know well.

Name of country	
Geographical areas	
Crops grown in each area	
Animals raised in each area	
Natural resources found in each area	
Birds or animals found in each area	
Languages spoken	
Art, handicrafts, or music created	

B WRITE Use the information to write an essay about the country. Use the passive. Try to avoid the common mistakes in the chart.

EXAMPLE: Turkey is both a European and an Asian country. European Turkey is separated from Asian Turkey by the Sea of Marmara, the Bosphorus, and the Dardanelles. Citrus fruits, such as lemon and oranges, and tobacco are grown in . . .

Common Mistakes in Using the Passive

Use the correct form of *be* + **past participle** to form the passive. Do not use the base form of the main verb.	Oranges **are grown** in Turkey. **NOT** Oranges are ~~grow~~ in Turkey.
Only mention the **agent** when it is important information. Do not mention the agent when it is unnecessary information.	Tobacco **is grown**. **NOT** Tobacco is grown ~~by tobacco farmers~~.

C CHECK YOUR WORK Read your essay. Underline all the passive forms. Circle *by* + agent. Use the Editing Checklist to check your work.

Editing Checklist

Did you use . . . ?

☐ passive sentences to focus on the object

☐ the correct form of the passive (*be* + past participle)

☐ *by* if you mentioned the agent

☐ the agent only when it was important information

D REVISE YOUR WORK Read your essay again. Can you improve your writing? Make changes if necessary. Give your essay a title.

UNIT 17 REVIEW

Test yourself on the grammar of the unit.

A Complete with active and passive sentences.

Active	Passive
1. They speak Spanish in Bolivia.	Spanish is spokcen in Bolivia
2. They play soccer in Bolivia	Soccer is played in Bolivia.
3. Reza Degatti took the photo	The photo was taken by Reza Deghati.
4. They translated the articles into Spanish.	The articles were translated into Spanish
5. They grow quinoa in the mountains.	Quenoa is grown in the mountains
6. They nane the main street elprado	The main street was named El Prado.

B Complete the sentences with the correct passive form of the verbs in parentheses.

1. Jamaica was discove _____ by Europeans in the sixteenth century.
(discover)

2. Today, Creole, a mixture of languages, are spoken _____ by many Jamaicans.
(speak)

3. Some of the best coffee in the world is grown _____ on the island.
(grow)

4. Sugar is exported _____ to many countries.
(export)

5. Many people are employed _____ by the sugar industry.
(employ)

6. Reggae music originated in Jamaica. It was made _____ popular by Bob Marley.
(make)

7. Since the summer of 1992, it has been performed at the Sumfest festival on the island.
(perform)

8. Every year, the festival is attended _____ by music lovers from around the world.
(attend)

C Find and correct six mistakes.

Photojournalist Alexandra Avakian was born and ~~raise~~ raised in New York. Since she began

her career, she has covered many of the world's most important stories. Her work have

been published in many newspapers and magazines including *National Geographic*, and her

photographs have being exhibited around the world. Avakian has also written a book, *Window

of the Soul: My Journey in the Muslim World*, which was been published in 2008. It has not yet been

translated by translators into other languages, but the chapter titles appear in both English and

Arabic. Avakian's book have be discussed on international TV, radio, and numerous websites.

Now check your answers on page 479.

UNIT 18

The Passive with Modals and Similar Expressions

INTERNATIONAL COOPERATION

OUTCOMES
- Express certainty, ability, possibility, impossibility, advice, or necessity with passive modals and similar expressions
- Identify key information in a social science article
- Identify details in a science-fiction movie dialog
- Discuss rules for group living in close quarters
- Discuss pros and cons of investing money in space projects
- Write about the ideal school for diplomacy

STEP 1 GRAMMAR IN CONTEXT

BEFORE YOU READ

Look at the article and at the photos on this page and on pages 288–289. Discuss the questions.

1. What do you know about the International Space Station?

2. What are some problems that can occur when people from different cultures must live and work together?

READ

⊙18|01 Read this article about an international space project.

Close Quarters[1]

"Will decisions be made too fast?" the Japanese astronauts wondered. "Can they be made quickly enough?" the Americans wanted to know. "Is dinner going to be taken seriously?" was the question worrying the French and the Dutch, while the Italians were nervous about their personal space: "How can privacy be maintained in such very close quarters?"

The year was 2000. It was the beginning of the new millennium,[2] and the focus of all these concerns was the International Space Station (ISS), the largest and most complex international project ever. At the time, many were asking themselves: "Can this huge undertaking really be accomplished by a multicultural group living in close quarters?"

In addition to their other concerns, all the astronauts were worrying about language. In the beginning, English was the official language on the ISS, and a great number of technical terms had to be learned by everyone on board. (Today, both English and Russian must be

---

1 *close quarters:* a small, crowed place where people live or work together
2 *millennium:* a time when a new 1,000-year period begins

learned by all astronauts before they go into space.) Another major concern was food. What time should meals be served? How should preparation and cleanup be handled?

Those worries had to be tested in space before anyone would know for sure. But by now the answer is clear. For almost two decades, ISS astronauts have been proving that great achievements in technology and science can be made by an international group working together. Since November 2000, when the first crew boarded the ISS, the station has been operated by astronauts from fifteen countries, including Brazil, Canada, Japan, Russia, the United States, and members of the European Union.

How did this international group of astronauts manage to work together and assemble the space station in just about ten years? How were they able to cooperate with one another to achieve their research goals during long periods in a "trapped environment"? All astronauts receive cross-cultural training, but often sensitivity and tolerance can't be taught from a textbook. They must be observed and experienced personally.

Two researchers suggested that a model for space station harmony[3] might be found in an unusual place—the popular TV series *Star Trek*, in which a multicultural crew has been getting along for eons.[4] However, real-life astronauts have found a more down-to-earth solution: the family dinner. Astronaut Nicole Stott reported, ". . . we always spend mealtimes together . . . it's a lot like bringing your family together." The dinner table is where the world's (and each other's) problems can be solved, and where the astronauts "listen to good music, eat good food, improve our vocabulary in other languages, and laugh a lot."

Astronauts also benefit from their unique perspective of Earth. They like to point out that national borders can't be seen from space. As Indian-American astronaut Sunita Williams says, "I consider myself a citizen of the universe. When we go up in space, all we can see is a beautiful Earth where there are no borders of nations and religions." Russian cosmonaut[5] Sergey Ryazansky says, "The ISS can't exist without international cooperation." This spirit of cooperation may turn out to be the project's greatest achievement.

---

3 *harmony:* a situation in which people are friendly and peaceful together
4 *eons:* very long immeasurable periods of time
5 *cosmonaut:* the Russian word for *astronaut*

AFTER YOU READ

A VOCABULARY **Complete the sentences with the words from the box.**

assemble	benefit	concern	cooperate	perspective	undertaking

1. It took years to _____ the many parts of the space station.

2. Money is a big _____. There has to be enough for this expensive project.

3. This book changed my _____. I see the problem differently now.

4. If we all _____ and work together, we'll get the job done quickly.

5. This is a big _____, and it requires a lot of planning.

6. How do we _____ from this change? How will it help us?

B COMPREHENSION **Read the statements. Check (✓) *True* or *False*.**

	True	False
1. Japanese and American astronauts worried about decision making.	☐	☐
2. Dutch astronauts worried about privacy.	☐	☐
3. The time of meals was also a big concern.	☐	☐
4. At first, all ISS astronauts had to learn technical language in English.	☐	☐
5. Today, English is the only official language on the ISS.	☐	☐
6. The ISS was completely assembled in around ten years.	☐	☐
7. Astronauts learn cross-cultural understanding most effectively from textbooks.	☐	☐
8. The astronauts can see individual countries from the ISS.	☐	☐

C DISCUSSION **Work with a partner. Compare your answers to the questions in B. Why did you choose *True* or *False*?**

THE PASSIVE WITH MODALS AND SIMILAR EXPRESSIONS

Statements

Subject	Modal	Be	Past Participle	
The decision	will (not) should (not) ought (not) to must (not) can (not) might (not) had better (not)	be	made	quickly.

Subject	*Have (got) to / Be going to*	Be	Past Participle	
The problem	has (got) to doesn't have to had to is (not) going to	be	solved	quickly.

Yes/No Questions

Modal	Subject	Be	Past Participle	
Will				
Should	it	be	made	quickly?
Must				
Can				

Short Answers

Affirmative			Negative		
Yes,	it	will. should. must. can.	No,	it	won't. shouldn't. doesn't have to be. can't.

Yes/No Questions

Auxiliary Verb	Subject	*Have to / Going to*	Be	Past Participle	
Does	it	have to	be	solved?	
Is		going to			

Short Answers

Affirmative			Negative		
Yes,	it	does. is.	No,	it	doesn't. isn't.

GRAMMAR NOTES

1 Passive Modals and Similar Expressions: Forms

Use **modal/expression + be + past participle** to form passive modals or expressions.

You can use all modals and similar expressions in the passive. For example:

• *will*	The labs *will* be used for experiments.
• *can*	The Earth *can* be seen from the ISS.
• *have to*	Sometimes decisions *have to* be made quickly.

CONTINUED ▶

Remember to use *by* before the **agent** if the agent is mentioned. However, only mention the agent when it is important information.	The repairs will be made **by a robot**.
IN WRITING The passive with modals is not common in conversation. It is more common in academic writing, especially with *may*, *must*, and *should*.	Lessons in cross-cultural understanding **should be introduced** early in the program. *(textbook)*

2 Certainty in the Future

Use *will* or a form of *be going to* with the passive to express **certainty in the future**.

• *will*	The ISS *will* **be used** for several more years.
• *be going to*	The ISS *is going to* **be used** for several more years.

3 Ability or Possibility

Use a form of *can* with the passive to express **ability or possibility**.

• **present ability**	Russian *can* **be understood** by all the astronauts.
• **present possibility**	Many languages *can* **be heard** aboard the ISS.
• **past ability**	Problems *could* **be solved** by the crew.
• **past possibility**	Last month, the ISS *could* **be seen** from Earth.

4 Future Possibility or Impossibility

Use *could*, *may*, *might*, and *can't* with the passive to express **future possibility or impossibility**.

• **future possibility**	The equipment *could* **be replaced** very soon. Some anxiety *may* **be experienced** on takeoff. New discoveries *might* **be made**.
• **future impossibility**	The job *can't* **be handled** by just one person.

5 Advice or Necessity

Use *should*, *ought to*, *had better*, *must*, and *have (got) to* with the passive to express **advice or necessity**.

• **advice**	The crew *should* **be told** to leave now. They *ought to* **be given** more training. Privacy *had better* **be taken** seriously.
• **necessity**	Everyone *must* **be treated** with respect. Technical language *has got to* **be learned**. The equipment *had to* **be repaired**.

REFERENCE NOTES

For a review of **modals and similar expressions**, see Unit 14 on page 222.

For information about **modals and their functions**, see Appendix 18 on page 461.

EXERCISE 1 DISCOVER THE GRAMMAR

A GRAMMAR NOTES 1–5 Read the interview with scientist Dr. Bernard Kay (BK) by *Comet Magazine* (CM). Underline the passive with modals and similar expressions. Circle *by* when it is used before the agent in a passive sentence.

CM: I understand that some parts of the ISS could not be built, and the building of other parts was delayed (by) various problems. But the whole station has finally been assembled. What an undertaking this has been! When was it completed?

BK: It was finished at the end of 2010. In February of that year, the last major sections—Tranquility and the Cupola—were attached. In Tranquility, oxygen can be produced and waste water can be recycled.[1] And life in the ISS will be supported by Tranquility's equipment if communication with Earth can't be maintained for a period of time.

CM: And the Cupola? I understand it was built by the European Space Agency.

BK: Yes, it was. It's amazing. It should be considered one of the most important parts of the station. It's got seven huge windows, and the views of Earth and space are spectacular.

CM: Why the big windows?

BK: Because maintenance outside the space station has to be performed by robots. The windows allow astronauts to observe and control them more easily. But I think that the perspective of Earth and space that we gain from these views might be considered just as important.

CM: Why is that?

BK: Observing the Earth and space keeps the astronauts in touch with the importance of their mission. Originally the station was going to include sleeping cabins with windows, but that part of the project couldn't be accomplished for a number of reasons. Now the sleeping cabins are windowless, and the Cupola is everyone's favorite hangout.[2]

---

1 *recycled:* cleaned or treated (such as water or paper) so that it can be used again
2 *hangout:* a place where people like to spend free time, especially with friends

CM: Now that the station is complete, will more scientific work be done on the ISS?

BK: Yes, it will. The ISS is the first step to further exploration of our solar system. On the ISS, ways to grow food in space can be developed, and new materials can be tested, for example. But most important of all, human interactions have got to be understood better. An international crew from fifteen different countries makes the ISS a wonderful laboratory for cross-cultural understanding. This could be one of the great benefits of the ISS.

CM: I guess we don't know what might be discovered, right?

BK: Right. That's what makes it so exciting.

B Answer the questions.

1. What will support life in the ISS if there's a problem? _____

2. Who built the Cupola? _____

3. Who performs maintenance outside the space station? _____

EXERCISE 2 AFFIRMATIVE AND NEGATIVE STATEMENTS

GRAMMAR NOTES 1–5 **Complete this article about zero-G (zero gravity or weightlessness) with the correct form of the words in parentheses.**

Living in Zero-G

Some tasks _____*can be accomplished*_____ more easily in zero-G. Inside the station,
        1. (can / accomplish)

astronauts _____*can be protected*_____ from the deadly conditions of space—but life in
      2. (can / protect)

almost zero-G still _____*can't be considered*_____ normal. What's it like to live on the ISS?
      3. (can't / consider)

Getting Rest: Sleeping _____*can be compared*_____ to floating in water. It's
      4. (can / compare)

relaxing, but sleeping bags _____*must be attached*_____ to the walls of the cabins.
      5. (must / attach)

Otherwise, astronauts will drift around as they sleep.

Keeping Clean: Showers _____*can't be used*_____ because in zero-G, water from
      6. (can't / use)

a shower flies in all directions and sensitive equipment _____*might be damage*_____
      7. (might / damage)

Instead, astronauts take sponge baths, and they use no-rinse soap and shampoo to wash their

hands and hair. Used bath water _____*it has to be sucked*_____ into a container by a
      8. (have to / suck)

vacuum machine. Clothes _____*can be washed*_____ by putting them into a bag with
      9. (can / wash)

water and soap, but astronauts really ___not have to be concerned___ with laundry. They

10. (not have to / concern)

usually put dirty clothes into a trash container which ___can be send___ back

11. (can / send)

toward Earth and _____ in Earth's atmosphere.

12. (burn up)

Eating Good Meals: From the beginning of the project, ISS planners have known that food

_____ very seriously. Unlike meals on early space missions, food

13. (should / take)

on the ISS _____ out of tubes. Frozen, dried, canned, and fresh

14. (not have to / squeeze)

food _____ and _____ at a

15. (can / heat)   16. (eat)

table. Regular utensils are used, but meals are packed into containers that

_____ to a tray so they don't float away.

17. (must / attach)

Taking It Easy: Not surprisingly, a stressed astronaut is a grouchy astronaut. Free time

_____ for relaxing and enjoying views from the Cupola. All crew

18. (have got to / provide)

members have laptops that _____ for listening to music, reading

19. (can / use)

e-books, and accessing the Internet. Before, the Internet _____

20. (could / access)

only for work, but now a direct Internet connection is available for astronauts' personal use. Emails

and texts _____ easily with friends and family. And blogs,

21. (can / exchange)

tweets, and videos from the astronauts _____ by millions of

22. (be going to / enjoy)

people back on Earth.

Staying Fit: Time also _____ for exercise. In low-gravity

23. (must / allow)

environments, muscle and bone _____ quickly without exercise.

24. (will / lose)

Astronauts spend two hours a day, five to six days a week, exercising.

EXERCISE 3 AFFIRMATIVE AND NEGATIVE STATEMENTS

(A) GRAMMAR NOTES 1–5 Some scientists who are going to join the space station have just completed a simulation[1] of life on the station. Complete each conversation using the modals or expressions in parentheses and correct verbs from the boxes.

Conversation 1

accept	do	~~keep~~	reject	send	train

CESAR: This simulation was great, but it was too warm in there. I think the temperature on the ISS _____*should be kept*_____ at 20 degrees Celsius—no warmer than that.
1. (should)

GINA: Shorts and T-shirts _____*can be sent*_____ to the station for you. That's what
2. (can)
most astronauts ask for.

CESAR: By the way, you know that woman who wants to visit the space station? I hear that she _____*might not be accepted*_____ on our mission. They're considering her application
3. (might not)
now. Her company wants her to do a spacewalk, and so far only astronauts have done that.

GINA: Her application _____*shouldn't be rejected*_____ just for that. But she ought to
4. (shouldn't)
complete a simulation first.

LYLE: Absolutely. She _____*has got to be trained*_____ to work while wearing a spacesuit.
5. (have got to)
That _____*can't be done*_____ except underwater in one of the space labs.
6. (can't)

Conversation 2

approve	do	send	share	surprise

HANS: ·Did you fill in your food-preference forms? They _____*should be sent*_____ to the
7. (should)
Food Systems Lab today.

HISA: I did. I'm glad the new dishes _____*have to be approved*_____ by everyone.
8. (have to)

HANS: You'll find that the food _____*will be shared*_____ by everyone, too. Everyone
9. (will)
enjoys trying different things, and we all benefit from the variety.

LUIS: That's great. But I have a concern about shaving in zero-G. The whisker dust from my beard and mustache keep flying back into my face. It's uncomfortable. I also wonder if it could be dangerous and if something _____*could be done*_____ about it.
10. (could)

HANS: I have a feeling we _____*are going to be surprised*_____ by a lot of unexpected problems.
11. (be going to)

▶18|02 (B) LISTEN AND CHECK Listen to the conversations and check your answers in A.

---

1 *simulation:* something you do in order to practice what you would do in a real situation

EXERCISE 4 EDITING

GRAMMAR NOTES 1–5 Read an astronaut's journal notes. There are seven mistakes in the use of the passive with modals and similar expressions. The first mistake is already corrected. Find and correct six more.

FLIGHT JOURNAL

October 4

6:15 a.m. In the past, astronauts used sleeping restraints, so their feet and hands didn't float around while they were sleeping. It was clear that sleeping arrangements had to be ~~make~~ *made* more comfortable. Luckily, things have improved a lot. Last night, I slept in a soft sleeping bag that's attached to the wall of my sleeping "pod." It seemed very natural. But maybe the sleeping quarters could designed differently. They're too small— it's kind of like sleeping in a closet.

1:00 p.m. Lunch was pretty good. Chicken teriyaki. It's nice and spicy, and the sauce can actually taste, even at zero gravity. More had better be fly in for us soon. It's the most popular dish in the freezer and will all be eaten up soon!

4:40 p.m. I'm worried about my daughter. Just before I left on this mission, she said she was planning to quit school at the end of the semester. That's only a month away. I want to call her and discuss it. But I worry that I might get angry and yell. I might overheard by the others. We really could use a little more privacy here.

10:30 p.m. The view of Earth is unbelievably breathtaking! Tonight I spent a long time just looking out the window and watching Earth pass below. At night, a halo of light surrounds the horizon. It's so bright that the tops of the clouds can see. It can't be described. It simply have to be experienced.

EXERCISE 5   LISTENING

▶18|03   Ⓐ   Some crew members aboard the ISS are watching a science-fiction movie. Listen to the conversations from the movie. Listen again and circle the words that you hear the movie characters say.

1. "It can / can't be repaired out here."

2. "Our messages could / should be misunderstood."

3. "We know that Lon will / won't be taken seriously down there."

4. "Oxygen must / mustn't be used in this situation."

5. "They can / can't be grown in space."

6. "As you know, we have to help / be helped with the repairs."

▶18|03   Ⓑ   Work with a partner. Listen again. Discuss the answers. Why do you think the movie characters made those statements?

EXAMPLE: A: For number 1, the answer is *can't*. The captain said "It can't be repaired out here."
         B: Right. Why do you think the spaceship can't be repaired in space?
         A: I don't know. Maybe they don't have the parts they need.
         B: That's possible. Maybe the parts have to be sent from Earth or another planet.

EXERCISE 6   IN CLOSE QUARTERS

Ⓐ   REACHING AGREEMENT   Work in a group. Imagine that in preparation for a space mission, your group is going to spend a week together in a one-room apartment. Discuss the rules that should be made for living in close quarters. Consider some of the issues listed below.

EXAMPLE: A: I think dinner should be served at 6:00 every night.
         B: 6:00? Isn't that a little early?
         C: Well, do meals always have to be eaten together? Perhaps people should be given a choice of time.
         A: Good idea. And what about choice of food? I think we should be given several choices.

• food	• noise	• privacy	• entertainment
• clothes	• neatness	• language	• sleep time
• room temperature	• cleanliness	• Other: _____	

Ⓑ   Make a list of rules that you've agreed on. Use the passive with modals and similar expressions.

Dinner will be served at 6:00 and 8:00 p.m.

A choice of at least two menus should be given for each meal.

C Compare your list with another group's list.

EXAMPLE: A: We decided that dinner should be served at 6:00 and then again at 8:00.

          B: And we also thought that a choice of at least two menu items should be given for each meal.

EXERCISE 7 A LOT SHOULD BE DONE HERE

PROBLEM SOLVING Work in a group. Look at the picture of an international student lounge. You are responsible for getting it in order, but you have limited time and money. Agree on five things that should be done.

EXAMPLE: A: The window has to be replaced.

          B: No. That'll cost too much. It can just be taped.

          C: That'll look terrible. It's really got to be replaced.

          A: OK. What else should be done?

EXERCISE 8 FOR OR AGAINST

DISCUSSION Sending people to the International Space Station costs millions of dollars. Should money be spent for these space projects, or could it be spent better on Earth? If so, how should it be spent? Discuss these questions with your classmates.

EXAMPLE: A: I think space projects are useful. A lot of new products are going to be developed in space.

          B: I don't agree. Some of that money should be spent on public housing.

FROM GRAMMAR TO WRITING

A BEFORE YOUR WRITE Diplomats are people who officially represent their country in a foreign country. Imagine that you are going to attend a school for future diplomats. Complete the information about some of the features of your ideal school.

Courses required: _____

Language(s) spoken: _____

Living quarters provided: _____

Food offered: _____

Trips taken: _____

Electronic devices provided: _____

B WRITE Use your information to write one or two paragraphs about your ideal school for diplomacy. Use the passive with modals and similar expressions. Try to avoid some of the common mistakes in the chart.

EXAMPLE: I think the ideal school for diplomacy should teach a lot about cross-cultural understanding. Courses should be required in ... More than one official language should be spoken. Classes could be offered in ...

Common Mistakes in Using the Passive with Modals and Similar Expressions

Use *be* + past participle after the modal. Do not leave out *be*.	Language classes **should *be* required**. NOT Language classes should required.
Use the **past participle after** *be*. Do not use the base form of the verb after *be*.	A lot **could be *learned***. NOT A lot could be learn.

C CHECK YOUR WORK Read your paragraph(s). Underline the passive with modals and similar expressions. Use the Editing Checklist to check your work.

Editing Checklist

Did you use ...?

☐ *be* + past participle to form the passive after modals or similar expressions

☐ *will* or *be going to* for certainty in the future

☐ *can* for present ability

☐ *could* for past ability or future possibility

☐ *may*, *might*, and *can't* for future possibility or impossibility

☐ *should*, *ought to*, and *had better* for advice

☐ *must* and *have (got) to* for necessity

D REVISE YOUR WORK Read your paragraph(s) again. Can you improve your writing? Make changes if necessary. Give your writing a title.

UNIT 18 REVIEW

Test yourself on the grammar of the unit.

A Circle the correct words to complete the sentences.

1. What should be <u>did / done</u> about the student lounge?

2. I think the furniture should <u>be replaced / replaced</u>.

3. Maybe some computer workstations <u>could / have</u> be provided.

4. The air conditioning <u>has / had</u> better be repaired.

5. It might not <u>be / being</u> fixed by the summer.

6. The lounge <u>don't / won't</u> be used by students while it's being painted.

7. The school office <u>has / had</u> got to be told about these problems.

8. In the future, problems will be <u>handle / handled</u> faster.

B Complete the sentences with the correct form of the verbs in parentheses.

1. Astronauts _____ in zero gravity.
                (should / train)

2. They _____ the chance to work in those conditions.
        (have to / give)

3. Equipment _____ in conditions similar to space.
           (must / test)

4. Zero gravity _____ underwater as well as on the ISS.
        (can / experience)

5. Underwater living space _____ by Aquatics Laboratory.
          (will / provide)

6. A lot more astronauts _____ there for training.
         (may / send)

7. Skills for Moon missions _____ also _____ underwater.
          (could / develop)

C Find and correct five mistakes.

    The new spacesuits are going to be testing underwater today. They've got to been improved before they can be used on the Moon or Mars. Two astronauts are going to be wearing them while they're working, and they'll watched by the engineers. This morning, communication was lost with the Earth's surface, and all decisions had to be make by the astronauts themselves. It was a very realistic situation. This crew will got to be very well prepared for space travel. They're going to the Moon in a few years.

Now check your answers on page 480.

19

The Passive Causative

PERSONAL SERVICES

OUTCOMES
- Describe services that people have done for them by others, using the passive causative
- Identify key information in an article about beauty
- Identify details in a conversation about tasks needing to be done
- Discuss preparations for a trip to another country
- Discuss steps people from different cultures take to improve their appearance
- Write about preparations for an upcoming event

STEP 1   GRAMMAR IN CONTEXT

BEFORE YOU READ

Look at the photos on this page and on pages 302–303. Discuss the questions.

1. Which forms of body art do you think are attractive?
2. Does body art have any disadvantages? What are they?

READ

▶ 19|01   Read this article from a fashion magazine.

Body Art

Each culture has a different ideal of beauty, and throughout the ages,[1] men and women have done amazing things to achieve the ideal. They have had their hair shaved, cut, colored, straightened, and curled; and they have had their bodies decorated with painting and tattoos. Here are some of today's many options:

Hair

Getting your hair done is the easiest way to change your appearance. Today, both men and women have their hair permed. This chemical procedure[2] can curl hair or just give it more body.[3]

---

1 *throughout the ages:* during different periods of time
2 *chemical procedure:* a technique that uses chemicals (for example, hydrogen peroxide) to change the appearance or texture of something
3 *body:* hair thickness

If your hair is long, you can, of course, get it cut. But did you know that you can also have short hair lengthened with hair extensions?[4] Of course you can have your hair colored and become a blonde, brunette, or redhead. But you can also have it bleached white or get it dyed blue, green, or orange!

Tattoos

This form of body art was created many thousands of years ago. Today, tattoos have again become popular. More and more people are having them done. However, caution is necessary. Although nowadays you can get a tattoo removed with less pain and scarring[5] than before, getting a tattoo is still a big decision.

Piercing

Pierced ears are an old favorite, but lately the practice of piercing has expanded. Many people now are getting their noses, lips, or other parts of the body pierced for jewelry. Piercing requires even more caution than tattooing, and aftercare is very important to avoid infection.

Body Paint

If a tattoo is not for you, you can have ornaments painted on your skin instead. Some people have necklaces and bracelets painted on their neck and arms or get a butterfly mask applied to their face for a special event. Sports fans often get their face painted with their team's colors or the name of their favorite player. Body paintings can be large, but unlike tattoos, they can be washed off.

---

4 *hair extensions:* pieces of hair (natural or synthetic) that people have attached to their own hair to make it longer

5 *scarring:* the creation of a permanent mark on the skin as a result of an accident, or a cosmetic or medical procedure

Cosmetic Surgery

You can get your nose shortened, or have your chin lengthened. You can even have the shape of your body changed. There is always some risk involved, so the decision to have cosmetic surgery requires a lot of thought.

Some of the ways of changing your appearance may be cheap and temporary. However, others are expensive and permanent. So, think before you act, and don't let today's choice become tomorrow's regret.

AFTER YOU READ

Ⓐ VOCABULARY Complete the sentences with the words from the box.

caution	expand	option	permanent	risk	temporary

1. Buying a new car isn't a(n) _____ for us now. It's much too expensive.
2. Miguel's job is just _____. He's leaving next month.
3. Be careful! _____ is always necessary when crossing the street.
4. My salon is small, but they are going to _____ next month.
5. Carly hates her new hair color. It's a good thing it isn't _____.
6. Piercing can be attractive, but there is always the _____ of infection.

Ⓑ COMPREHENSION Read the statements. Check (✓) *True* or *False*.

	True	False
1. Changing your hair is an easy way to change your appearance.	☐	☐
2. Only women perm their hair.	☐	☐
3. It's possible to lengthen short hair.	☐	☐
4. Tattoos are very popular.	☐	☐
5. Tattoos are permanent.	☐	☐
6. People usually pierce only their ears for jewelry.	☐	☐
7. You can have surgery to make your chin longer.	☐	☐

Ⓒ DISCUSSION Work with a partner. Compare your answers in B. Why did you check *True* or *False*?

THE PASSIVE CAUSATIVE

Statements

Subject	*Have/Get*	Object	Past Participle	*(By* + Agent)	
She	**has**	*her hair*	**cut**	*by André*	every month.
He	**has had**	*his beard*	**trimmed**		before.
I	**get**	*my nails*	**done**		at André's.
They	**are going to get**	*their ears*	**pierced.**		

Yes/No Questions

Auxiliary Verb	Subject	*Have/Get*	Object	Past Participle	*(By* + Agent)	
Does	she	**have**	*her hair*	**cut**	*by André?*	
Has	he	**had**	*his beard*	**trimmed**		before?
Do	you	**get**	*your nails*	**done**		at André's?
Are	they	**going to get**	*their ears*	**pierced?**		

Wh- Questions

Wh- Word	Auxiliary Verb	Subject	*Have/Get*	Object	Past Participle	*(By* + Agent)	
How often	**does**	she	**have**	*her hair*	**cut**	*by André?*	
Where	**did**	he	**get**	*his beard*	**trimmed**		before?
When	**do**	you	**get**	*your nails*	**done**		at André's?
Why	**are**	they	**going to get**	*their ears*	**pierced?**		

GRAMMAR NOTES

1   Forms of the Passive Causative

Form the **passive causative** with the appropriate form of *have* or *get* + **object** + **past participle**. *Have* and *get* have the same meaning.

• *have*	I **have** *my hair* **cut** by André.
• *get*	I **get** *my hair* **cut** by André.

CONTINUED ▶

You can use the **passive causative** with:

• **all verb tenses** (simple present, simple past, etc.)	I **get** *my car* **checked** every year. I **had** *it* **washed** yesterday.
• **all modals** (*can, could, must, should, will*, etc.)	I **can get** *the oil* **changed** tomorrow. You **should have** *the tires* **checked**, too.
• **gerunds**	I love **having** *my hair* **done**.
• **infinitives**	I want **to get** *it* **colored**.
BE CAREFUL! The **object** always goes right **after** *have* or *get*. Do not put the object after the past participle.	She **gets** *her nails* **done**. **NOT** She ~~gets done her nails.~~

2 Meaning of the Passive Causative

Use the **passive causative** to describe services that you arrange for someone to do for you.

There is a big difference in meaning between an active sentence and a passive causative sentence. • **active** • **passive causative**	I **color** my hair. *(I do it myself.)* I **have** *my hair* **colored**. *(Someone does it for me.)*
BE CAREFUL! Do not confuse the passive causative with *had* with the past perfect. The meaning is very different.	**PASSIVE CAUSATIVE WITH *HAD*** I **had** *it* **colored** last week. *(Someone did it for me.)* **PAST PERFECT** I **had colored** it before. *(I did it myself.)*
IN WRITING The regular passive is more common in writing. The **passive causative** is more common in **conversation**.	**REGULAR PASSIVE** The operation **was done** on Monday. *(report)* **PASSIVE CAUSATIVE** She **had it done** on Monday. *(conversation)*

3 The Passive Causative with *By* + Agent

Use *by* when it is necessary to mention the **agent** (the person doing the service).

When it is new or important information, use *by* + **agent** to express who is doing the service.	This week, Lee **is getting her hair done** *by a new stylist*.
BE CAREFUL! Do not use *by* + agent when it is clear who is doing the service or when it is not important information.	**NOT** When does Lee get her hair done ~~by a stylist~~? *(Because of the causative, it is already clear that a stylist does her hair.)*

EXERCISE 1 DISCOVER THE GRAMMAR

GRAMMAR NOTES 1–3 **Read the conversations. Decide if the statement that follows each conversation is *True* (*T*) or *False* (*F*).**

1. DEBRA: We should start planning for our party.
   JAKE: OK. In fact, I'm going to get my hair cut by Roberto tomorrow for the big event.

   __F__ Jake cuts his own hair.

2. JAKE: Speaking about hair—Amber, *your* hair's getting awfully long.
   AMBER: I know, Dad. I'm going to cut it tomorrow.

   _____ Amber cuts her own hair.

3. DEBRA: And what about your party dress? Are you going to have it shortened?
   AMBER: Yes, Mom. But not until next week.

   _____ Amber is going to shorten her dress herself.

4. AMBER: Mom, why didn't you get your nails done last time you went to the hair salon?
   DEBRA: Because I did them just before my appointment.

   _____ Debra did her own nails.

5. AMBER: I was thinking of painting a butterfly on my forehead for the party.
   DEBRA: A butterfly! Well, OK. At least paint is just temporary.

   _____ Someone is going to paint a butterfly on Amber's forehead for her.

6. DEBRA: Jake, do you think we should get the floors waxed before the party?
   JAKE: I think they look OK. We'll get them done afterward.

   _____ Debra and Jake are going to hire someone to wax their floors after the party.

7. DEBRA: I'm going to watch some TV and then go to bed. What's on the agenda for tomorrow?
   JAKE: I have to get up early. I'm getting the car washed before work.

   _____ Jake is going to wash the car himself.

8. DEBRA: You know, I think it's time to change the oil, too.
   JAKE: You're right. I'll do it this weekend.

   _____ Jake is going to change the oil himself.

EXERCISE 2 STATEMENTS

GRAMMAR NOTES 1–2 Today is February 15. Look at the Santanas' calendar and write sentences about when they *had/got things done* and when they *are going to have/get things done*. Use the correct form of the words in parentheses.

FEBRUARY

SUNDAY	MONDAY	TUESDAY	WEDNESDAY	THURSDAY	FRIDAY	SATURDAY
1	2	3	4	5	6	7 Deb – hair salon
8	9	10	11	12 Jake – haircut	13 carpets	14 dog groomer
15 TODAY	16 windows	17	18	19	20 food and drinks	21 party!! family pictures
22	23	24	25 Amber – ears pierced	26	27	28

1. *The Santanas are going to have family pictues taken on the 21st.*
   (The Santanas / have / family pictures / take)

2. _____
   (Debra / get / her hair / perm)

3. _____
   (Amber / have / the dog / groom)

4. _____
   (They / get / the windows / wash)

5. _____
   (They / have / the carpets / clean)

6. _____
   (Amber / have / her ears / pierce)

7. _____
   (Jake / get / his hair / cut)

8. _____
   (They / have / food and drinks / deliver)

EXERCISE 3 STATEMENTS AND QUESTIONS

GRAMMAR NOTES 1–3 Debra and Jake are going to have a party. Complete the conversations with the passive causative of the appropriate verbs in the box.

color	cut	dry clean	paint	remove	repair	~~shorten~~	wash

1. AMBER: I bought a new dress for the party, Mom. What do you think?

   DEBRA: It's pretty, but it's a little long. Why don't you _____ *get or have it shortened* _____?

   AMBER: OK. They do alterations at the cleaners. I'll take it in tomorrow.

2. AMBER: By the way, what are *you* planning to wear?

   DEBRA: Me? My white silk suit. But I have to _____. It has a stain on

   the sleeve. I hope it's not permanent.

   AMBER: I can drop it off at the cleaners with my dress.

3. JAKE: The house is ready, except for the windows. They look pretty dirty.

   DEBRA: Don't worry. We _____ tomorrow.

4. DEBRA: Amber, your hair is getting really long. I thought you were going to cut it.

   AMBER: I decided not to do it myself this time. I _____ by André.

5. DEBRA: My hair's getting a lot of gray in it. Should I _____?

   JAKE: Well, I guess that's an option. But it looks fine to me the way it is.

6. AMBER: Mom, I've been thinking about getting a butterfly tattoo instead of having one painted. I

   can always _____ if I decide I don't like it.

   DEBRA: No! That's *not* an option! There are too many risks involved in the procedure.

7. AMBER: Someone's at the door, and it's only 6 o'clock!

   DEBRA: No, it's not. I guess my mother's antique clock stopped again.

   JAKE: Oh no, not again. I don't believe it! I _____ twice this

   year, and it's only February!

8. GUEST: The house looks really beautiful, Jake. I love the colors you chose. _____ you

   _____?

   JAKE: No, actually we did it ourselves last summer.

EXERCISE 4 EDITING

GRAMMAR NOTES 1–3 **Read Amber's Facebook post. There are seven mistakes in the use of the passive causative. The first mistake is already corrected. Find and correct six more.**

Amber's thoughts...

February 21: The party was tonight. It went really well! The house looked

great. Last week, Mom and Dad had the floors waxed and all the windows ~~clean~~ *cleaned*

professionally so everything sparkled. And of course we had the whole house

painted ourselves last summer. (I'll never forget that. It took us two weeks!) I wore

my silver dress that I have shortened by Bo; and my best friend, Alicia, wore her

new black gown. Right before the party, I got cut my hair by André. He did a great

job. There were a lot of guests at the party. We had almost fifty people invited,

and they almost all showed up for our

family event! The food was great, too.

Mom made most of the main dishes

herself, but she had the rest of the

food prepare by a caterer. Mom

and Dad had hired a professional

photographer, so at the end of

the party we took our pictures.

Here's one of me and Alicia.

EXERCISE 5   LISTENING

▶19|02 **A** Ji-woo has just gone away to college. Read the list of tasks. Then listen to the phone call between Ji-woo and her father. Listen again and check (✓) *Does the Job Herself* or *Hires Someone to Do the Job*.

	Does the Job Herself	Hires Someone to Do the Job
1. change the oil in her car	✓	☐
2. change the locks	☐	☐
3. paint the apartment	☐	☐
4. put up bookshelves	☐	☐
5. bring new furniture to the apartment	☐	☐
6. paint her hands	☐	☐
7. cut her hair	☐	☐
8. color her hair	☐	☐

▶19|02 **B** Listen again. Then work with a partner. What do you think? Answer the questions and give reasons for your opinions. Do you and your partner agree?

1. Is Ji-woo handy? (good at making, maintaining, and repairing things)

   EXAMPLE: A: I think she's pretty handy. She changed the oil in her car by herself.
   B: Right. She didn't have to have it done for her. And she . . .

2. Why does Ji-woo tell her father not to worry?
3. Why does Ji-woo turn down her father's offer to paint her apartment?
4. Why didn't Ji-woo have to get her new desk and lamps delivered?
5. Why does Ji-woo's father ask, "Will we be able to recognize you?"

EXERCISE 6   GETTING READY

A ROLE PLAY Work in a group. Imagine that you are taking a car trip together to another country. You'll be gone for several weeks. Decide where you're going. Then make a list of things you have to do and arrange before the trip. Use the ideas below and ideas of your own.

EXAMPLE: A: I have to get my passport renewed.
B: Me too. And we should apply for visas right away.

- passport and visa
- car (oil, gas, tires, brake fluid)
- home (pets, plants, mail, newspaper delivery)
- personal (clothing, hair, nails)
- medical (teeth, eyes, prescriptions)
- Other: _____

B Now compare your list with that of another group. Did you forget anything?

EXERCISE 7 BEFORE AND AFTER

A PICTURE DISCUSSION Work with a partner. Look at the *Before* and *After* pictures of a fashion model. Discuss all the things the model had done to change her appearance.

EXAMPLE: A: Well, her nose looks different.
B: You're right. She had it shortened! And look at her . . .

Before   After

B Do you think the woman looks better? Why or why not?

EXAMPLE: A: I don't know why she had her nose fixed.
B: Neither do I. I think it looked fine before.

EXERCISE 8 BODY ART AROUND THE WORLD

CROSS-CULTURAL COMPARISON Work in a group. Think about other cultures. Discuss the types of things men and women do or get done in order to change or improve their appearance. Report back to your class.

EXAMPLE: A: In India, women get their hands painted for special occasions. I think it looks nice.
B: In Japan, . . .

Some procedures to think about:

- **hands/feet:** painting nails, painting hands or bottom of feet

- **eyes:** lengthening eyelashes, coloring eyebrows

- **teeth:** straightening, whitening

- **face:** shortening nose, plumping lips

- **hair:** coloring, lengthening, styling, curling, straightening, braiding

- **skin:** whitening, tanning, tattooing, painting

A BEFORE YOU WRITE Think about an event in your life (a party, a wedding, moving into a new home, looking for a job, a trip). What did you do to prepare for it? What did you have done to prepare for it? Complete the outline.

The Event: _____

Things I did myself	Things I had done
_____	_____
_____	_____
_____	_____

B WRITE Use your outline to write one or two paragraphs about the preparations for your event. Try to avoid the mistakes in the chart.

EXAMPLE: Last month, I moved into a new apartment. It's an old apartment, and it needed a lot of work. Because the apartment is small, I was able to do quite a few things myself. For example, before I moved in, I painted the kitchen and living room, but I had to have carpet installed and some windows replaced. I didn't have any furniture, so I bought a bed and a couch and had them delivered. I also got... Although I've already been there a month, there are still a lot of things I have to get done!

Common Mistakes in Using the Passive Causative

Use the correct word order, ***have something done***. Do not use *have done something*.	I **had *the apartment* painted** by Colorama. **NOT** I ~~had painted the apartment~~ by Colorama.
Use ***by* + agent** only when it is important to mention the agent. Do not mention the agent when it is obvious or unimportant information.	I **had *the apartment* painted** by Colorama. **NOT** I had the apartment painted ~~by a painter~~.

C CHECK YOUR WORK Read your paragraph(s). Underline once the words that express things you did yourself. Underline twice the words that express things someone did for you. Circle the *by* + agent if you used it. Use the Editing Checklist to check your work.

Editing Checklist

Did you use...?

☐ the passive causative for services someone did for you

☐ the passive causative with the appropriate form of *have* or *get* + object + past participle

☐ the correct word order for the passive causative

☐ *by* only when it was important to mention the agent

D REVISE YOUR WORK Read your paragraph(s) again. Can you improve your writing? Make changes if necessary. Give your paragraph(s) a title.

UNIT 19 REVIEW

Test yourself on the grammar of the unit.

Ⓐ Circle the correct words to complete the sentences.

1. I don't cut my own hair. I <u>have it cut / have cut it</u>.

2. My friend has her hair <u>did / done</u> every week.

3. We should <u>get / gotten</u> the house painted again this year.

4. Did you have <u>painted your house / your house painted</u>?

5. I want to have the job done <u>by / from</u> a professional.

Ⓑ Complete each sentence with the correct passive causative form of the verbs in parentheses and a pronoun.

1. My computer stopped working. I have to _____ .
   (get / repair)

2. I don't clean the windows myself. I _____ once a year.
   (have / clean)

3. Your pants are too long. You should _____ .
   (have / shorten)

4. Does Monica color her own hair or does she _____ ?
   (get / color)

5. I can't fix this vacuum cleaner myself. I'll have to _____ .
   (get / fix)

6. Todd used to have a tattoo, but he _____ last year.
   (have / remove)

7. My passport is going to expire soon. I need to _____ .
   (get / renew)

8. The car has been making a strange noise. I _____ tomorrow.
   (have / check)

Ⓒ Find and correct seven mistakes.

I'm going on vacation next week. I'd like to have done some work in my office, and this seems like a good time for it. Please have my carpet clean while I'm gone. And could you have my computer and printer looked at? It's been quite a while since they've been serviced. Ted wants to have my office painted by a painter while I'm gone. Please tell him any color is fine except pink! Last week, I had designed some new brochures by Perfect Print. Please call the printer and have them delivered directly to the sales reps. And could you also get made up more business cards? When I get back, it'll be time to plan the holiday party. I think we should have it catered this year from a professional. While I'm gone, why don't you call around and get some estimates from caterers? Has the estimates sent to Ted. Thanks.

Now check your answers on page 480.

Conditional Sentences

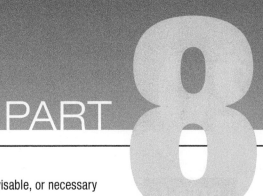

OUTCOMES

- Describe present real conditions and results that are certain, possible, advisable, or necessary
- Express instructions, commands, or invitations that depend on a condition
- Identify specific information in an article about shopping online
- Infer correct information from announcements
- Discuss different types of shopping
- Write about things to do in one's city or town

OUTCOMES

- Describe future real conditions and results that will be certain, possible, advisable, or necessary
- Identify specific information in a magazine article
- Identify and discuss details in an interview
- Discuss common problems and possible solutions
- Discuss superstitions, giving opinions and making cross-cultural comparisons
- Write a speech about what one will do if elected class or school president

OUTCOMES

- Describe present or future unreal conditions and results that are untrue, impossible, or possible
- Give advice with *If I were you*
- Express wishes about the present or the future
- Identify key details in a written and a recorded fairy tale
- Discuss hypothetical questions and wishes
- Write about a wish one has for oneself or society

OUTCOMES

- Describe past unreal conditions and results that are untrue, imagined, impossible, or possible
- Express regret about things that happened or didn't happen in the past
- Extract specific information from an article
- Infer correct information from conversations
- Speculate about past events or hypothetical situations
- Discuss a past decision one regrets
- Write about an event that changed one's life

Present Real Conditional Sentences

SHOPPING

OUTCOMES
• Describe present real conditions and results that are certain, possible, advisable, or necessary
• Express instructions, commands, or invitations that depend on a condition
• Identify specific information in an article about shopping online
• Infer correct information from announcements
• Discuss different types of shopping
• Write about things to do in one's city or town

STEP 1 GRAMMAR IN CONTEXT

BEFORE YOU READ

Look at the photo and at the title of the article. Discuss the questions.

1. What is a cyber mall?

2. Have you ever purchased something online? If *yes*, what?

3. What are some steps people should take to shop safely online?

READ

20|01 Read this article about cyber malls.

Pick and Click: Shopping@Home

Where is the largest mall[1] in the world? If you think it's in Dubai or China, you're wrong! It's in cyberspace![2] And you can get there from home on your very own computer.

Cyber shopping is fast, convenient, and often less expensive. It doesn't matter if it's a book or a diamond necklace—with just a click of your mouse, you can buy anything without getting up from your chair. If you're looking for the best price, you can easily compare prices and read other buyers' reviews of products. Shopping online can save you time and money—but

---

1 *mall:* a very large building or outdoor area with a lot of stores in it
2 *cyberspace:* all the connections between computers in different places (people think of it as a real place where information, messages, pictures, etc., exist)

you need to surf[3] and shop safely. Here are some tips to make your trip to the cyber mall a good one:

- You are less likely to have a problem if you shop with well-known companies.
- If you don't know the company, ask them to send you information. **What is their address? Their phone number?**
- Always pay by credit card if you can. If you are unhappy with the product (or if you don't receive it), then you can dispute the charge.
- **Only enter your credit card information on a secure site.** If you see a closed lock 🔒 or complete key 🔑 symbol at the bottom of your screen, the site is secure. **Also, the web address will change from `http://www` to `https://www`.** This means that your credit card number will be encrypted (changed so that others can't read it). If the site isn't secure, don't enter your credit card information.
- If you have kids, don't let them give out personal information.
- If you have any doubts about a site's security, contact the store by phone or email.
- **Find out the return policy.** What happens if you don't like the product?
- **Print out and save a record of your purchase.** If there is a problem, the receipt gives you proof of purchase.
- If you change your mind about an order, contact the company immediately.

As you can see, many of these steps are similar to the ones you follow in a "store with doors." **Just use common sense.** If you take some basic precautions, you shouldn't have any problems.

Internet shopping has literally[4] brought a world of opportunity to consumers. Today, we can shop 24 hours a day, 7 days a week in stores that are halfway around the globe without ever having to leave home or stand in line. As with many things in life, there are some risks. Just remember that online or off, if an offer seems too good to be true, it probably is. **Happy cyber shopping!**

---

3 *surf:* go quickly from one website to another in order to find information that interests you
4 *literally:* according to the most basic meaning of a word or expression

AFTER YOU READ

Ⓐ VOCABULARY **Complete the sentences with the words from the box.**

| consumer | dispute | policy | precaution | secure | site |

1. You should ask about a store's return _____.

2. A smart _____ always compares prices before making a purchase.

3. As a safety _____, you should never give your password to anyone.

4. My friend never shops online. He doesn't think it's _____ enough.

5. I don't like that store's online _____. It's very confusing.

6. I need to _____ that charge. I ordered one shirt, but they charged me for two.

B COMPREHENSION Choose the word or phrase that best completes each sentence.

1. The largest mall in the world is in _____ .
   a. China
   b. Dubai
   c. cyberspace

2. The process of shopping for a book online is _____ shopping for a diamond necklace.
   a. the same as
   b. faster than
   c. different from

3. It's a good idea to shop with a company that has _____ .
   a. a nice website
   b. a name you know
   c. products for children

4. If possible, you should pay for Internet purchases _____ .
   a. by credit card
   b. by check
   c. with cash

5. A closed lock at the bottom of the computer screen means _____ .
   a. you can't shop there
   b. the site is safe
   c. the product is sold out

6. You can avoid problems by _____ .
   a. shopping in "real" stores
   b. using cash
   c. being careful

7. An offer that seems unbelievably good is probably not _____ .
   a. safe
   b. expensive
   c. cheap

C DISCUSSION Work with a partner. Compare your answers in B. Why did you choose each answer?

STEP 2   GRAMMAR PRESENTATION

PRESENT REAL CONDITIONAL SENTENCES

Statements

If-Clause	Result Clause
If I **shop** online,	I **save** time.
If the mall **is** closed,	I **can shop** online.

Statements

Result Clause	If-Clause
I **save** time	*if* I **shop** online.
I **can shop** online	*if* the mall **is** closed.

Yes/No Questions

Result Clause	If-Clause
Do you **save** time	*if* you **shop** online?
Can you **shop** online	*if* the mall **is** closed?

Short Answers

Affirmative		Negative	
Yes,	I do.	No,	I don't.
	I can.		I can't.

Wh- Questions

Result Clause	If-Clause
What **happens**	*if* I **don't like** it?

GRAMMAR NOTES

1 Present Real Conditional Sentences

Use present real conditional sentences to describe **real conditions** and **results** that are **certain**. When these conditions happen, the results are always the same.

The *if*-clause describes a **real** or **true condition**. The **result clause** describes **what always happens** when this condition occurs.	IF-CLAUSE RESULT CLAUSE **If** it's a holiday, the store is closed. *(When there is a holiday, the store is always closed.)*
You can use present real conditional sentences to express:	
• **general truths**	**If** you use a credit card, it's faster. *(When you use a credit card, it's always faster.)*
• **habits** or things that happen again and again	**If** Bill shops online, he spends a lot of money. *(Every time Bill shops on line, he always spends a lot of money.)*
For **general truths**, use the **simple present** in both clauses.	PRESENT PRESENT **If** you **see** a closed lock symbol, the site **is** secure.
For **habits** or things that happen again and again, use the **simple present or present progressive** in the *if*-clause. Use the **simple present** in the result clause.	PRESENT PRESENT **If** I **surf** the Web, I **use** Google. PRESENT PROG. PRESENT **If** I'm **surfing** the Web, I **use** Google.
USAGE NOTE We often use *even if* when the **result is surprising**.	**Even if** it's a holiday, this store stays open.

2 With a Modal in the Result Clause

You can use **modals** or similar expressions in the **result clause** to express **possibility** (*can, may, could*), **advice** (*should, ought to*), or **necessity** (*must, have to*).

• *can*	IF-CLAUSE RESULT CLAUSE If you don't like the gift, you *can* **return** it.
• *should*	If it's not too expensive, you *should* **buy** it.
• *must*	If you use their website, you *must* **have** a password.
USAGE NOTE We sometime use *then* to **emphasize the result** in present real conditional sentences with modals or similar expressions.	If you don't like the gift, *then* you **can return** it.

3 With an Imperative in the Result Clause

Use an **imperative** in the result clause to give **instructions**, **commands**, and **invitations** that depend on a condition.

	IF-CLAUSE	RESULT CLAUSE
• instructions	If you change your mind, **call** the company.	
• command	If you get home very late, **don't make** noise.	
• invitation	If you want to come along, **meet** us at noon.	

USAGE NOTE We sometimes use *then* to **emphasize the result** in present real conditional sentences with imperatives.	If you change your mind, ***then* call** the company.

4 Position of the *If*-Clause

The *if*-clause can come **at the beginning or the end** of the sentence. The meaning is the same.

• at the **beginning**	***If* I shop online**, I save time.
• at the **end**	I save time ***if* I shop online**.

IN WRITING Use a **comma after the *if*-clause** when it comes at the **beginning** of the sentence. Do not use a comma after the result clause when the result clause comes first.	***If* I shop online**, I use my credit card. **NOT** I use my credit card, if I shop online.

5 Present Real Conditional Sentences with *When* Instead of *If*

In present real conditional sentences, you can often use *when* instead of *if*. The meaning is the same.

• **general truths**	***If* you **use** a credit card, it**'s** faster.** ***When* you **use** a credit card, it**'s** faster.**
• **habits** or things that happen again and again	***If* Bill **shops** online, he **spends** a lot of money.** ***When* Bill **shops** online, he **spends** a lot of money.**

USAGE NOTE We sometimes use *when* with the **present progressive** in both clauses to describe actions that happen **at the same time**.	***When* stores **are opening** in Los Angeles, they **are closing** in Johannesburg.**

USAGE NOTE We sometimes use *whenever* instead of *when*. It means *every time*.	***Whenever* Bill shops online, he spends a lot of money.** *(Every time Bill shops online, he spends a lot of money.)*

EXERCISE 1 DISCOVER THE GRAMMAR

GRAMMAR NOTES 1–5 **Read these shopping tips. In each present real conditional sentence, underline once the result clause. Underline twice the clause that talks about the condition.**

SHOP Smart

YOU'RE SHOPPING in a foreign city. Should you pay full price, or should you bargain? If you don't know the answer, you can pay too much or miss a fun experience. Bargaining is one of the greatest shopping pleasures if you know how to do it. The strategies are different in different places. Check out these tips before you go.

HONG KONG Hong Kong is one of the world's greatest shopping cities. If you like to bargain, you can do it anywhere except the larger department stores. The trick is not to look too interested. If you see something you want, pick it up along with some other items and ask the prices. Then make an offer below what you are willing to pay. If the seller's offer is close to the price you want, then you should be able to reach an agreement quickly.

ITALY When Italians shop at outdoor markets, they often bargain. You can try this, too, if you want to get a better price. In stores, you can politely ask for a discount if you want to bargain. Take your time. Make conversation if you speak Italian. Show your admiration for the object by picking it up and pointing out its wonderful features. When you hear the price, look sad. Make your own offer. Then end the bargaining politely if you don't agree.

MEXICO In Mexico, people truly enjoy bargaining. There are some clear rules, though. You should bargain only if you really are interested in buying the object. If the vendor's price is far more than you want to pay, then politely stop the negotiation. If you know your price is truly reasonable, walking away often brings a lower offer.

Remember, bargaining is always a social interaction, not an argument. And it can still be fun even if you don't get the item you want at the price you want to pay.

EXERCISE 2 PRESENT REAL CONDITIONAL SENTENCES

Ⓐ GRAMMAR NOTES 1–2, 4 Complete the interview with Claudia Leggett, a fashion buyer. Combine the two sentences in parentheses to make a present real conditional sentence. Keep the same order and decide which clause begins with *if*. Make necessary changes in capitalization and punctuation.

INTERVIEWER: Is understanding fashion the most important thing for a career as a buyer?

LEGGETT: It is. *If you don't understand fashion, you don't belong in this field.*
 1. (You don't understand fashion. You don't belong in this field.)

But buyers need other skills, too.

INTERVIEWER: Such as?

LEGGETT: _If you have good bussines skills, you can make better_
 2. (You can make better decisions. You have good business skills.)

INTERVIEWER: "People skills" must be important, too.

LEGGETT: True. _If _____, she's _____
 3. (A buyer needs great interpersonal skills. She's negotiating prices.)

INTERVIEWER: Do you travel in your business?

LEGGETT: A lot! _If there's a big _____
 4. (There's a big international fashion fair. I'm usually there.)

INTERVIEWER: Why fashion fairs?

LEGGETT: Thousands of professionals attend. _If I go to a fair ____
 5. (I go to a fair. I can see hundreds of products in a few days.)

INTERVIEWER: You just got back from the Milan fair, didn't you?

LEGGETT: Yes, and I went to Paris and Madrid, too. _If _____
 6. (I usually stay two weeks. I'm traveling to Europe.)

INTERVIEWER: Does your family ever go with you?

LEGGETT: Often. _If _____
 7. (My husband has the time to come. He and our son, Pietro, do things together.)

 _If _____
 8. (Pietro comes to the fair with me. My husband doesn't have time.)

Next week, we're all going to Hong Kong.

INTERVIEWER: What do you do when you're not at a fashion fair?

LEGGETT: _If _____
 9. (I always go shopping. I have free time.)

Ⓑ 20|02 Ⓑ LISTEN AND CHECK Listen to the interview and check your answers in A.

EXERCISE 3 PRESENT REAL CONDITIONAL SENTENCES WITH MODALS AND IMPERATIVES

GRAMMAR NOTES 1–3 Read this Q & A about shopping around the world. Write conditional sentences to summarize the advice. Start with the *if*-clause and use appropriate punctuation.

1. Hong Kong

Q: I want to buy some traditional crafts. Any ideas?

A: You ought to visit the Western District on Hong Kong Island. It's famous for its crafts.

If you want to buy some traditional crafts, (then)

you ought to visit the Western District on Hong

Kong Island.

2. Barcelona

Q: I want to buy some nice but inexpensive clothes. Where can I go?

A: Take the train to outdoor markets in towns *outside* of the city. They have great stuff.

_____

_____

_____

3. Istanbul

Q: I want to go shopping in the Grand Bazaar. Is it open on Sunday?

A: No. You have to go during the week.

_____

_____

_____

4. Bangkok

Q: My son wants to buy computer games. Where should he go?

A: He should try the Pantip Plaza. The selection is huge.

_____

_____

_____

5. **Mexico City**

   Q: I plan to buy some silver jewelry in Mexico. Any tips?

   A: Try bargaining. That way, you may get something nice at a very good price.

   _____

   _____

   _____

6. **London**

   Q: I want to find some nice secondhand clothing shops. Can you help me?

   A: Try Portobello Market on the weekend. Happy shopping!

   _____

   _____

   _____

EXERCISE 4 PRESENT REAL CONDITIONAL SENTENCES WITH *WHEN*

GRAMMAR NOTE 5 Look at the map. Write sentences about the cities with clocks. Use the words in parentheses and *when*. The white clocks show daylight hours; the gray clocks show evening or nighttime hours.

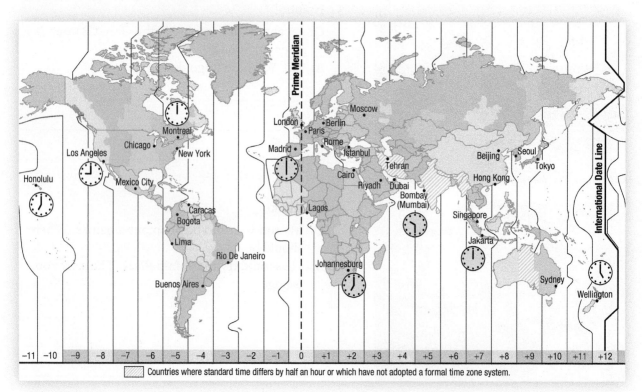

1. <u>When it's noon in Montreal, it's midnight in Jakarta.</u>
   (be noon / be midnight)

2. <u>When stores are opening in Los Angeles, they're closing in Johannesburg.</u>
   (stores open / stores close)

3. _____
   (people watch the sunrise / people watch the sunset)

4. _____
   (be midnight / be 6:00 p.m.)

5. _____
   (people eat lunch / people eat dinner)

6. _____
   (people get up / people go to bed)

7. _____
   (be 7:00 a.m. / be 7:00 p.m.)

8. _____
   (be 5:00 a.m. / be 9:00 a.m.)

EXERCISE 5 EDITING

GRAMMAR NOTES 1–5 **Read Claudia's email message. There are seven mistakes in the use of present real conditional sentences. The first mistake is already corrected. Find and correct six more. Don't forget to check punctuation.**

● ● ●

Tomorrow, I'm flying to Hong Kong for a fashion show! My son, Pietro, is flying

with me, and my husband is already there. When Pietro's off from school, I

~~liked~~ *like* to take him on trips with me. If my husband comes too, they are going

sightseeing during the day. Our plane leaves Los Angeles around midnight. If

we flew at night, we can sleep on the plane. (At least that's the plan!)

I love Hong Kong. We always have a great time, when we will go there. The

shopping is really fantastic. When I'm not working I'm shopping.

I'll be arriving at the hotel around 7:00 a.m. When it will be 7:00 a.m. in Hong

Kong, it's midnight in London. That's probably too late to call you, so I'll just

text. OK?

EXERCISE 6 LISTENING

▶20|03 **A** Claudia Leggett and her son, Pietro, are flying from Los Angeles to Hong Kong. Listen to the announcements they hear in the airport and aboard the plane. Read the statements. Then listen again and check (✓) *True* or *False*.

	True	False
Announcement 1: Claudia has two pieces of carry-on luggage, and Pietro has one. They can take them all on the plane.	☐	☑
Announcement 2: Look at their boarding passes. They can board now.	☐	☐

UPAir *Boarding Pass*
01 of 02

NAME OF PASSENGER
LEGGETT/PIETRO

FROM
X/O Los Angeles

TO
X/O Hong Kong

CARRIER
UPAIR

CODE	FLIGHT	CLASS	DATE	TIME
UP	398	V	13Aug	11:45P

GATE	BOARDING TIME	SEAT
8C	11:15PM	16A

1 037 2171281950 2

UPAir *Boarding Pass*
02 of 02

NAME OF PASSENGER
LEGGETT/CLAUDIA

FROM
X/O Los Angeles

TO
X/O Hong Kong

CARRIER
UPAIR

CODE	FLIGHT	CLASS	DATE	TIME
UP	398	V	13Aug	11:45P

GATE	BOARDING TIME	SEAT
8C	11:15PM	16B

1 037 2171281950 2

	True	False
Announcement 3: Look at their boarding passes again. They can board now.	☐	☐
Announcement 4: Pietro is only ten years old. Claudia should put his oxygen mask on first.	☐	☐
Announcement 5: Claudia is sitting in a left-hand window seat. She can see the lights of Tokyo.	☐	☐
Announcement 6: Passengers who are taking connecting flights can get this information on the plane.	☐	☐

▶20|03 **B** Work with a partner. Listen again to the announcements. Discuss your answers.

EXAMPLE: A: OK. So, why is the answer to number 1 *False*?
B: The announcement says if you have more than one piece of carry-on luggage, you must check the extra pieces at the gate.
A: Right. And they have three pieces, so they can't take them all on the plane with them. Now, what did you choose for number 2?

Passengers on Flight 398 to Hong Kong

EXERCISE 7 WHAT SHOULD WE GET?

A REACHING AGREEMENT Work with a partner. You are going to buy some T-shirts for a friend—an eighteen-year-old male or female. Look at part of a store's website and discuss the selections. Agree on a purchase. Think about the following issues.

- color
- size
- style
- quantity
- price
- shipping

EXAMPLE:
A: Let's get a cherry red, short-sleeve, V-neck T-shirt.
B: But what if she doesn't like red?
A: Well, if she doesn't like it, she can always exchange it for another color.
B: OK. And, if we order it today, ...

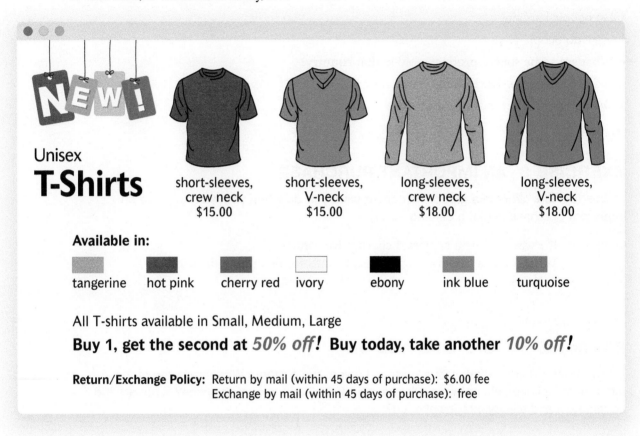

Unisex
T-Shirts

| short-sleeves, crew neck $15.00 | short-sleeves, V-neck $15.00 | long-sleeves, crew neck $18.00 | long-sleeves, V-neck $18.00 |

Available in:

tangerine   hot pink   cherry red   ivory   ebony   ink blue   turquoise

All T-shirts available in Small, Medium, Large

Buy 1, get the second at *50% off*! Buy today, take another *10% off*!

Return/Exchange Policy: Return by mail (within 45 days of purchase): $6.00 fee
Exchange by mail (within 45 days of purchase): free

B Work with your partner. Complete the order form for the item(s) you decided on.

	QUANTITY	COLOR	SIZE
short-sleeved, crew neck T			○ S ○ M ○ L
short-sleeved, V-neck T			○ S ○ M ○ L
long-sleeved, crew neck T			○ S ○ M ○ L
long-sleeved, V-neck T			○ S ○ M ○ L

Shipping Method   ○ Standard: 5–9 business days **$5.00**
○ Express: 2 business days **$10.00**

EXERCISE 8 SHOPPING HERE AND THERE

CROSS-CULTURAL COMPARISON Work with a partner. Compare shopping in a place you've lived in or one you have visited. Choose two different places and consider the questions below.

EXAMPLE: A: If you're in a small city or town in Mexico, stores are usually open from Monday to Friday between 9:00 a.m. and 2:00 or 4:00 p.m.
B: In South Korean cities, stores usually stay open until 10:00 p.m. And if you want to go shopping after that, you can find many stores that are open 24 hours.

- What days and hours are stores open?
- What kinds of stores are there: malls? small stores? indoor or outdoor markets?
- Do people bargain?
- How do people pay?
- What are some special products sold in that country?
- Is there a sales tax for clothing? If *yes*, how much is it?
- Do stores allow refunds or exchanges?

EXERCISE 9 AN IMPORTANT PURCHASE

CONVERSATION Work in a group. Talk about what you do when you want to make an important purchase (a gift, a camera, a car).

EXAMPLE: A: If I want to buy a camera, I check prices online.
B: When I buy a camera, I always ask friends for recommendations.
C: I always...

EXERCISE 10 OFF-LINE AND ON

PICTURE DISCUSSION Work with a partner. Look at the cartoon. What are some of the differences between shopping in a "store with doors" and shopping online? What are the advantages and disadvantages of each?

EXAMPLE: A: If you shop for clothes in a store, you can try them on first.
B: But you have a lot more choices if you shop online.

FROM GRAMMAR TO WRITING

A BEFORE YOU WRITE **Work with a partner. Brainstorm information for tourists visiting your city or town. Then complete the list of tips for visitors.**

What to Do if You Visit _____
(name of city or town)

Shopping _____   Weather _____

Food _____   Interesting Sights _____

Transportation _____   Outdoor Activities _____

B WRITE **Use your list to write a short article about things to do in your city or town. Use present real conditional sentences. Try to avoid the mistakes in the chart.**

EXAMPLE: There are many things to do if you visit Jamestown. If you enjoy swimming, you can go to one of the many beautiful beaches in and around town. The weather is great in the summer, but remember to bring a sweater if you plan to go out in the evening. If you forget to pack one, don't worry. You can go shopping for one at . . .

Common Mistakes in Using Present Real Conditional Sentences

Use the **simple present** in both clauses for **general truths**. Do not use the future in the *if/when* clause.	**If** you **shop** online, it**'s** faster. NOT If you ~~will shop~~ online, it's faster.
Use the **simple present or present progressive** in the *if/when* clause for **habits** and things that happen again and again. Do not use the future in the *if/when* clause.	**When** I **visit** Jamestown, I always eat at Joe's. NOT When I ~~will visit~~ Jamestown, I always eat at Joe's.
Use a **comma after the *if/when* clause** when it comes first. Do not use a comma after the result clause when the result clause comes first.	**If** it**'s** nice out**,** go to the beach. NOT Go to the beach_x if it's nice out.

C CHECK YOUR WORK **Read your article. Underline the *if* or *when* clauses once and the result clauses twice. Circle *if* or *when*. Use the Editing Checklist to check your work.**

Editing Checklist

Did you use . . . ?

☐ the simple present in both clauses for general truths

☐ the simple present or present progressive in the *if/when* clause for habits and things that happen again and again

☐ a comma after the *if/when* clause when it comes first

D REVISE YOUR WORK **Read your article again. Can you improve your writing? Make changes if necessary. Give your article a title.**

UNIT 20 REVIEW

Test yourself on the grammar of the unit.

A Complete the present real conditional sentences in the conversation with the correct form of the verbs in parentheses.

A: What _____ you _____ when you _____ too busy
                              1. (do)   **2.** (be)

   to shop?

B: It depends. If a store _____ open late, I _____ in the evening.
                                 3. (be)   **4.** (shop)

A: What _____ if a store _____ open late?
             5. (happen)   **6.** (not stay)

B: If it _____ early, I _____ to its website. It's really easy.
          7. (close)   **8.** (go)

A: Great idea! When I _____ rushed, I never _____ of that.
                9. (feel)   **10.** (think)

B Combine each pair of sentences to make a present real conditional sentence. Keep the same order.

1. It's 7:00 a.m. in Honolulu. What time is it in Mumbai?

   _____

2. You love jewelry. You should visit an international jewelry show.

   _____

3. A tourist may have more fun. She tries bargaining.

   _____

4. You're shopping at an outdoor market. You can always bargain for a good price.

   _____

5. But don't try to bargain. You're shopping in a big department store.

   _____

C Find and correct five mistakes. Remember to check punctuation.

1. If I don't like something I bought online, then I returned it.

2. Don't buy from an online site, if you don't know anything about the company.

3. When he'll shops online, Frank always saves a lot of time.

4. I always fell asleep if I fly at night. It happens every time.

5. Isabel always has a wonderful time, when she visits Istanbul.

Now check your answers on page 480.

Future Real Conditional Sentences

CAUSE AND EFFECT

OUTCOMES
- Describe future real conditions and results that will be certain, possible, advisable, or necessary
- Identify specific information in a magazine article
- Identify and discuss details in an interview
- Discuss common problems and possible solutions
- Discuss superstitions, giving opinions and making cross-cultural comparisons
- Write a speech about what one will do if elected class or school president

---

STEP 1	GRAMMAR IN CONTEXT

BEFORE YOU READ

Look at the pictures on this page and on page 332. Discuss the questions.

1. What is a superstition? Can you give an example of one?

2. Do you believe in any superstitions?

3. Do you wear or carry things that make you feel lucky?

READ

▶ 21|01   Read this magazine article about superstitions.

Knock on Wood!

- If you knock on wood, you'll keep bad luck away.

- You'll get a good grade on the test if you wear your shirt inside out.

- You'll get a bad grade unless you use your lucky pen.

Superstitions may sound silly to some, but millions of people all over the world believe in their power to bring good luck or prevent bad luck. In fact, different cultures share many similar superstitions:

- If you break a mirror, you'll have seven years of bad luck.

- If the palm of your hand itches, you're going to get some money.

- If it rains when you move to a new house, you'll get rich.

All superstitions are based on a cause-and-effect relationship: If X happens, then Y will also happen. However, in superstitions, the cause is magical and unrelated to the effect. In our scientific age, why are these beliefs so powerful and widespread? The Luck Project, an online survey of superstitious behaviors, gives us some fascinating insight. Read some of their findings on the next page.

- Emotions can influence superstitions, especially in uncertain situations where people do not have control. People will react in a more superstitious way if they are worried. They will react in a less superstitious way if they don't feel a strong need for control.

- We make our own luck. If you believe you're lucky, you will carry out rituals[1] that make you feel good (crossing your fingers for luck, for example). As a result, you probably won't fear bad luck signs (such as breaking a mirror), and you might perform better in stressful situations. In contrast, if you think you're unlucky, you will anticipate the worst and look for signs of bad luck that confirm your belief. Your attitude makes a difference.

- More people than you might think believe in superstitions. Of the 4,000 people surveyed, 84 percent knocked on wood for good luck. Almost half feared walking under a ladder. And 15 percent of the people who studied or worked in the sciences feared the number 13.

Clearly, higher education doesn't eliminate[2] superstition—college students are among the most superstitious people. Other superstitious groups are performers, athletes, gamblers,[3] and stock traders. People in these groups often have lucky charms[4] or personal good luck rituals.

Deanna McBrearty, a New York City Ballet member, has lucky hair bands. "If I have a good performance when I'm wearing one, I'll keep wearing it," she says. Baseball player Wade Boggs would only eat chicken before a game. Brett Gallagher, a stock trader, believes he'll be more successful if he owns pet fish. "I had fish for a while, and after they died, the market didn't do so well," he points out.

Will you do better on the test if you use your lucky pen? Maybe. If the pen makes you feel more confident, you might improve your score. So go ahead and use it. But don't forget: Your lucky pen will be powerless unless you study. The harder you work, the luckier you'll get.

---

1 *rituals:* sets of actions always done in the same way
2 *eliminate:* get rid of something completely
3 *gamblers:* people who risk money in a game or race (cards, horse race) because they might win more money
4 *lucky charms:* very small objects worn on a chain that will bring good luck (horseshoes, four-leaf clovers, etc.)

AFTER YOU READ

Ⓐ VOCABULARY **Match the words with their definitions.**

_____ 1. widespread   **a.** to expect that something will happen

_____ 2. insight   **b.** sure

_____ 3. percent   **c.** the usual way someone thinks or feels about something

_____ 4. confident   **d.** the ability to understand something clearly

_____ 5. anticipate   **e.** happening in many places

_____ 6. attitude   **f.** equal to a certain amount in every hundred

B COMPREHENSION Read the statements. Check (✓) *True* or *False*.

	True	False
1. A superstition expresses a cause and effect.	☐	☐
2. If you are worrying about something, you might act less superstitiously.	☐	☐
3. If you feel lucky, you'll have more good luck rituals.	☐	☐
4. If you feel unlucky, you won't believe in superstitions.	☐	☐
5. If you study science, you won't be superstitious.	☐	☐
6. If you don't study, your good luck pen won't work.	☐	☐

C DISCUSSION Work with a partner. Compare your answers in B. Why did you check *True* or *False*?

STEP 2　**GRAMMAR PRESENTATION**

FUTURE REAL CONDITIONAL SENTENCES

Statements

If-Clause: Present	Result Clause: Future
If she **studies**,	she **won't fail** the test. she**'s going to pass** the test. she **might get** an A.
If she **doesn't study**,	she**'ll fail** the test. she **isn't going to pass** the test. she **might not get** an A.

Yes/No Questions

Result Clause: Future	*If*-Clause: Present
Will she **pass** the test	*if* she **studies**?
Is she **going to pass** the test	

Short Answers

Affirmative		Negative	
Yes,	she **will**. she **is**.	No,	she **won't**. she **isn't**.

Wh- Questions

Result Clause: Future	*If*-Clause: Present
What **will** she **do** What **is** she **going to do**	*if* she doesn't **pass** the test?

Future Real Conditional Sentences　**333**

GRAMMAR NOTES

1 Future Real Conditional Sentences

Use future real conditional sentences to describe **real conditions** and **results** that are **certain**.

The *if*-clause describes a **real** or **true condition**. The **result clause** describes the **certain result**.

IF-CLAUSE	RESULT CLAUSE
If I use this pen, I'll pass the test.	
(If I use this pen, I'll certainly pass the test.)	

Use the **simple present** in the *if*-clause. Use the **future** with *will* or *be going to* in the **result clause**.

PRESENT	FUTURE
If you **feel** lucky, you'**ll expect** good things.	
If you **feel** unlucky, you'**re going to expect** bad things to happen.	

BE CAREFUL! Even though the *if*-clause refers to the future, use the simple present. Do not use the future.

If she **gets** an A on her test, she **will stop** worrying.

NOT If she ~~will get~~ an A on her test, she will stop worrying.

2 With a Modal in the Result Clause

You can use **modals** or similar expressions in the **result clause** to express **possibility** (*may, might, could*), **advice** (*should, ought to*), or **necessity** (*must, have to*).

	IF-CLAUSE	RESULT CLAUSE
• *may*	If they have time tomorrow, they *may go* to the park.	
• *should*	If you want to pass that test, you *should* study more.	
• *must*	If she wants to do well here, she *must* work harder.	

USAGE NOTE We sometimes use *then* to **emphasize the result** in future real conditional sentences with **modals** or similar expressions or with *will*.

If she studies hard, *then* she **might get** an A.
If she studies hard, *then* she'**ll get** an A.

3 Position of the *If*-Clause

The *if*-clause can come **at the beginning or the end** of the sentence. The meaning is the same.

• at the **beginning**	*If* she uses that pen, she'll feel lucky.
• at the **end**	She'll feel lucky *if* she uses that pen.

IN WRITING Use a **comma after the** *if*-clause when it comes at the **beginning** of the sentence. Do not use a comma after the result clause when the result clause comes first.

If she gets a good grade, she'll be happy.

NOT She'll be happy~~,~~ if she gets a good grade.

You can use *if* or *unless* in future real conditional sentences, but their **meanings are very different**.

Use *if* to express an **affirmative condition**.	*If* he studies, he will pass the test.
Use *unless* to express a **negative condition**.	*Unless* he studies, he will fail the test. *(If he doesn't study, he will fail the test.)*
Unless often means *if . . . not*.	*Unless* you're superstitious, you won't be afraid of black cats. or *If* you aren't superstitious, you won't be afraid of black cats.

STEP 3   FOCUSED PRACTICE

EXERCISE 1   DISCOVER THE GRAMMAR

Ⓐ GRAMMAR NOTES 1–2, 4 **Match each condition with its result.**

Condition

___d___ **1.** If I lend someone my baseball bat,

_____ **2.** Unless you take an umbrella,

_____ **3.** If I give my boyfriend a new pair of shoes,

_____ **4.** If the palm of your hand itches,

_____ **5.** If I use my lucky pen,

_____ **6.** If you wear your sweater backwards,

Result

a. you'll want to scratch it.

b. people might laugh at you.

c. I'll get 100 percent on the test.

~~**d.**~~ I won't hit a home run.

e. you're going to get wet.

f. he'll walk out of the relationship.

Ⓑ **Now write the sentences that describe superstitions.**

1. *If I lend someone my baseball bat, I won't hit a home run.*

2. _____

3. _____

EXERCISE 2 *IF* OR *UNLESS*

A GRAMMAR NOTE 4 Two students are talking about a test. Complete their conversations with *if* or *unless*.

Conversation 1

YUKI: It's midnight. _____Unless_____ we get some sleep, we won't do well tomorrow.
1.

EVA: But I won't be able to sleep _____Unless_____ I stop worrying about the test.
2.

YUKI: Here's my lucky charm. _____If_____ you wear it, you'll do fine!
3.

Conversation 2

EVA: I found my blue shirt! _____If_____ I wear it, I'm sure I'll pass!
4.

YUKI: Great. Now _____If_____ we just clean up the room, we can leave for school.
5.

EVA: We can't clean up! There's a Russian superstition that says _____If_____ you clean
6.

your room, you'll get a bad test grade!

Conversation 3

YUKI: _____If_____ we finish the test by noon, we can go to the job fair.
7.

EVA: I want to get a job, but nobody is going to hire me _____Unless_____ I pass this test.
8.

Conversation 4

EVA: I'm looking for my lucky pen. _____Unless_____ I find it, I won't pass the test!
9.

YUKI: Don't worry. _____If_____ you use the same pen that you used to study with, you'll
10.

do great! The pen will remember the answers.

Conversation 5

EVA: I was so nervous without my lucky pen. It'll be a miracle[1] _____If_____ I pass.
11.

YUKI: That's the wrong attitude! There aren't any miracles. _____If_____ you study, you'll
12.

do well. It's that simple.

Conversation 6

EVA: Do you think a company like ZY3, Inc. will offer me a job _____If_____ I fill out
13.

an application?

YUKI: Only _____If_____ you use your lucky pen. I'm kidding! You won't know
14.

_____Unless_____ you try!
15.

▶21|02 **B** LISTEN AND CHECK Listen to the conversations and check your answers in A.

---

1 *miracle:* something lucky that happens when you didn't think it was possible

EXERCISE 3 SIMPLE PRESENT OR FUTURE

GRAMMAR NOTE 1 Complete these sentences describing superstitions from around the world. Use the correct form of the verbs in parentheses.

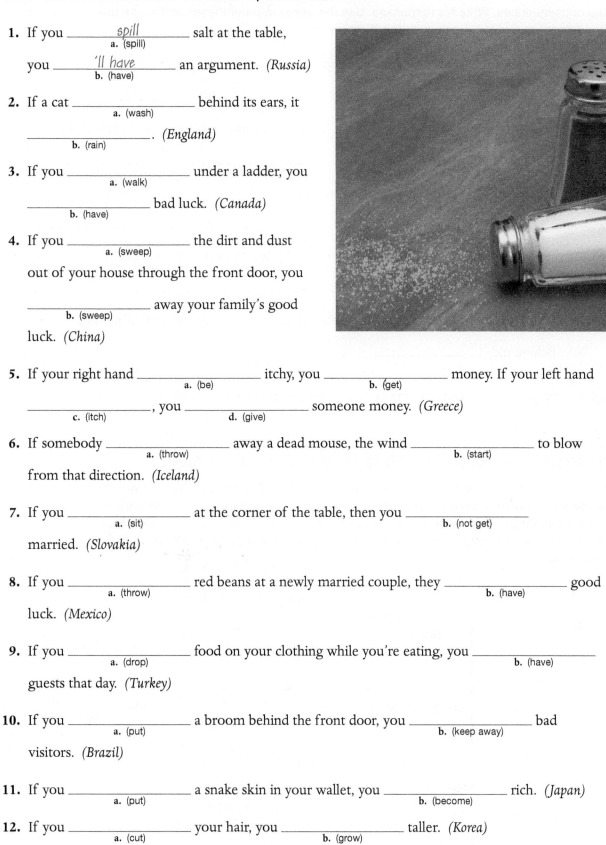

1. If you _____spill_____ salt at the table,
   a. (spill)

   you _____'ll have_____ an argument. *(Russia)*
   b. (have)

2. If a cat _____ behind its ears, it
   a. (wash)

   _____. *(England)*
   b. (rain)

3. If you _____ under a ladder, you
   a. (walk)

   _____ bad luck. *(Canada)*
   b. (have)

4. If you _____ the dirt and dust
   a. (sweep)

   out of your house through the front door, you

   _____ away your family's good
   b. (sweep)

   luck. *(China)*

5. If your right hand _____ itchy, you _____ money. If your left hand
   a. (be)   b. (get)

   _____, you _____ someone money. *(Greece)*
   c. (itch)   d. (give)

6. If somebody _____ away a dead mouse, the wind _____ to blow
   a. (throw)   b. (start)

   from that direction. *(Iceland)*

7. If you _____ at the corner of the table, then you _____
   a. (sit)   b. (not get)

   married. *(Slovakia)*

8. If you _____ red beans at a newly married couple, they _____ good
   a. (throw)   b. (have)

   luck. *(Mexico)*

9. If you _____ food on your clothing while you're eating, you _____
   a. (drop)   b. (have)

   guests that day. *(Turkey)*

10. If you _____ a broom behind the front door, you _____ bad
    a. (put)   b. (keep away)

    visitors. *(Brazil)*

11. If you _____ a snake skin in your wallet, you _____ rich. *(Japan)*
    a. (put)   b. (become)

12. If you _____ your hair, you _____ taller. *(Korea)*
    a. (cut)   b. (grow)

EXERCISE 4 AFFIRMATIVE AND NEGATIVE SENTENCES

A GRAMMAR NOTES 1, 3 Eva is thinking of working for a company called ZY3, Inc. Her best friend Don, who used to work there, thinks it's a terrible idea and is explaining to her the consequences. Write his responses. Use the words in parentheses and future real conditional sentences. Begin with the *if*-clause.

1. EVA: If I work for ZY3, I'm going to be happy. I'm sure of it.

   DON: *If you work for ZY3, you're not going to be happy. You're going to be miserable.*
   (miserable)

2. EVA: You have such a pessimistic attitude! I'll have the chance to travel a lot if I take this job.

   DON: Not true. _____
   (never leave the office)

3. EVA: But I'll get a raise every year if I stay at ZY3.

   DON: _____
   (every two years)

4. EVA: Well, if I join ZY3, I'm going to have wonderful health care benefits.

   DON: Stay healthy! _____
   (terrible health care benefits)

5. EVA: I don't believe you! If I accept ZY3's offer, it'll be the best career move of my life.

   DON: Believe me, _____
   (the worst)

21|03 **B** LISTEN AND CHECK Listen to the conversation and check your answers in A.

EXERCISE 5 SENTENCES WITH *WILL* AND MODALS

GRAMMAR NOTES 1–3 Yuki Tamari is not sure if she should go to law school or not. She made a decision tree to help her decide. In the tree, arrows connect the conditions and the results. Write future real conditional sentences about her decision. Use *will* if the result is certain. Use *may*, *might*, or *could* if the result is possible. Remember to use commas where necessary.

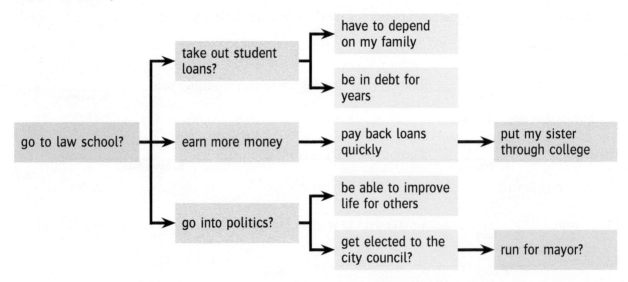

1. *If I go to law school, I might take out students loans.* _____

2. *I'll be in debt for years if I take out student loans.* _____

3. _____

4. _____

5. _____

6. _____

7. _____

8. _____

9. _____

10. _____

EXERCISE 6 EDITING

GRAMMAR NOTES 1–4 **Read Yuki's blog. There are seven mistakes in the use of future real conditional sentences. The first mistake is already corrected. Find and correct six more. Don't forget to check punctuation.**

OCTOBER 1

Should I campaign for student council president? I'll have to decide soon if I ~~wanted~~ *want*
to run. If I'll be busy campaigning, I won't have much time to study. That's a problem
because I'm not going to get into law school if I get good grades this year. On the
other hand, the problems in this school are widespread, and nothing is getting done
if Todd Laker becomes president again. I'm 100 percent certain of that, and most
people agree with me. But will I know what to do if I'll get the job? Never mind. I
shouldn't anticipate difficulties. I really need to have a better attitude. I'll deal with
that problem, if I win. I know what I'll do. If I become president, I cut my hair. That
always brings me good luck!

EXERCISE 7 LISTENING

▶21|04 **A** Yuki is talking about her campaign platform. Read the list of issues. Then listen to the interview. Listen again and check (✓) the things that Yuki promises to work for if she is elected.

☑ **1.** have contact with a lot of students

☐ **2.** improve the student council's newsletter

☐ **3.** publish teacher evaluations on the student council's website

☐ **4.** get the college to provide a bus service between the airport and the college

☐ **5.** get the college to offer a major in environmental science

☐ **6.** reduce tuition costs

▶21|04 **B** Listen again to the interview. Work with a partner. Discuss Yuki's platform. Do you think she is a good candidate for student council president? Why or why not?

EXAMPLE: A: I think she'll improve things if she gets elected.
          B: I agree. I like the fact that she thinks communication is very important. If she's elected, she'll communicate more with students. For example, she'll have . . .

EXERCISE 8
IT'S A REAL PROBLEM!

PROBLEM SOLVING **Work in a group. Read this list of problems. Discuss possible solutions for each one. Use** *if, if . . . not,* **or** *unless.*

1. Your neighbors are always playing music so loudly that you can't fall asleep.

EXAMPLE: A: What will you do if they don't stop?
          B: If they don't stop, I'll call the police.
          C: Unless they stop, I'll call the landlord.
          D: I'll consider moving if they continue to bother me.

2. You've had a headache every day for a week. You can't concentrate.

3. You keep phoning your parents, but there's no answer. It's now midnight, and you're worried.

4. You like your job, but you just found out that other workers are making much more money than you are.

5. You live in an apartment building. It's winter, and the building hasn't had any heat for a week. You're freezing.

6. You're ten pounds overweight. You've been trying for months to lose weight, but so far you haven't lost a single pound.

7. You bought a phone at a local store. It doesn't work, but when you tried to return it, the salesperson refused to take it back.

8. Your roommates don't clean up after they cook. You've already reminded them several times, but they always "forget."

9. You paid for a parking space near school or work. For the past week, the same car has taken your space.

EXERCISE 9 LUCK AROUND THE WORLD

CROSS-CULTURAL COMPARISON Work in a group. Read the list of superstitions below. Compare each one with a similar superstition in a country or culture you know well.

EXAMPLE: A: In Germany, people press the thumbs of both their hands to wish themselves or another person good luck.
B: In Mexico, . . .
C: In Russia, . . .

- If you cross your fingers, you'll have good luck.

- If you touch blue, your dreams will come true.

- If you break a mirror, you will have seven years of bad luck.

- If you put a piece of clothing on inside out, you will have good luck.

- If your palm itches, you're going to find some money soon.

EXERCISE 10 IT'S HOW YOU LOOK AT IT

DISCUSSION Work with a partner. What is your attitude about superstitions? Are superstitions good or bad? Discuss and give examples to support your opinions.

EXAMPLE: A: I think some superstitions are bad. For example, if you think a lucky pen will help you do well on a test, you may not study enough. And if you don't study enough, you probably won't get a good grade.
B: I don't know about that. If you believe a special pen will give you good luck, you may have more confidence. If you have more confidence, you might actually do better on the test.

A BEFORE YOU WRITE Imagine you are running for class or school president. Make a list of five things you will do if you become president.

1. _____

2. _____

3. _____

4. _____

5. _____

B WRITE Use your list to write a short speech. What will you do if you become class or school president? What may, might, or could happen if you don't win the election? Try to avoid the common mistakes in the chart.

EXAMPLE: We have a wonderful school, but there are always opportunities for improvement. If I become school president, I will ask for ten new computers. . . . If I'm not elected, classroom conditions might . . .

Common Mistakes in Using Future Real Conditional Sentences

Use the **simple present** in the *if*-clause. Do not use the future in the *if*-clause.	*If* I **become** president, I will ask for more money. NOT If I ~~will become~~ president, I will ask for more money.
Use *unless* or *if . . . not* to state a **negative condition**. Do not use *if*.	*Unless* you **vote** for me, I won't get the job done. *If* you **don't vote** for me, I won't get the job done. NOT ~~If you vote~~ for me, I won't get the job done.
Use a **comma after the** *if/unless* **clause** when it comes first. Do not use a comma after the result clause when the result clause comes first.	*If* I **win,** I will make changes. NOT I will make changes͵ if I win.

C CHECK YOUR WORK Read your speech. Underline the *if* or *unless* clauses once and the result clauses twice. Circle *if* or *unless*. Use the Editing Checklist to check your work.

Editing Checklist

Did you use . . . ?

☐ the simple present in the *if*-clause

☐ the future with *will* or *be going to* in the result clause for results that are certain

☐ *may, might,* or *could* in the result clause for results that are possible

☐ *unless* or *if not* to express a negative condition

☐ a comma after the *if/unless* clause when it comes first

D REVISE YOUR WORK Read your speech again. Can you improve your writing? Make changes if necessary. Give your speech a title.

UNIT 21 REVIEW

Test yourself on the grammar of the unit.

Ⓐ Match each condition with its result.

Condition	Result
_____ **1.** If it rains,	**a.** you might have good luck.
_____ **2.** Unless you study,	**b.** I could pay you back tomorrow.
_____ **3.** If you cross your fingers,	**c.** I may not buy it.
_____ **4.** Unless they lower the price,	**d.** I'll take an umbrella.
_____ **5.** If you lend me $10,	**e.** you could rent one.
_____ **6.** If you don't own a car,	**f.** you won't pass.

Ⓑ Complete the future real conditional sentences in these conversations with the correct form of the verbs in parentheses.

1. A: Are you going to take the bus?

   B: No. If I _____ the bus, I _____ late.
                           a. (take)   **b.** (be)

2. A: What _____ you _____ if you _____ the job?
                                  a. (do)   **b.** (not get)

   B: I _____ in school unless I _____ the job.
               c. (stay)   **d.** (get)

3. A: If I _____ the test, I _____ .
               a. (pass)   **b.** (celebrate)

   B: Good luck, but I'm sure you'll pass. You've studied really hard for it.

   A: Thanks!

Ⓒ Find and correct six mistakes. Remember to check punctuation.

    It's been a hard week, and I'm looking forward to the weekend. If the weather will be nice tomorrow Marco and I are going to go to the beach. The ocean is usually too cold for swimming at this time of year, so I probably don't go in the water unless it's really hot outside. But I love walking along the beach and breathing in the fresh sea air.

    If Marco has time, he might makes some sandwiches to bring along. Otherwise, we'll just get some pizza. I hope it'll be a nice day. I just listened to the weather report, and there may be some rain in the afternoon. Unless it rains, we probably go to the movies instead. That's our Plan B. But I really want to go to the beach, so I'm keeping my fingers crossed!

Now check your answers on page 480.

Present and Future Unreal Conditional Sentences

WISHES

OUTCOMES
- Describe present or future unreal conditions and results that are untrue, impossible, or possible
- Give advice with *If I were you*
- Express wishes about the present or the future
- Identify key details in a written and a recorded fairy tale
- Discuss hypothetical questions and wishes
- Write about a wish one has for oneself or society

STEP 1   GRAMMAR IN CONTEXT

BEFORE YOU READ

Read the first sentence of the story and look at the picture. Discuss the questions.

1. Is this a true story? What makes you think so?
2. How do fairy tales begin in your culture?

READ

▶ 22|01   Read this version of a famous fairy tale.

The Fisherman and His Wife

O nce upon a time, there was a poor fisherman and his wife who lived in a pigpen[1] near the sea. Every day, the man went to fish. One day, after waiting a very long time, he caught a very big fish. To his surprise, the fish spoke and said, "Please let me live. I'm not a regular fish. If you knew my real identity, you wouldn't kill me. I'm an enchanted prince."

"Don't worry. I won't kill you," responded the kind-hearted fisherman. With these words, he threw the fish back into the clear water and went home to his wife.

"Husband," said the wife, "didn't you catch anything today?"

"I caught a fish, but it said it was an enchanted prince, so I let it go."

"You mean you didn't wish for anything?" asked the wife.

"No," said the fisherman. "What do I need to wish for?"

---

1 *pigpen:* a small building where pigs are kept

"Just look around you," said the wife. "We live in a pigpen. I wish we had a nice little cottage.[2] If we had a cottage, I would be a lot happier. You saved the prince's life. He's sure to grant your wish. Go back and ask him."

"I'm not going to ask for a cottage! If I asked for a cottage, the fish might get angry." But in the end, he consented because he was much more afraid of his wife's anger.

When he got to the sea, it was all green and yellow. "My wife wishes we had a cottage," said the fisherman. "Just go on back," said the fish. "She already has it."

When he returned home, the fisherman found his wife sitting outside a lovely little cottage. The kitchen was filled with food and all types of cooking utensils.[3] Outside was a little garden with vegetables, fruit trees, hens, and ducks.

Things were fine for a week or two. Then the wife said, "This cottage is much too crowded. I wish we lived in a bigger house. If we lived in a big stone castle, I would be much happier. Go and ask the fish for it."

The fisherman didn't want to go, but he did. When he got to the sea, it was dark blue and gray. "My wife wishes we lived in a big stone castle," he said to the fish.

"Just go on back. She's standing in front of the door," said the fish.

When he returned home, the fisherman found his wife on the steps of a great big stone castle. The inside was filled with beautiful gold furniture, chandeliers,[4] and carpets. There were servants everywhere.

The next morning, the wife woke up and said, "I wish I were king of all this land."

"What would you do if you were king?" asked her husband.

"If I were king, I would own all this land. Go on back and ask the fish for it."

This time, the sea was all blackish gray, and the water was rough and smelled terrible. "What does she want now?" asked the fish.

"She wants to be king," said the embarrassed fisherman.

"Just go on back. She already is."

---

2 *cottage:* a small house, usually in the country
3 *cooking utensils:* tools used for cooking or preparing food
4 *chandeliers:* large structures that hang from the ceiling and hold many lights or candles

When the fisherman returned home, he found an enormous palace.[5] Everything inside was made of marble and pure gold, and it was surrounded by soldiers with drums and trumpets. His wife was seated on a throne, and he said to her, "How nice for you that you are king. Now we won't need to wish for anything else."

But his wife was not satisfied. "I'm only king of *this* country," she said. "I wish I were emperor of the whole world. If I were emperor, I would be the most powerful ruler on Earth."

"Wife, now be satisfied," responded the fisherman. "You're king. You can't be anything more."

The wife, however, wasn't convinced. She kept thinking and thinking about what more she could be. "If I were emperor, I could have anything—and you wouldn't have to ask the fish for anything more. Go right now and tell the fish that I want to be emperor of the whole world."

"Oh, no," said the fisherman. "The fish can't do that. If I were you, I wouldn't ask for anything else." But his wife got so furious that the poor fisherman ran back to the fish. There was a terrible storm, and the sea was pitch black[6] with waves as high as mountains.

"Well, what does she want now?" asked the fish.

"She wishes she were emperor of the whole world," said the fisherman.

"Just go on back. She's sitting in the pigpen again."

And they are still sitting there today.

---

5 *palace:* a very large house where the ruler of a country lives
6 *pitch black:* very dark black; the color of coal or tar

AFTER YOU READ

A VOCABULARY Choose the word or phrase that best completes each sentence.

1. If something is **enchanted**, it has been _____.
   a. changed by magic   b. broken   c. stolen

2. When you **consent**, you _____ to do something.
   a. refuse   b. agree   c. like

3. Someone who is **furious** is very _____.
   a. kind-hearted   b. poor   c. angry

4. Someone who is **embarrassed** feels _____.
   a. uncomfortable   b. powerful   c. frightened

5. If you **grant** someone's request, you say _____ to it.
   a. yes   b. maybe   c. no

6. If you have a **regular** day, your day is _____.
   a. special   b. ordinary   c. surprising

COMPREHENSION   Read the statements. Check (✓) *True* or *False*.

	True	False
1. Before the fisherman caught the fish, he and his wife lived in a nice little cottage.	☐	☐
2. As soon as he caught the fish, the fisherman knew its real identity.	☐	☐
3. The wife wanted to have a cottage.	☐	☐
4. The fisherman didn't want to ask for a cottage because he didn't want to make the fish angry.	☐	☐
5. The wife was satisfied with the stone castle.	☐	☐
6. The man advised his wife not to ask to be emperor of the whole world.	☐	☐

C DISCUSSION   Work with a partner. Discuss your answers in B. Why did you check *True* or *False*?

STEP 2   GRAMMAR PRESENTATION

PRESENT AND FUTURE UNREAL CONDITIONAL SENTENCES

Statements

If-Clause: Simple Past	Result Clause: *Would (not)* + Base Form
If Mia **had** money, *If* she **were*** rich,	she **would live** in a palace. she **wouldn't live** in a cottage.
If Mia **didn't have** money, *If* she **weren't** rich,	she **wouldn't live** in a palace. she **would live** in a cottage.

*With the verb *be*, use *were* for all subjects.

Contractions

I would	=	**I'd**
you would	=	**you'd**
he would	=	**he'd**
she would	=	**she'd**
it would	=	**it'd**
we would	=	**we'd**
they would	=	**they'd**
would not	=	**wouldn't**

Yes/No Questions

Result Clause	*If*-Clause
Would she **live** here	*if* she **had** money?
	if she **were** rich?

Short Answers

Affirmative	Negative
Yes, she **would**.	**No**, she **wouldn't**.

Wh- Questions

Result Clause	*If*-Clause
What **would** she **do**	*if* she **had** money?
	if she **were** rich?

GRAMMAR NOTES

1 Present and Future Unreal Conditional Sentences

Use present and future unreal conditional sentences to describe **unreal conditions and their results**. A condition and its result may be untrue, imagined, or impossible.

The *if*-clause describes an **unreal** or **untrue** condition. The **result clause** describes the **unreal** or **untrue result** of that condition.

IF-CLAUSE	RESULT CLAUSE
If I had more time, I would read fairy tales.	
(But I don't have time, so I don't read fairy tales.)	

The sentence can be about:

- the **present**

If I lived in a palace **now**, I would give parties.
(I don't live in a palace. I don't give parties.)

- the **future**

If I moved **next month**, I would buy a car.
(I won't move. I won't buy a car.)

2 Verb Forms in Present and Future Unreal Conditional Sentences

Use the **simple past** in the *if*-clause. Use *would* + **base form** of the verb in the **result clause**.

SIMPLE PAST   *WOULD* + BASE FORM
If he **had** a nice house, he **wouldn't move**.

BE CAREFUL! The *if*-clause uses the simple past, but it's **not about the past**. It's about the present or the future. Do not use the simple present or *will* in the *if*-clause.

If I **had** more money *now*, I would take a big trip.
NOT If I ~~have~~ more money now, . . .
If I **got** money *tomorrow*, I would take a big trip.
NOT If I'~~ll get~~ money tomorrow, . . .

BE CAREFUL! Use *would* only in the **result clause**. Do not use *would* in the *if*-clause.

If I **lived** there, I **would move**.
NOT If I ~~would live~~ there, I would move.

Use *were* for **all subjects** when the verb in the *if*-clause is a form of *be*. Do not use *was*.

If I **were** king, I would solve the problem.
NOT If I ~~was~~ king, . . .

USAGE NOTE Some people use *was* with *I, he, she*, and *it*. However, this is usually considered incorrect, especially in formal or written English.

3 With a Modal in the Result Clause

You can use the **modals** *might* or *could* in the **result clause** to express **possibility**.

- *might*
- *could*

IF-CLAUSE   RESULT CLAUSE
If they took a trip, they *might* **go** to China.

If I knew Chinese, I *could* **translate** for them.

BE CAREFUL! Do not use *may* or *can* in unreal conditional sentences.

If they had time, they *might* **take** a trip.
NOT If they had time, they ~~may~~ take a trip.
If they went there, they *could* **see** the Great Wall.
NOT If they went there, they ~~can~~ see . . .

4 Position of the *If*-Clause

The *if*-clause can come **at the beginning or the end** of the sentence. The meaning is the same.

• at the **beginning**	*If* **I had more money**, I would move.
• at the **end**	I would move *if* **I had more money**.

IN WRITING Use a **comma after the *if*-clause** when it comes at the **beginning** of the sentence. Do not use a comma after the result clause when the result clause comes first.	*If* **I had time,** I would go fishing. **NOT** I would go fishing, if I had time.

5 With *If I Were You* to Give Advice

Use *If I were you* to **give advice**.	*If I were you*, I wouldn't ask for more. *(My advice is: Don't ask for more.)*
BE CAREFUL! Use *were* in the *if*-clause. Do not use *was*.	*If I were you*, I'd try harder. **NOT** If I was you, I'd try harder.

6 With *Wish* to Express Wishes

Use *wish* + **simple past** to express things that you **want to be true now**, but that are **not true**.	I *wish* I **lived** in a castle. *(I don't live in a castle now, but I want to.)*
BE CAREFUL! Use *were* after *wish*. Do not use *was*.	I **wish** I *were* a child again. **NOT** I wish I was a child again.
Use *wish* + *would/could* + **base form** of the verb for **wishes about the future**.	I **wish** she *would* **visit** us next summer. She **wishes** she *could* **travel** around the world.
USAGE NOTE We often use *wish* + *would/could* to express a **wish for change**.	My neighbors are loud. I **wish** they *would* **be** quiet. I don't like my apartment, I **wish** I *could* **move**.
BE CAREFUL! Use *would* or *could* after *wish*. Do not use *will* or *can*.	I **wish** she *would* **call** me. **NOT** I wish she will call me. I **wish** I *could* **buy** a car. **NOT** I wish I can buy a car.

EXERCISE 1   DISCOVER THE GRAMMAR

GRAMMAR NOTES 1–3, 5–6   **Read the numbered statements. Decide if the sentences that follow are** *True (T)* **or** *False (F)***.**

1. If I had time, I would read fairy tales in English.

   _F_   **a.** I have time.

   _F_   **b.** I'm going to read fairy tales in English.

2. If it weren't so cold, I would go fishing.

  _____   **a.** It's cold.

  _____   **b.** I'm going fishing.

3. If I caught an enchanted fish, I would make three wishes.

  _____   **a.** I believe I'm going to catch an enchanted fish.

  _____   **b.** I'm going to make three wishes.

4. If I had three wishes, I wouldn't ask for a palace.

  _____   **a.** I have three wishes.

  _____   **b.** I don't want a palace.

5. If my house were too small, I would try to find a bigger one.

  _____   **a.** My house is big enough.

  _____   **b.** I'm not looking for a bigger house right now.

6. I could buy a new car if I got a raise.

  _____   **a.** I recently got a raise.

  _____   **b.** I want a new car.

7. If I didn't earn enough money babysitting, I might look for a regular job.

  _____   **a.** I don't earn enough money.

  _____   **b.** I'm looking for a regular job.

8. Your friend tells you, "If I were you, I wouldn't change jobs."

  _____   **a.** Your friend is giving you advice.

  _____   **b.** Your friend thinks you shouldn't change jobs.

9. I wish I were a princess.

  _____   **a.** I'm a princess.

  _____   **b.** I want to be a princess.

10. I wish I could live in a big house.

  _____   **a.** I want to live in a big house.

  _____   **b.** I don't live in a big house.

EXERCISE 2 VERB FORMS IN THE *IF* AND RESULT CLAUSES

GRAMMAR NOTES 1–3, 6 Complete this article from a popular psychology magazine. Use the correct form of the verbs in parentheses to form unreal conditional sentences.

Marty Hadad has always wanted to invite his whole family over for the holidays, but his apartment is small, his family is very large, and he doesn't want to feel embarrassed. "If I _____*invited*_____ them all for dinner, there _____*wouldn't be*_____ enough
   1. (invite)   **2.** (not be)

room for everyone to sit down," he told a friend. If Marty _____ a
                                                              3. (be)

complainer, he _____ about the size of his apartment and spend the
                   4. (moan)

holiday at his parents' house. But Marty is a problem solver. This year he is hosting an open house.

People can drop in at different times during the day, and there will be room for everyone.

   "If life _____ a fairy tale, we _____
               5. (be)   **6.** (can / wish)

problems away," noted psychologist Joel Grimes. "What complainers are really saying is, 'If I

_____ a magical solution, I _____ with this
   7. (have)   **8.** (not have to deal)

myself.' I wish it _____ that easy," says Grimes. He gives an example of a
                      9. (be)

very wealthy client who is convinced that he has almost no time for his family. "He's waiting for a

miracle to give him the time he needs. But he _____ the time if he
                                                   10. (can / find)

_____ about the problem creatively," says Grimes.
   11. (think)

   Even very wealthy people have limited time, money, and space. If complainers

_____ this, then they _____
   12. (realize)   **13.** (understand)

that there will always be problems. Then they could stop complaining and try to

find possible solutions. Marty, who is still a student in college,

_____ for years before inviting his
   14. (may / have to wait)

family over if he _____ on a bigger
                     15. (insist)

apartment for his party. Instead, he is creatively solving his

problems right now.

   There is an old sixteenth-century English saying: "If

wishes _____ horses, then beggars
            16. (be)

_____." But wishes aren't horses. We
   17. (will / ride)

have to learn to create our own good fortune and not wait for a

genie with three wishes to come along and solve our problems.

EXERCISE 3 STATEMENTS

GRAMMAR NOTES 1–4 Psychologist Joel Grimes hears all types of excuses from his clients. Rewrite each excuse as a present unreal conditional statement. Keep the same order and decide which clause begins with *if*. Use commas where necessary.

1. I'm so busy. That's why I don't read bedtime stories to my little girl.

   If I weren't so busy, I would read bedtime stories to my little girl.

2. My husband won't ask for a raise. It's because he's not ambitious.

   _____

3. I don't play sports. But only because I'm not in shape.

   _____

4. I don't have enough time. That's why I'm not studying for the exam.

   _____

5. I'm too old. That's why I'm not going back to school.

   _____

6. I can't do my job. The reason is, my boss doesn't explain things properly.

   _____

7. I'm not good at math. That's why I don't balance my checkbook.

   _____

8. I can't stop smoking. The problem is, I feel nervous all the time.

   _____

9. I'm so tired. That's why I get up so late.

   _____

EXERCISE 4 WISHES ABOUT THE PRESENT OR FUTURE

GRAMMAR NOTE 6 Remember the fish from the fairy tale on pages 344–346? Read the things the fish would like to change. Then write sentences with *wish*.

1. I'm a fish. *I wish I weren't a fish.*

2. My life doesn't change. *I wish my life would change.*

3. I'm not a handsome prince. _____

4. I live in the sea. _____

5. I don't live in a castle. _____

6. The fisherman comes here every day. _____

7. He'll return tomorrow. _____

8. His wife always wants more. _____

9. She'll ask for a bigger house. _____

10. She can't be satisfied. _____

11. They don't leave me alone. _____

12. I can't grant my own wishes. _____

EXERCISE 5
QUESTIONS

GRAMMAR NOTES 1–4

Marty is having his open-house holiday party. His nieces and nephews are playing a fantasy question game. Use the words in parentheses to write present and future unreal conditional questions. Use commas where necessary. Keep the same order.

1. *What would you do if you were a millionaire?* _____
(what / you / do / if / you / be a millionaire)

2. _____
(if / you / be the leader of this country / what / you / do)

3. _____
(how / you / feel / if / you / never need to sleep)

4. _____
(what / you / do / if / you / have more free time)

5. _____
(if / you / have three wishes / what / you / ask for)

6. _____
(what / you / do / if / you / not have to work)

7. _____
(if / you / have a ticket for anywhere in the world / where / you / travel)

8. _____
(if / you / can build anything / what / it / be)

9. _____
(if / you / can meet a famous person / who / you / want to meet)

10. _____
(who / you / have dinner with / if / you can invite three famous people)

EXERCISE 6 EDITING

GRAMMAR NOTES 1–6 **Read part of a book report that Marty's niece wrote. There are eight mistakes in the use of present and future unreal conditional sentences. The first mistake is already corrected. Find and correct seven more.**

NAME: Laila Hadad   CLASS: English 4

The Disappearance

What would happen to the women if all the men in the world ~~would disappear~~ *disappeared*?

What would happen to the men when there were no women in the world?

Philip Wylie's 1951 science-fiction novel, *The Disappearance*, addresses these

fascinating questions. The answers show us how society has changed since

the 1950s.

According to Wylie, if men and women live in different worlds, the results

would be a disaster. In Wylie's vision, men are too aggressive to survive on

their own, and women are too helpless. If women didn't control them, men

will start more wars. If men aren't there to pump gas and run the businesses,

women wouldn't be able to manage.

If Wylie is alive today, would he write the same novel? Today, a lot of men

take care of their children, and a lot of women run businesses. In 1951, Wylie

couldn't imagine these changes because of his opinions about men and women.

I wish that Wylie was here today. If he were, then he might learns that men are

not more warlike than women, and women are not more helpless than men.

His story might be very different.

STEP 4   COMMUNICATION PRACTICE

EXERCISE 7   LISTENING

▶ 22|02 **A** Listen to a modern fairly tale about Cindy, a clever young girl. Then read the statements. Listen again to the fairy tale and check (✓) *True* or *False*.

		True	False
1.	Cindy wishes she had a new soccer ball.	☐	☑
2.	The toad wishes Cindy would marry him.	☐	☐
3.	If Cindy married the toad, he would become a prince again.	☐	☐
4.	Cindy wishes she could become a beautiful princess.	☐	☐
5.	If Cindy became a princess, she'd have plenty of time to study science.	☐	☐
6.	The toad doesn't know how to use his powers to help himself.	☐	☐
7.	Cindy wants to become a scientist and help the prince.	☐	☐
8.	Cindy wishes she didn't have to work.	☐	☐

B Work with a partner. Discuss your answers in A. Why did you check *True* or *False*?

EXAMPLE: **A:** Number 1 is false. Cindy doesn't wish she had a new soccer ball.
　　　　 B: Right. She already has one, but she can't find it.
　　　　 A: She just wishes she could find it.

EXERCISE 8   WHAT ABOUT YOU?

CONVERSATION Work in a group. Answer the questions in Exercise 5 on page 353. Then talk about your answers with the whole class.

EXAMPLE: **A:** What would you do if you were a millionaire?
　　　　 B: If I were a millionaire, I'd donate half my money to charity.
　　　　 C: With half the money, you could . . .

EXERCISE 9 IF I WERE YOU...

PROBLEM SOLVING Work in a group. One person describes a problem. Group members give advice with *If I were you, I would/wouldn't...* Use the problems below and write three more.

1. You need $500 to pay this month's rent. You only have $300.

    EXAMPLE: A: I can't pay the rent this month. I only have $300, and I need $500. I wish I knew what to do.
    B: If I were you, I'd try to borrow the money.
    C: If I were you, I'd call the landlord right away.

2. You're lonely. You work at home and never meet new people.

3. You never have an opportunity to practice English outside of class.

4. You've been invited to dinner. The main dish is going to be shrimp. You hate shrimp.

5. _____

6. _____

7. _____

EXERCISE 10 JUST THREE WISHES

Ⓐ CONVERSATION In fairy tales, people are often given three wishes. Imagine that you had just three wishes. What would they be? Write them down.

1. *I wish I were famous.*
2. *I wish I spoke perfect English.*
3. *I wish I knew how to fly a plane.*

Ⓑ Talk about your wishes with a partner.

EXAMPLE: A: I wish I were famous.
B: What would you do if you were famous?
A: I would...

Ⓒ There is an old saying: "Be careful what you wish for; it may come true." Look at your wishes again. Work with a partner. Talk about the results—negative as well as positive— that might happen if they came true.

EXAMPLE: A: If I were famous, I might not have enough free time to do regular things. I wouldn't have a private life because...
B: Yes, but if you were famous, maybe you could travel a lot and meet a lot of interesting people.

A BEFORE YOUR WRITE Think about a wish you have for yourself or for society. Then think about both positive and negative results if your wish came true. Complete the outline.

Your Wish: _____

Positive Results	Negative Results
_____	_____
_____	_____

B WRITE Use your outline to write a paragraph about your wish. First, state your wish and describe its positive results. Then, describe its possible negative results. Use present and future unreal conditional sentences. Try to avoid the common mistakes in the chart.

EXAMPLE: I wish people lived forever and didn't have to die. If people lived forever, they would be able to accomplish much more.... On the other hand, if people lived forever, there might be some serious problems. For example,...

Common Mistakes in Using Present and Future Unreal Conditional Sentences

Use the **simple past** in the *if*-clause. Do not use the simple present or the future in the *if*-clause.	**If** I **lived** forever, I would be happy. NOT If I ~~live~~ forever, I would be happy. NOT If I ~~will live~~ forever, I will be happy.
Use *would* + **base form** of the verb in the **result clause**. Do not use *would* in the *if*-clause.	If I lived forever, I **would get** a lot more done. NOT If I ~~would live~~ forever . . .
Use *wish* + **simple past** for wishes about the **present**. Do not use *would* after *wish*.	I **wish** I **had** more friends. NOT I wish I ~~would have~~ more friends.
Use a **comma after the *if*-clause** when it comes first. Do not use a comma after the result clause when it comes first.	**If** I **had more time,** I would travel. NOT I would travel~~,~~ if I had more time.

C CHECK YOUR WORK Read your paragraph. Underline the *if*-clauses once and the result clauses twice. Circle *wish*. Use the Editing Checklist to check your work.

Editing Checklist

Did you use . . . ?

- ☐ the simple past in the *if*-clause
- ☐ *would/might/could* + base form of the verb in the result clause
- ☐ *wish* + simple past for wishes about the present
- ☐ a comma after the *if*-clause when it comes first

D REVISE YOUR WORK Read your paragraph again. Can you improve your writing? Make changes if necessary. Give your paragraph a title.

UNIT 22 REVIEW

Test yourself on the grammar of the unit.

A Circle the correct words to complete the conversation.

A: If I lived in another city, <u>I'd feel / I'm feeling</u> much happier.
  1.

B: Then if I <u>am / were</u> you, I'd move.
  2.

A: I wish I <u>can / could</u> move, but that's just impossible right now.
  3.

B: Would it be impossible if <u>you found / you'll find</u> a job somewhere else?
  4.

A: No, I think Harry <u>can / could</u> help me find a job if I asked him. But I hate to ask.
  5.

B: If he <u>isn't / weren't</u> an old friend, he might not want to help. But he's been your friend for ages.
  6.

A: That's true. You know, I thought that if I talked to you, <u>I'll / I'd</u> get some good ideas. Thanks!
  7.

B Complete the present and future unreal conditional sentences in this paragraph with the correct form of the verbs in parentheses.

What _____ you _____ if you _____ a wallet
                         1. (do)   **2. (find)**

lying in the middle of the street? _____ you _____ the money if
                                                    3. (take)

you _____ no one would ever find out? When Lara faced that situation, she first
       4. (know)

said to herself, "Our life _____ a lot easier if I just _____ this
                           5. (become)   **6. (put)**

money in my pocket." Then she brought the wallet to the police. Her family needed the money,

but she's not sorry. "If we _____ bad choices, our kids _____ the
                            7. (make)   **8. (learn)**

wrong lessons," she told reporters. "So we always try to do the right thing."

C Find and correct five mistakes.

1. Pablo wishes he can speak German.

2. If he had the time, he'll study in Germany. But he doesn't have the time right now.

3. He could get a promotion when he spoke another language.

4. His company may pay the tuition if he took a course.

5. What would you do if you are in Pablo's situation?

Now check your answers on page 481.

Past Unreal Conditional Sentences
ALTERNATE HISTORIES

OUTCOMES
• Describe past unreal conditions and results that are untrue, imagined, impossible, or possible
• Express regret about things that happened or didn't happen in the past
• Extract specific information from an article
• Infer correct information from conversations
• Speculate about past events or hypothetical situations
• Discuss a past decision one regrets
• Write about an event that changed one's life

STEP 1 GRAMMAR IN CONTEXT

BEFORE YOU READ

Look at the title of the article and at the pictures on this page and on page 360. Discuss the questions.

1. What is an example of a *What if* question?
2. Do you think *What if* questions are useful?

READ

▶23|01 Read this article about alternate histories.

What if...

What would have happened if I had stayed in my own country? What would have happened if I had never met my husband? It's human nature to wonder how life would have been different if certain events had (or had not) occurred. There's even a name for the stories we create to answer these *What if* questions—alternate histories. Scientists, historians, fiction writers, and everyday people are always asking *What if* questions. Read some typical examples on the next page.

Science

More than 65 million years ago, dinosaurs roamed[1] our planet. Then a meteor[2] hit the Earth, changing the climate, causing the complete extinction[3] of most types of dinosaurs, and making the development of other kinds of animals possible. But what if the meteor had missed? Phil Currie, a scientist from the University of Alberta, Canada, believes that if the meteor had not struck the Earth, some types of dinosaurs would have become even more intelligent and would have

continued dominating the world, the way humans do today. Would humans have been able to develop alongside these "supersaurs"? If yes, what would our lives have been like if most types of dinosaurs had survived?

History

The seventeenth-century French philosopher Blaise Pascal said, "If Cleopatra's nose had been shorter, the whole face of the world would have been changed." Like Cleopatra, many famous people have changed the course of history,[4] and there has been much speculation on what would have occurred if they hadn't lived. One of the most common questions, for example, is "What would have happened if Adolf Hitler had never been born or if the assassination[5] attempt on his life had been successful?" Many people believe that World War II could have been avoided or at least might have been shortened, saving tens of millions of lives and countless cities from destruction.

Everyday Life

A woman rushes to catch a subway train. Just as she gets there, the doors close. The train pulls away, leaving the woman on the platform.

---

1 *roamed:* traveled freely over a wide area
2 *meteor:* a rock that falls from space into the Earth's atmosphere
3 *extinction:* the disappearance of a whole group of animals so that no more animals of that kind exist any more
4 *the course of history:* the direction history takes
5 *assassination:* the murder of an important person, usually for political reasons

What would have happened if she had gotten on the train? The film *Sliding Doors* explores this question by showing us two parallel stories: the life of the woman if she had gotten on the train, and the life of the same woman if she had missed the train. In one version of the story, the woman meets a man on the train, and the two end up falling in love. In the other, she gets mugged[6] while running to catch a taxi and has to go to the hospital. The outcomes of this everyday occurrence—catching or missing a train—show us how a single ordinary moment can change the direction of our lives.

Some people argue that there is no way of ever really knowing what would have happened if a single event had been different. To those people, speculating about the past is just a game, an amusing way to pass the time. Yet to others, it is obvious that alternate histories have a lot to offer. To them, while we can never know exactly how a small change could have affected an outcome, exploring the results of an alternate past—in books, movies, or our own lives—can teach us important lessons.

---

6 *gets mugged:* is attacked and robbed in a public place

AFTER YOU READ

Ⓐ VOCABULARY Match the words with their definitions.

_____ **1. alternate**   **a.** to happen

_____ **2. dominate**   **b.** one person's description of an event

_____ **3. occur**   **c.** a result

_____ **4. outcome**   **d.** happening at the same time

_____ **5. parallel**   **e.** different

_____ **6. version**   **f.** to have power and control over other people or things

Ⓑ COMPREHENSION Check (✓) the events which, according to the article, can lead to an alternate history.

☐ **1.** staying in one's own country

☐ **2.** a meteor hitting the Earth

☐ **3.** missing one's train

☐ **4.** reading fiction

☐ **5.** the survival of an animal species

☐ **6.** a person's appearance

☐ **7.** playing a game

Ⓒ DISCUSSION Work with a partner. Compare your answers in B. Why did you choose each answer?

PAST UNREAL CONDITIONAL SENTENCES

Statements

If-Clause: Past Perfect	Result Clause: *Would (not) have* + Past Participle
If I **had missed** the train,	I **would have been** late. I **wouldn't have come** on time.
If I **had not gotten** that job,	I **would have felt** very bad. I **wouldn't have met** my wife.

Yes/No Questions

Result Clause	*If*-Clause
Would you **have walked**	**if** you **had had** the time?

Short Answers

Affirmative	Negative
Yes, I **would have**.	**No**, I **wouldn't have**.

Wh- Questions

Result Clause	*If*-Clause
What **would** you **have done**	**if** you **had missed** the train?

Contractions

would have	= **would've**
would not have	= **wouldn't have**

GRAMMAR NOTES

1 Past Unreal Conditional Sentences

Use past unreal conditional sentences to describe **past unreal conditions and their results**. A condition and its result may be untrue, imagined, or impossible.

The *if*-clause describes the **unreal** or **untrue condition**. The **result clause** describes the **unreal** or **untrue result** of that condition.

IF-CLAUSE   RESULT CLAUSE

If I had missed the train, I would have been late.
   (*But I didn't miss the train, so I wasn't late.*)
If I hadn't taken that job, I wouldn't have met my wife.
   (*But I took the job, so I met my wife.*)

2 Verb Forms in Past Unreal Conditional Sentences

Use the **past perfect** in the *if*-clause. Use *would have* + **past participle** of the verb in the **result clause**.

PAST PERFECT   *WOULD HAVE* + PAST PART.

If it **had won** an award, it **would have become** a famous movie.

BE CAREFUL! Sometimes speakers use *would have* in the *if*-clause. However, this is usually considered incorrect, especially in formal or written English.

If I **had had** time, I **would have watched** the movie.
NOT If I ~~would have had~~ time . . .

3 With a Modal in the Result Clause

You can use the **modals** *might have* or *could have* in the **result clause** to express **possibility**.

	IF-CLAUSE *RESULT CLAUSE*
• *might have*	If Ed had studied hard, he *might have* become a teacher.
• *could have*	If Ed had studied hard, he *could have* become a teacher.
BE CAREFUL! Use *might have* or *could have* if the result is **not certain**. Do not use *may have* or *can have*.	If I had known about the party, I *might have* gone. NOT . . . I ~~may have~~ gone . . . If I had gone, I *could have* seen you there. NOT . . . I ~~can have~~ seen . . .

4 Position of the *If*-Clause

The *if*-clause can come **at the beginning or the end** of the sentence. The meaning is the same.

• at the **beginning**	**If he had won a million dollars**, he would have traveled around the world.
• at the **end**	He would have traveled around the world **if he had won a million dollars**.
IN WRITING Use a **comma after the *if*-clause** when it comes at the **beginning** of the sentence. Do not use a comma after the result clause when the result clause comes first.	**If I had known**, I would have told you. NOT I would have told you͓ if I had known.

5 Past Unreal Conditional Sentences to Express Regret

Past unreal conditional sentences are often used to express **regret** about what really **happened in the past**.	**If** I **had been** free, I **would have gone** with you. *(I regret that I didn't go with you.)*

6 With *Wish* to Express Regret or Sadness

Use *wish* + **past perfect** to express **regret or sadness** about things in the past that you **wanted to happen but didn't**, or about things you **didn't want to happen but happened**.	Glen *wishes* he **had studied** history. *(He didn't study history, and now he thinks that was a mistake.)* He *wishes* he **hadn't taken** that job. *(He took that job, and now he regrets it.)*

EXERCISE 1 DISCOVER THE GRAMMAR

GRAMMAR NOTES 1–3, 5–6 **Read the numbered statements. Decide if the sentences that follow are** *True (T)* **or** *False (F)*.

1. If a girl hadn't stepped in front of her, Helen wouldn't have missed her train.

    _T_ **a.** A girl stepped in front of Helen.

    _T_ **b.** Helen missed her train.

2. If she had gotten on the train, she would've met James.

    _____ **a.** She met James.

    _____ **b.** She got on the train.

3. She wouldn't have gotten her new job if James hadn't told her about it.

    _____ **a.** She got a new job.

    _____ **b.** James didn't tell her about it.

4. If I had gotten home before 10:00, I could've watched the movie *Sliding Doors*.

    _____ **a.** I got home before 10:00.

    _____ **b.** I regret missing the movie.

5. I would have called you if I hadn't fallen asleep.

    _____ **a.** I called you.

    _____ **b.** I fell asleep.

6. If I hadn't had a history test the next day, I wouldn't have gone to bed so late.

    _____ **a.** I had a history test the next day.

    _____ **b.** I went to bed late.

7. I wish I had studied hard for the test.

    _____ **a.** I studied hard for the test.

    _____ **b.** I feel bad about not studying hard.

8. Ana would've helped me if I had asked.

    _____ **a.** Ana helped me.

    _____ **b.** I asked Ana for help.

9. If I had studied more, I might have gotten a good grade.

    _____ **a.** I definitely would have gotten a good grade.

    _____ **b.** I possibly would have gotten a good grade.

10. If I had gotten a good grade, I would've been happy.

    _____ **a.** I didn't get a good grade.

    _____ **b.** I wasn't happy.

EXERCISE 2 VERB FORMS IN *IF* AND RESULT CLAUSES

GRAMMAR NOTES 1–3 George is a character from the movie *It's a Wonderful Life* by Frank Capra. Circle the correct form of the verbs to complete George's thoughts about the past.

1. I didn't go into business with my friend Sam. If I went / (had gone) into business with him, I might become / (might have become) a success.

2. I couldn't go into the army because I was deaf in one ear. I would have gone / would go into the army if I hadn't lost / didn't lose the hearing in that ear.

3. Mary and I weren't able to go on a honeymoon. We could have gone / could go away if my father had gotten / hadn't gotten sick.

4. My uncle lost $8,000 of the company's money. I would have felt / wouldn't have felt so desperate if he had found / hadn't found the money.

5. I'm really feeling depressed. So many things seem to be going wrong. Sometimes I wish I had / would never been / would be born.

6. Clarence showed me how the world would look without me. I didn't know / wouldn't have known that I was so important to a lot of people if Clarence had shown / hadn't shown me.

7. If I hadn't rescued / wouldn't have rescued my little brother Harry from drowning in a pond, Harry would have saved / wouldn't have saved all those lives, later on, when he was a soldier.

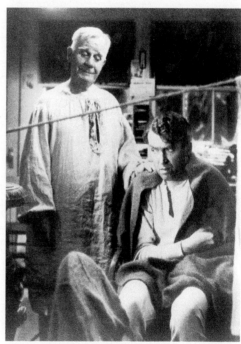

8. My old boss once almost made a terrible mistake in his shop. If I didn't help / hadn't helped him, my boss might have gone / might go to jail.

George with his angel, Clarence

9. My wife, Mary, hadn't been / wouldn't have been happy if she hadn't met / had met me.

10. Clarence showed me that life here in Bedford Falls really were / would have been worse if I hadn't been / wouldn't have been born.

EXERCISE 3 STATEMENTS

GRAMMAR NOTES 1–3 Complete this article about a two-car accident. Use the correct form of the verbs in parentheses. Use contractions when possible.

Accidents Happen

"Everything _____ *could've turned out* _____ very differently if just one small thing
                    1. (can / turn out)

_____ different." That's what Officer Rosa Ortiz said about
        2. (be)

yesterday's collision between a Honda Civic and a Volkswagen Jetta at 6:15 p.m. on Route 1.

"I guess that can be said about all accidents," she added. This is what other first responders,

eyewitnesses, and the drivers themselves said:

▪ "If the accident _____ a little earlier in the day, there
                        3. (happen)

_____ many more cars on the road." —Jake O'Neill, police officer
        4. (be)

▪ "If the ambulance _____ a little earlier, the victims
                        5. (arrive)

_____ medical treatment sooner." —Angela DuBois, witness
        6. (can / receive)

▪ "If the driver of the VW _____ his seatbelt on, his injuries
                              7. (not have)

_____ much worse." —Lucy Chen, emergency medical technician
        8. (be)

▪ "If the driver of the Honda _____ the speed limit, she
                                9. (not ignore)

_____ to stop in time." —Luke Adams, witness
        10. (may / be able to)

▪ "If I _____ this morning, I _____
          11. (not oversleep)   **12.** (take)

the train. And if I _____ the train, I _____
                        13. (take)   **14.** (not be)

on the road when the VW got to the intersection." —Michelle Johnson, driver of the Honda

▪ "If I _____ for a donut and cup of coffee on the way home,
          15. (not stop)

I _____ the accident. I was just in the wrong place at the wrong
      16. (may / avoid)

time." —Jason Hill, driver of the VW

   "Accidents happen," said Officer Ortiz. "Sometimes just a little thing like stopping for a cup

of coffee can determine the outcome of events. But there *are* things we can do to help avoid

accidents or reduce their seriousness, such as obeying the speed limit and wearing a seatbelt.

Luckily, in this case both drivers are going to be fine."

EXERCISE 4 AFFIRMATIVE AND NEGATIVE STATEMENTS

GRAMMAR NOTES 1–4 Read these stories from an Internet message board about how people met their wives, husbands, boyfriends, or girlfriends. Using the words in parentheses, combine each pair of sentences to make one past unreal conditional sentence.

● ● ●

My temp became permanent. I'd already planned this great vacation to Jamaica when my boss canceled my time off. "Sorry," she told me, "I'm going to be away, but I'll hire a temp to help you out." I was so furious that I almost quit right on the spot. I thought, *if she had planned ahead, we wouldn't have needed that temp*
1. She didn't plan ahead. We needed that temp. (would)   .
Now I know that _____ .
2. She didn't plan ahead. I met the love of my life. (might)
When Vlad, the temp, walked in that first morning, I nearly ran into her office to thank her.

_____ .
3. She was so disorganized. My next trip to Jamaica was for my honeymoon. (would)

She knocked me off my feet.[1] I was skiing with some friends in Colorado. I met my wife when she knocked me down on a ski slope. It's a good thing I was OK because

_____ .
4. I didn't break my leg. I accepted her dinner invitation. (could)
Actually, I only accepted because she felt so bad about the accident. But after the first few minutes, I knew I had to see her again. She was pretty, funny, and really intelligent.

_____ .
5. I went skiing that day. She knocked me over. (would)
And _____ !
6. She knocked me over. We got married. (would)

Best in the universe. I met my boyfriend online. We write stories on a *Star Trek* fan site.

_____ .
7. He was such a good writer. I thought about contacting him. (would)
because I'm very careful about online privacy. In fact, I didn't even know he was a guy!

_____ .
8. I didn't know. I was brave enough to write to him. (might)
But I thought he was another Isaac Asimov,[2] so I wanted to discuss his writing. We just emailed for a long time. Then we decided to meet at a *Star Trek* conference. I'm really glad we waited. He isn't the most handsome Klingon[3] in the universe, but to me he's Mr. Right.

_____ .
9. We didn't meet right away. I realized that. (might)

---

1 *knocked me off my feet:* made a very big impression on me
2 *Isaac Asimov:* a famous science-fiction writer
3 *Klingon:* in *Star Trek* stories, a race of people from another planet

EXERCISE 5 REGRETS ABOUT THE PAST

Ⓐ GRAMMAR NOTE 6 These characters from the movie *Sliding Doors* feel bad about some things that occurred. Read the facts. Then write their regrets about the past. Use *wish*.

Helen and James after
their first meeting

1. **HELEN:** I took supplies from my office. My boss fired me.

   I wish I hadn't taken supplies from my office. I wish my boss hadn't fired me.

2. **HELEN:** I didn't catch my train. I had to find a taxi.

   _____

3. **TAXI DRIVER:** She got mugged near my taxi. She needed to go to the hospital.

   _____

4. **GERRY** *(Helen's old boyfriend)*: Helen saw me with Lydia. Helen left me.

   _____

5. **LYDIA** *(Gerry's old girlfriend)*: I started seeing Gerry again. I didn't break up with him.

   _____

6. **JAMES** *(Helen's new boyfriend)*: I didn't tell Helen about my wife. I lost her trust.

   _____

7. **HELEN:** James didn't call me. I got so depressed.

   _____

8. **ANNA** *(Helen's best friend)*: James lied to Helen. He hurt her.

   _____

▶23|02 **Ⓑ** LISTEN AND CHECK Listen to the characters' regrets and check your answers in A.

EXERCISE 6 EDITING

GRAMMAR NOTES 1–6 Read this student's journal essay. There are ten mistakes in the use of past unreal conditional sentences. The first mistake is already corrected. Find and correct nine more.

It Changed My Life

Have you ever made a small decision that changed the rest of your life? Has an unimportant event, like missing a bus, ever altered the course of your personal history? What would have happened if you had ~~decide~~ *decided* to do something different? How would your life had been different if you hadn't missed your bus? Will your life have been better or worse?

Several years ago, I went to see *Sliding Doors*, a movie about parallel lives. At first, I wasn't going to go because I had too much school work to do. But, at the last minute, my friend convinced me to take a break. I rushed out of the house just in time to see my bus pull away. I was upset with myself. "I wish I have left earlier!" I thought. I got to the movie theater late, and in my rush, I dropped my jacket. A friendly-looking guy picked it up and handed it to me. We started talking, met for coffee after the movie, and, five months later, we were married.

I often think of that day. When I hadn't gone to the movies, I wouldn't have met my husband-to-be. Also, if I had missed my bus, I probably won't have met him, either. And, if I haven't dropped my jacket, he might not have noticed me. (Of course in *his* version of the story, he says he would have noticed me even if there were a hundred other people in the theater lobby that day!)

The movie *Sliding Doors* is about alternate histories. It is ironic that a film about alternate histories ended up changing *my* history. If I hadn't went to see *Sliding Doors*, my life would have been very different.

EXERCISE 7 LISTENING

⏵23|03 **A** Read the statements. Listen again to the conversations and check (✓) *True* or *False*.

	True	False
Conversation 1		
1. The man missed his train.	✓	☐
2. The train was in an accident.	☐	☐
3. The man was injured in the accident.	☐	☐
Conversation 2		
1. The woman always wanted to be an English teacher.	☐	☐
2. The woman's friend got sick one day and couldn't teach a class.	☐	☐
3. The woman became a teacher as a result of her friend's illness.	☐	☐
Conversation 3		
1. The man was having trouble finding an apartment.	☐	☐
2. One day, he saw a For Rent sign in front of a building.	☐	☐
3. The man found an apartment when he got lost.	☐	☐
Conversation 4		
1. The woman went to the movies with the man.	☐	☐
2. The man really liked the movie.	☐	☐
3. The woman regrets that she missed the movie.	☐	☐
Conversation 5		
1. The man lost his wallet.	☐	☐
2. The man got a call from the police.	☐	☐
3. The man had definitely planned to call the police.	☐	☐
Conversation 6		
1. The man used to work at a bank.	☐	☐
2. On the day that he lost his job, he went to a café.	☐	☐
3. The man doesn't regret losing his job.	☐	☐

⏵23|03 **B** Work with a partner. Listen again. Discuss your answers in A. Each conversation describes a bad event that led to a good result. What was the bad event? What would have happened differently if that event hadn't happened?

EXAMPLE: A: In the first conversation, the man missed his train and was late for his meeting. Usually missing a train is bad luck.

B: But in this case, it turned out to be good luck. The train he missed was in an accident. If he had been on that train, he could have been injured.

EXERCISE 8 THINGS WOULD HAVE BEEN VERY DIFFERENT!

CONVERSATION Work in a group. Tell your classmates how a single decision or event changed your life or the life of someone you know. What would have happened if that decision or event hadn't occurred?

EXAMPLE: A: Four years ago, I was going to take a 5:15 train home from work, but I was two minutes late, and I missed the train.
B: Oh. And what happened as a result?
A: Well, the train was in an accident. If I had been on it, I could have been injured, or worse.
C: Something like that happened to me, too. Ten years ago, . . .

EXERCISE 9 WHAT WOULD *YOU* HAVE DONE?

PROBLEM SOLVING Work in a group. Read the following situations. Did the person make the right decision? What would *you* have done in each situation? Why? What *might have* or *could have* happened as a result?

1. Zeke started his business making and selling energy bars[1] when he was a teenager. Ten years later, a large company offered to buy the business. Zeke turned the offer down because he wanted to make sure Zeke's Bars were always very high quality. If he had accepted, he could have retired rich by age thirty-five. What would you have done?

   EXAMPLE: A: I wouldn't have rejected the offer. I would've sold the business.
   B: If he'd sold the business, he could've started a new one.
   C: He might've . . .

2. A man was walking down the street when he found ten $100 bills lying on the ground. There was no one else around. He picked them up and put them in his pocket.

3. A woman came home late and found her apartment door unlocked. She was sure she had locked it. No one else had the keys. She went inside.

---

1 *energy bars:* food that gives you energy and that is in the shape of candy bars

EXERCISE 10 A REGRET

CONVERSATION Work with a partner. Talk about a decision you made at one point in your life and that you now regret. Describe the situation and talk about what you wish had happened and why.

EXAMPLE: A: Someone asked me to go to a party the night before a test. I didn't like the course, and I didn't really feel like studying, so I decided to go.
B: And what happened? Did you do OK on the test?
A: No. I failed it.
B: Oh, that's too bad.
A: It's even worse than that. I had to repeat the course! I wish I hadn't gone to the party. If I'd stayed home, I'd have studied for the test. If I'd been prepared, I would've passed.
B: But you shouldn't let regrets dominate your life. Everyone makes mistakes.

FROM GRAMMAR TO WRITING

Ⓐ BEFORE YOU WRITE Think about an event that changed your life (or the life of someone you know). Answer these questions.

1. What was the event? _____

2. When did it happen? _____

3. What happened as a result of the event? _____

Ⓑ WRITE Use your answers to write one or two paragraphs about the event. If the event hadn't happened, what would have been different? Would the result have been better or worse? Use past unreal conditional sentences. Try to avoid the common mistakes in the chart.

EXAMPLE: Two years ago, I was in a serious car accident that changed my life. I was in the hospital for a long time, and my friends and family were always there for me. If I hadn't been so badly injured, I might never have realized what good friends and family I had. . . .

Common Mistakes in Using Past Unreal Conditional Sentences

Use the **past perfect** in the *if*-clause. Do not use *would have* in the *if*-clause.	**If** I **hadn't been** in that accident, I wouldn't have known how great my friends are. **NOT** If I ~~wouldn't have been~~ in that accident . . .
Use *wish* + **past perfect**. Do not use the simple past or *would have* after *wish*.	I **wish** I **had known** you in 2015. **NOT** I wish I ~~knew~~ you in 2015. **NOT** I wish I ~~would have known~~ you in 2015.
Use a **comma after the *if*-clause** when it comes first. Do not use a comma after the result clause when the result clause comes first.	**If** I **had had more time,** I would have traveled. **NOT** I would have traveled͇ if I had had more time.

Ⓒ CHECK YOUR WORK Read your paragraph(s). Underline the *if*-clauses once and the result clauses twice. Circle *wish*. Use the Editing Checklist to check your work.

Editing Checklist

Did you use . . . ?

☐ the past perfect in the *if*-clause

☐ *would have, might have,* or *could have* + past participle in the result clause

☐ *wish* + past perfect to express regret or sadness

☐ a comma after the *if*-clause when it comes first

Ⓓ REVISE YOUR WORK Read your paragraph(s) again. Can you improve your writing? Make changes if necessary. Give your paragraph(s) a title.

UNIT 23 REVIEW

Test yourself on the grammar of the unit.

A Circle the correct words to complete the sentences.

1. If you <u>didn't tell / hadn't told</u> us about the movie, we wouldn't have seen it.

2. I wish I <u>had / hadn't</u> gone to the movie, too. I hear it's great.

3. We <u>had been / would have been</u> late if we had taken the bus.

4. <u>If / When</u> you had called me, I might have driven you there.

5. I would've <u>gone / went</u> to the movies if I had had the time.

B Complete the past unreal conditional sentences in these conversations with the correct form of the verbs in parentheses.

1. A: Sorry I'm late. I _____ on time if I _____ my train.
   a. (be)   b. (not miss)

   B: Well, if you _____ on time, I _____ that great café.
      c. (be)   d. (not discover)

2. A: I wish I _____ this job offer.
   a. (not accept)

   B: But, if you _____ another job instead, we _____!
      b. (take)   c. (not meet)

3. A: It's hard to believe that birds are a type of dinosaur!

   B: I know. If I _____ that science program on TV, I _____ it.
      a. (not see)   b. (not believe)

C Find and correct six mistakes.

Tonight, we watched the movie *Back to the Future* starring Michael J. Fox. I might never had seen it if I hadn't read his autobiography, *Lucky Man*. His book was so good that I wanted to see his most famous movie. Now, I wish I saw it in the theater when it first came out, but I hadn't even been born yet! It would have been better if we would have watched it on a big screen. Fox was great. He looked really young—just like a teenager. But I would have recognized him even when I hadn't known he was in the film.

In real life, when Fox was a teenager, he was too small to become a professional hockey player. But if he hadn't looked so young, he can't have gotten his role in the TV hit series *Family Ties*. In Hollywood, he had to sell his furniture to pay his bills, but he kept trying to find an acting job. If he would have given up, he might never have become a star.

Now check your answers on page 481.

Indirect Speech and Embedded Questions

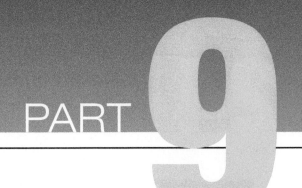

PART 9

OUTCOMES
- Report what others said, using direct or indirect speech
- Identify key information in a social science article
- Identify and discuss details in conversations
- Discuss lying and telling the truth
- Discuss and interpret literary quotes and international proverbs
- Write about a past conversation, reporting what was said, using direct and indirect speech

OUTCOMES
- Report other people's statements using indirect speech, making necessary tense and time-word changes
- Match quotations with speakers, based on information in a scientific article
- Identify specific information in a conversation
- Discuss extreme weather events and report other people's statements
- Write about an extreme weather event, reporting another person's experience

OUTCOMES
- Report other people's instructions, commands, advice, requests, and invitations, using indirect speech
- Identify specific information in an interview transcript
- Identify medical advice reported in a conversation
- Discuss health issues and possible home remedies
- Report how someone followed instructions
- Write about a health problem one had and about the health advice one received

OUTCOMES
- Report other people's questions, using indirect speech
- Identify specific information in a business article
- Identify and discuss details in a conversation
- Role-play and discuss a job interview
- Complete a questionnaire about work values, discuss the answers, and report conversations
- Write a report on a job interview

OUTCOMES
- Ask for information or express something you don't know, using embedded questions
- Extract key information from an interview transcript
- Identify and discuss details in a call-in radio show
- Discuss tipping around the world, giving opinions
- Discuss problems one had during a first-time experience
- Role-play a conversation between a hotel clerk and a guest asking for information
- Write about a confusing or surprising situation

Direct and Indirect Speech

TRUTH AND LIES

OUTCOMES
• Report what others said, using direct or indirect speech
• Identify key information in a social science article
• Identify and discuss details in conversations
• Discuss lying and telling the truth
• Discuss and interpret literary quotes and international proverbs
• Write about a past conversation, reporting what was said, using direct and indirect speech

STEP 1 GRAMMAR IN CONTEXT

BEFORE YOU READ

Look at the title of the article and at the photo, and read what the woman is saying. Discuss the questions.

1. Do you think the woman's hair looks great?

2. Is it ever all right to tell a lie? If *yes*, in what situations?

READ

24|01 Read this article about lying.

The Truth About Lying

At 9:00, Rick Spivak's landlord[1] called and said Rick's rent was late. "The check is in the mail," Rick replied quickly. At 11:45, Rick left for a 12 o'clock meeting across town. Arriving late, Rick told his client that traffic had been bad. That evening, Rick's wife, Ann, came home with a new hairstyle. Rick hated it. "It looks great," he said.

Three lies in one day! Does Rick have a problem? Or is he just an ordinary guy? Each time, he told himself that sometimes the truth causes too many problems. Like Rick, most of us tell white lies— harmless untruths that help us avoid trouble. In fact, one social psychologist[2] estimates that the average American tells about 200 lies a day! He says that lying is a habit, and we are often not even aware that we are doing it. When we do notice, we justify the lie by telling ourselves it was for a good purpose.

He said my hair looked great this way!

---

1 *landlord:* someone who owns a building or other property and rents it to other people

2 *social psychologist:* a psychologist who studies how social groups affect the way people behave

These are our six most common excuses:

- **To be polite:** "I'd love to go to your party, but I have to work."

- **To protect someone else's feelings:** "Your hair looks great that way!"

- **To feel better about yourself:** "I'm looking good these days."

- **To appear more interesting to others:** "I run five miles every day."

- **To get something more quickly:** "I have to have that report today."

- **To avoid uncomfortable situations:** "I was going to call you, but my phone battery was dead."

How do we get away with all those white lies? First of all, it's difficult to recognize a lie because body language usually doesn't reveal dishonesty. But even when we suspect[3] someone is lying, we often don't want to know the truth. If an acquaintance says she's fine, but she clearly isn't, a lot of people find it easier to take her statement at face value.[4] And when someone tells you, "You did a great job!" you probably don't want to question the compliment!

Is telling lies a new trend? In one survey, the majority of people who answered said that people were more honest in the past. Nevertheless, lying wasn't really born yesterday. In the eighteenth century, the French philosopher[5] Vauvenargues told the truth about lying when he wrote, "All men are born truthful and die liars."

-----

3 *suspect:* think that something—usually something bad—is probably true
4 *take her statement at face value:* accept what she says without looking for hidden meanings
5 *philosopher:* someone who thinks a lot and questions the meaning of life and ideas about the world

AFTER YOU READ

A VOCABULARY **Choose the word or phrase that best completes each sentence.**

1. I enjoy reading **survey** results. It's interesting learning other people's _____.
   a. stories   **b.** opinions   **c.** secrets

2. Ed was **aware** that Sid lost his job. He _____ it.
   a. suspected   **b.** didn't know about   **c.** knew about

3. Some people **justify** lying. They _____ it.
   a. always avoid   **b.** find good reasons for   **c.** never recognize

4. The **majority** of people are honest. _____ of them don't tell lies.
   a. None   **b.** All   **c.** Most

5. Hamid **revealed** his plans yesterday. He _____ about them.
   a. refused to say anything   **b.** told everyone   **c.** didn't tell the truth

6. I really didn't like the meal. **Nevertheless**, I said that the food was _____.
   a. delicious   **b.** terrible   **c.** healthy

B COMPREHENSION Read the statements. Check (✓) *True* or *False*.

		True	False
1.	Rick's rent check is in the mail.	☐	☐
2.	Rick likes Ann's new hairstyle.	☐	☐
3.	Rick thinks some lies are all right.	☐	☐
4.	We often lie to avoid hurting another person.	☐	☐
5.	It's easy to know when a person is lying.	☐	☐
6.	Lying is a new trend.	☐	☐
7.	Vauvenargues thinks people get more dishonest with age.	☐	☐

C DISCUSSION Work with a partner. Compare your answers in B. Why did you choose *True* or *False*?

STEP 2 GRAMMAR PRESENTATION

DIRECT AND INDIRECT SPEECH

Direct Speech

Direct Statement	Subject	Reporting Verb	Noun/Pronoun
"The check **is** in the mail," "Your hair **looks** great," "The traffic **was** bad,"	he	**told**	the bank. Ann. her.
		said.	

Indirect Speech

Subject	Reporting Verb	Noun/Pronoun	Indirect Statement	
He	**told**	the bank Ann her	**(that)**	the check **was** in the mail. her hair **looked** great. the traffic **had been** bad.
	said			

GRAMMAR NOTES

1 Direct Speech

Direct speech states the exact words that the speaker used.	**"I always pay on time,"** he said. **"I like that tie,"** she told him.
IN WRITING Put **quotation marks** before and after the speech you are quoting. That speech (called the **quotation**) can go at the **beginning** or at the **end** of the sentence.	**"The traffic is bad,"** he said. He said, **"The traffic is bad."**
Use a **comma** to separate the quotation from the rest of the sentence.	Rick said, "It looks great." "It looks great," Rick said.
After a **quotation at the beginning**, the word order is **verb + subject** or **subject + verb**. With pronouns, verb + subject is rare.	"That's great," **said Chen.** *(more common)* "That's great," **Chen said.** *(less common)* "That's great," **said he.** *(rare)*

2 Indirect Speech

Indirect speech (also called *reported speech*) **reports** what a speaker **said without using the exact words** that the speaker used.	Rick said **he always paid on time.**
	   (Rick: "I always pay on time.")
	Ann told him **she liked that tie.**
	   (Ann: "I like that tie.")

The word *that* can introduce the indirect speech statement.	He said *that* **he always paid on time.** He said **he always paid on time.**
IN WRITING Do not use quotation marks or a comma in indirect speech.	She said **that she had to work.** **NOT** She said that, *×*she had to work.*×*

3 Reporting Verbs

We use **reporting verbs** (such as *say* and *tell*) with both direct and indirect speech. The reporting verb is usually in the simple past tense.

• **direct speech**	"It looks great," he **said.** "I'm sorry to be late," Rick **told** Ann.
• **indirect speech**	He **said** it looked great. He **told** Ann that he was sorry to be late.
Use *say* when you **do not mention the listener**.	"It looks great," he **said.** He **said** it looked great.
Use *tell* or *say to* when you **mention the listener**.	"It looks great," he **told** *Ann.* "It looks great," he **said to** *Ann.* He **told** *her* that it looked great. He **said to** *Ann* that it looked great.
BE CAREFUL! Do not confuse *say* and *tell*. Do not use *say* without *to* when you mention the listener. Do not use *tell* with *to* when you mention the listener.	He **said to me** it was great. **NOT** He said me it was great. He **told me** it was great. **NOT** He told to me it was great.

4 Change of Tense in Indirect Speech

When the **reporting verb** is in the **simple past** (*said, told*), we often **change the verb tense** in the indirect speech statement.

The **simple present** in direct speech becomes the **simple past** in indirect speech. Notice that the indirect speech uses the simple past, but the meaning is present.	She **said**, "I only *buy* shoes on sale." She **said** that she only *bought* shoes on sale. *(She only buys shoes on sale.)*
The **simple past** in direct speech becomes the **past perfect** in indirect speech.	She **said**, "I *found* a great store." She **said** she *had found* a great store.
BE CAREFUL! When the **reporting verb** is in the **simple present**, do **not change the verb tense** in the indirect speech statement.	Ann **says**, "I *run* a mile every day." Ann **says** that she *runs* a mile every day. **NOT** Ann says that she ~~ran~~ a mile every day.

5 Optional Change of Tense in Indirect Speech

You do not always have to change the tense in indirect speech.

The tense in indirect speech can **remain the same** when you report:	
• something that was **just said**	A: **I'm** tired from all this shopping. B: What did you say? A: I **said** I**'m** tired. **or** I **said** I **was** tired.
• something that is **still true**	Rick **said** the bank **wants** a check. Rick **said** the bank **wanted** a check.
• a **general truth** or **scientific law**	He **told** us that water **freezes** at 0° Celsius. He **told** us that water **froze** at 0° Celsius.

6 Other Changes in Indirect Speech

We often make changes in indirect speech to **keep the speaker's original meaning**.

To keep the original meaning, change:	
• **subject pronouns**	Ann told her boss, "**I** love the job." Ann told the boss that **she** loved the job.
• **object pronouns**	Ann said, "Jon texts **me** all the time." Ann told us that Jon texts **her** all the time.
• **possessive adjectives**	Ann said, "**Your** new tie is great!" Ann told me that **my** new tie was great.

REFERENCE NOTES

For **punctuation rules for direct speech**, see Appendix 28 on page 466.

For **additional tense changes in indirect speech**, see Unit 25 on page 395.

For a list of **reporting verbs**, see Appendix 19 on page 462.

EXERCISE 1   DISCOVER THE GRAMMAR

A GRAMMAR NOTES 1–6   Read this magazine article about lying at a job interview. Circle the reporting verbs. Underline once the examples of direct speech. Underline twice the examples of indirect speech.

"Lying during a job interview is risky business," says Martha Toledo, director of the management consulting firm Maxwell. "The truth has a funny way of coming out." Toledo tells the story of one woman, Jane, applying for a job as an office manager. The woman told the interviewer that she had a B.A. degree. Actually, she was eight credits short. She also said that she had made $50,000 at her last job. The truth was $10,000 less. "Many firms really do check facts," warns Toledo. In this case, a call to the applicant's company revealed the truth. "She was a strong applicant," says Toledo, "and most of the information on the résumé was true. Nevertheless, those details cost her the job."

Toledo relates a story about another job applicant, George. During an interview, George reported that he had quit his last job. George got the new job and was doing well until the company hired another employee, Pete. George and Pete had worked at the same company. Pete later told his boss that his old company had fired George. After George's supervisor became aware of the lie, he stopped trusting George, and their relationship became difficult. Eventually, George quit.

B Choose the correct answer to complete each statement.

1. _____ Jane told the job interviewer.
   a. "I had a B.A. degree,"   b. "I have a B.A. degree,"

2. She said, _____
   a. "She had made $50,000 at her last job."   b. "I made $50,000 at my last job."

3. George said, _____
   a. "He had quit his last job."   b. "I quit my last job."

4. _____ Pete told his boss.
   a. "My old company fired George,"   b. "His old company fired George,"

EXERCISE 2 *SAID* AND *TOLD*; VERB AND PRONOUN CHANGES

GRAMMAR NOTES 2–6 Complete this student's essay with the correct words.

The Broken Bowl

Once when I was a teenager, I went to my Aunt Leah's house. Aunt Leah

collected pottery, and as soon as I got there, she said / told me she wants / wanted

to show me my / her lovely new bowl. She said / told she has / had just bought it. I

admired it and said / told her it is / was very beautiful.

When Aunt Leah left the room, she handed me the bowl. To my horror, as I was

looking at it, it slipped from my hands and broke into pieces on the floor. When she

came back, I said / told the cat had broken her / your bowl. Aunt Leah gave me a

strange look, but said / told me that it isn't / wasn't important. She said / told that

people were much more important than things.

I didn't sleep at all that night, and the next morning I called my aunt and

said / told her that I have / had broken the bowl. I apologized and said / told that

I feel / felt really terrible about it. She laughed and said that I / she had known all

along. We still laugh about it today. The bowl broke that day, but my relationship

with my aunt is stronger than ever.

EXERCISE 3 INDIRECT SPEECH

GRAMMAR NOTES 1–4, 6 Look at the pictures. Rewrite the statements as indirect speech.
Use *said* as the reporting verb and make all necessary changes in the verbs and pronouns.

1. a. <u>She said it was her own recipe. "</u>

   b. <u>He said it looked great! "</u>

2. a. <u>The man said, "My car broke down, Mr. Brown!"</u>

   b. <u>Mr Brown said, "You missed the meeting!"</u>

3. a. <u>The man said, "I have to drive my aunt to the airport."</u>

   b. <u>Tina said "I already bought movie tickets!"</u>

4. a. <u>The woman said, "I exercise every day"</u>

   b. <u>The man said, "You look very fit."</u>

5. a. <u>Mr Morgan said, "Your bill is overdue."</u>

   b. <u>The man said, "I just mailed the check, Mr. Morgan."</u>

6. a. <u>The man said, "I am 35."</u>

   b. <u>The woman said, "You don't look 35."</u>

EXERCISE 4 INDIRECT SPEECH

GRAMMAR NOTE 2–4, 6 Rewrite Lisa and Ben's conversation using indirect speech. Use the reporting verbs in parentheses. Make necessary changes in the verbs and pronouns.

1. LISA: I just heard about a job at a scientific research company.

   (tell) *She told him she had just heard about a job at a scientific research company.*

2. BEN: Oh, I majored in science at Florida State.

   (say) *He said that he had majored in science at Florida State.*

3. LISA: They didn't mention the starting salary.

   (say) She said that they didn't mentiond the starting salary

4. BEN: I need a lot of money to pay off my student loans.

   (say) he said that he needed a lot of money to pay off his student loans.

5. LISA: They want someone with some experience as a programmer.

   (say) She said that they wanted someone with some experience as a programmer

6. BEN: Well, I work as a programmer for Data Systems.

   (tell) he told her that he worked as a programmer for data Systems

7. LISA: Oh—they need a college graduate.

   (say) She said that oh they needed a college graduate

8. BEN: Well, I graduated from Florida State.

   (tell) he told her that he had graduated from Florida State

9. LISA: But they don't want a recent graduate.

   (say) Lisa said that the don't wanted a recent graduate

10. BEN: I got my degree four years ago.

    (tell) he told d that he gotten my degree foor years ago

11. LISA: Great—I wasn't aware of that.

    (tell) She told that she hadn't been aware of that

12. BEN: I really appreciate the information.

    (say) he said that he really appreciated the information

13. LISA: My boss just came in, and I have to go.

    (tell) Lisa told him that her boss had just come She had to go

EXERCISE 5 EDITING

GRAMMAR NOTES 2–4 Read the article. There are ten mistakes in the use of direct and indirect speech. The first mistake is already corrected. Find and correct nine more. Mistakes with quotation marks count as one mistake for the sentence.

WARNING!!!! THIS MESSAGE IS A HOAX!!!!!

Everyone gets urgent email messages. They tell you that billionaire Bill

Gates now ~~wanted~~ *wants* to give away his money—to YOU! They say you that

a popular floor cleaner kills family pets. They report that your computer

monitor had taken photographs of you. Before I became aware of Internet

hoaxes, I used to forward these emails to all my friends. Not long ago,

a very annoyed friend explains that the story about killer bananas was

a hoax (an untrue story). He said me "that the majority of those scary

emails were hoaxes." He told me about these common signs of hoaxes:

- The email always says that it was very urgent. It has lots of

  exclamation points.

- It tells that it is not a hoax and quotes important people.

  (The quotations are false.)

- It urges you to send the email to everyone you know.

He also told that a lot of Internet sites reveal information about Internet

hoaxes. With this information, you can avoid forwarding all your friends a

false warning. So, before *you* announce that sunscreen had made people

blind, check out the story on a reliable website.

EXERCISE 6 LISTENING

▶ 24|02 **A** Read the sentences. Then listen to Lisa's conversations. Listen again and circle the correct word or phrase to complete each sentence.

Conversation 1

1. Lisa said to Alex, "I didn't / (don't) like to eat meat."

2. Lisa told Alex, "My parents are / were in town."

Conversation 2

3. Ben told Lisa, "I used to like / like to go to the gym."

4. Lisa told Ben, "I take / took aerobics on Sunday."

Conversation 3

5. Lisa told Mark that her boss said it wasn't / was urgent.

6. Lisa told Mark the staff meeting wasn't / was on Monday.

Conversation 4

7. Katy told Lisa, "I want / wanted to make something special for you."

8. Katy's mother said, "I always use / used two kinds of meat."

▶ 24|02 **B** Work with a partner. Read Lisa's weekly planner. Lisa wasn't always honest in her conversations. Listen to the conversations again and notice the differences between what Lisa said and the truth. Discuss the differences with your partner.

EXAMPLE: A: Lisa said her parents were in town for the weekend, but that's not true.
B: Right. She said she wanted to spend time with her parents on Saturday night, but she really had a date with Ben on Saturday night.

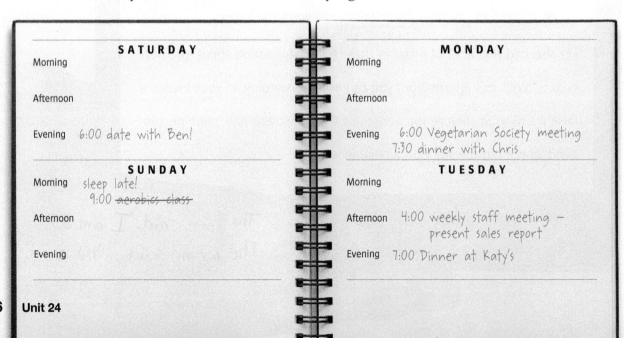

SATURDAY		**MONDAY**	
Morning		Morning	
Afternoon		Afternoon	
Evening	6:00 date with Ben!	Evening	6:00 Vegetarian Society meeting 7:30 dinner with Chris
SUNDAY		**TUESDAY**	
Morning	sleep late! 9:00 ~~aerobics class~~	Morning	
Afternoon		Afternoon	4:00 weekly staff meeting — present sales report
Evening		Evening	7:00 Dinner at Katy's

EXERCISE 7 TO LIE OR NOT TO LIE?

DISCUSSION Review the six excuses for lying described in "The Truth About Lying" on page 377. Then work in a group. Is it OK to lie in these circumstances? Give examples from your own experience to support your ideas.

- To be polite
- To protect someone else's feelings
- To feel better about yourself
- To appear more interesting to others
- To get something more quickly
- To avoid uncomfortable situations

EXAMPLE: A: Once, my friend told me that my haircut looked great, but it really looked awful. I know she wanted to protect my feelings, but I think she should have told me the truth. Now it's hard for me to believe anything she says.

B: I think at times it's OK to lie to protect someone's feelings. Once, I told my best friend that . . .

C: I think . . .

EXERCISE 8 QUOTABLE QUOTES

DISCUSSION Work in a group. Discuss these famous quotations about lying. Do you agree with them? Give examples to support your opinion. Use *says* to report the proverbs and *said* to report the ideas of individuals.

1. All men are born truthful and die liars.

   —*Vauvenargues (French philosopher, 1715–1747)*

   EXAMPLE: A: Vauvenargues said that all men are born truthful and die liars.

   B: I agree because babies don't lie, but children and adults do.

   C: I don't believe that *everyone* lies. . . .

2. A half-truth is a whole lie.

   —*Jewish proverb*

3. A little inaccuracy saves tons of explanation.

   —*Saki (British short story writer, 1870–1916)*

4. A liar needs a good memory.

   —*Quintilian (first-century Roman orator)*

5. The man who speaks the truth is always at ease.

   —*Persian proverb*

6. The cruelest lies are often told in silence.

   —*Robert Louis Stevenson (Scottish novelist, 1850–1894)*

Robert Louis Stevenson

EXERCISE 9 HONESTLY SPEAKING

A QUESTIONNAIRE Complete the questionnaire. Check (✓) your answers.

		Always	Usually	Sometimes	Rarely	Never
1.	I tell the truth to my friends.	☐	☐	☐	☐	☐
2.	I tell the truth to my family.	☐	☐	☐	☐	☐
3.	It's OK to lie on the job.	☐	☐	☐	☐	☐
4.	"White lies" protect people's feelings.	☐	☐	☐	☐	☐
5.	Most people are honest.	☐	☐	☐	☐	☐
6.	It's best to tell the truth.	☐	☐	☐	☐	☐
7.	I tell people my real age.	☐	☐	☐	☐	☐
8.	My friends are honest with me.	☐	☐	☐	☐	☐
9.	It's difficult to tell a convincing lie.	☐	☐	☐	☐	☐
10.	Politicians are honest.	☐	☐	☐	☐	☐
11.	Doctors tell patients the whole truth.	☐	☐	☐	☐	☐
12.	I answer questionnaires honestly.	☐	☐	☐	☐	☐

B Work in a group. Compare your answers to the questionnaire. Summarize your group's results and report them to the rest of the class.

EXAMPLE: A: Five of us said that we usually told the truth.
B: Only one of us said it was always best to tell the truth.
C: Everyone in our group said that they tell people their real age.

EXERCISE 10 TO TELL THE TRUTH

(A) GAME Work in a group of three. Each student tells the group an interesting fact about his or her life. The fact can *only* be true for this student.

EXAMPLE: A: Once I climbed a mountain that was 7,000 meters high.
B: I speak four languages.
C: I scored the winning goal for my soccer team at a big tournament.

(B) The group chooses a fact and goes to the front of the class. Each student states the same fact, but, remember: Only one student is telling the truth.

EXAMPLE:

Once I climbed a mountain that was 7,000 meters high.

Once I climbed a mountain that was 7,000 meters high.

Once I climbed a mountain that was 7,000 meters high.

(C) The class asks the three students questions to find out who is telling the truth.

EXAMPLE: A: Alice, how long did it take you to climb the mountain?
B: Justin, who did you climb the mountain with?
C: Kate, did you train for a long time?

(D) As a class, decide who was telling the truth. Explain your reasons.

EXAMPLE: A: I didn't believe Alice. She said it had taken two weeks to climb the mountain.
B: I think Justin was lying. He told us he'd climbed the mountain alone.
C: I think Kate was telling the truth. She said that she'd trained for several months.

FROM GRAMMAR TO WRITING

A BEFORE YOU WRITE Think about a short conversation you once had when you thought someone was not telling the truth. When and where was it? Who were you speaking to? What were you speaking about? Write three direct quotations from the conversation.

1. _____

2. _____

3. _____

B WRITE Use the situation and the direct quotations in A to write one or two paragraphs about your conversation. Use both direct and indirect speech. Try to avoid the common mistakes in the chart.

EXAMPLE: Two years ago, I wanted to buy a used car. I was talking to a woman who owned a Honda Civic, and we were discussing the price. She told me that it was a great car and that it had only 10,000 miles on it. She also said, "It was brand new when I bought it." I didn't believe her because . . .

Common Mistakes in Using Direct and Indirect Speech

Use **quotations marks** with direct speech, before and after the speech you are quoting. Do not use quotation marks with indirect speech.	She said, "The car is new." **NOT** She said that "the car is new."
Use a **comma** to separate a direct quotation from the rest of the sentence. Do not use a comma before the statement in indirect speech.	She said, "It's a great car." **NOT** She said, that it's a great car.
Change the verb tenses and the pronouns in indirect speech to keep the speaker's original meaning.	"I love your new car," he told Ina. He told Ina that he loved her new car. **NOT** He told Ina that I love your new car.

C CHECK YOUR WORK Read your paragraph(s). Underline once all the examples of direct speech. Underline twice all the examples of indirect speech. Circle all the reporting verbs. Use the Editing Checklist to check your work.

Editing Checklist

Did you use . . . ?

☐ quotation marks before and after the quotation in direct speech

☐ a comma to separate a direct quotation from the rest of the sentence

☐ the verb *say* when you didn't mention the listener

☐ the verb *tell* when you mentioned the listener

☐ the correct verb tenses and pronouns in indirect speech

D REVISE YOUR WORK Read your paragraph(s) again. Can you improve your writing? Make changes if necessary. Give your writing a title.

UNIT 24 REVIEW

Test yourself on the grammar of the unit.

A Circle the correct words to complete the sentences.

1. My friend Ryan always <u>says</u> / <u>tells</u> that white lies are OK.

2. When Talia invited him to dinner last month, he said, <u>"I'd love to."</u> / <u>"That he'd love to."</u>

3. Then Talia told him that she <u>plans</u> / <u>planned</u> to cook a Chinese meal.

4. Ryan said that <u>he</u> / <u>I</u> loved Chinese food. That was a white lie—he really dislikes it.

5. Talia served a wonderful meal. She told Ryan that <u>she'd cooked</u> / <u>I cooked</u> it all herself.

6. Ryan really liked it! When he finished dinner, he <u>told</u> / <u>said</u> Talia, "That was great."

7. After they got married, Talia told Ryan that the Chinese meal <u>is</u> / <u>had been</u> takeout.

8. Today, Ryan always says it was the best meal of <u>my</u> / <u>his</u> life—and that's the truth.

B Rewrite each direct statement as an indirect statement. Keep the original meaning.
(The direct statement was said one week ago.)

Direct Speech	**Indirect Speech**
1. "I always get up early."	She said _____ .
2. "Water boils at 100 degrees Celsius."	He told them _____ .
3. "I like your haircut."	He told me _____ .
4. "I loved the pasta."	She said _____ .
5. "It's my own recipe."	He said _____ .
6. "I mailed you the check."	She told him _____ .
7. "My boss liked my work."	He said _____ .

C Find and correct five mistakes. Remember to check punctuation.

1. A psychologist I know often tells me "that people today tell hundreds of lies every day."

2. Yesterday, Mia's boyfriend said her that he liked her new dress.

3. When she heard that, Mia said she didn't really believe you.

4. I didn't think that was so bad. I said that her boyfriend tells her a little white lie.

5. But Mia hates lying. She said that to me, all lies were wrong.

Now check your answers on page 481.

Direct and Indirect Speech   **391**

Tense Changes in Indirect Speech
EXTREME WEATHER

OUTCOMES
- Report other people's statements using indirect speech, making necessary tense and time-word changes
- Match quotations with speakers, based on information in a scientific article
- Identify specific information in a conversation
- Discuss extreme weather events and report other people's statements
- Write about an extreme weather event, reporting another person's experience

---

STEP 1   GRAMMAR IN CONTEXT

BEFORE YOU READ

Look at the photos and at the title of the article. Discuss the questions.

1. What do you think a *force of nature* is?
2. What is another example of a force of nature?

READ

25|01   Read this article about tornadoes.

Force of Nature

It was March 18, 1925. The weather forecaster said that there was going to be rain and strong winds. No one, however, was prepared for the extreme weather event that killed almost 700 people and destroyed 15,000 homes in the region of the United States known as the Midwest. The cause of this mass destruction? A tornado.

Tornadoes are extremely violent storms. They spin very quickly in the shape of a funnel.[1] Tornadoes occur mostly in North America and strike without much warning. They move quickly across both land and water, and their powerful winds, which often exceed 60 mph (96.5 kph), can destroy entire towns. Sadly, that's what happened in 1925, when the "Great Tri-State Tornado" hit the states of Missouri, Illinois, and Indiana, leaving death and destruction in its path. The tornado took everyone by surprise.

Judith Cox was having lunch in Gorham, Illinois, when the twister reached the town. She told a local newspaper that there had been a great roar[2] like a train, but much louder. She said that the air had been full of everything—boards, tree branches, clothing, pans, stoves, and even parts of houses.

Tornado destruction

---

1 *funnel:* a tube with a wide top and a narrow bottom, used for pouring liquids into a container
2 *roar:* a deep and loud continuous sound

Lela Hartman was just a four-year-old child on March 18, 1925, but she remembered that day well. She had been visiting her grandmother's farm in Illinois. Years later, she recounted the events of that terrible day. She said that the day had started out nice, but that then it had kept getting darker and darker. The worried family found shelter in the basement of the house. When they came out afterwards, the world looked very different to the young girl. As usual, her father had parked his car in the barn. Hartman said the storm had totally destroyed the barn, had taken the roof off her father's car, and had moved the car closer to the house. The house itself had been turned around on its foundation.[3] At the end of her account, when asked if she had anything else to say, Hartman replied simply that she hoped they would never have another tornado.

Tri-State Tornado 1925 Statistics	
Duration: 3½ hours	
Distance Traveled: 219 miles (352 km)	
Average Speed: 62 mph (99.7 kph)	
Highest Speed: 73 mph (117.5 kph)	
Deaths: 695 people	
Injuries: more than 2,000	
Homes Destroyed: 15,000	
Financial Loss: $1.5 billion	

---

3 *foundation:* the solid base that is built underground to support a building

In May, 2011, almost ninety years after the Tri-State Tornado, a tornado hit the state of Missouri again. This time, however, things were different. Whereas it took days for the world to learn about the 1925 disaster, this time news traveled much faster. Newspaper editor Joe Hadsall reported that it had taken only minutes for people to find out about the tornado through sites like Facebook and Twitter. He said that people's friends and family had known instantly about the disaster and that his newspaper had used these sites to spread more information.

Can a tornado like the Tri-State hit again? When asked this question, one meteorologist[4] answered that not only could one strike again, but that one would strike again. He said that it was not a question of *if*, it was a question of *when*. In other words, it is inevitable. However, thanks to advances in science, technology, and communication, the devastation of this force of nature will probably not be as great as on that tragic day in 1925.

_____

4 *meteorologist:* a scientist who studies weather

AFTER YOU READ

Ⓐ VOCABULARY **Complete the sentences with the words from the box.**

devastation	exceed	extreme	inevitable	shelter	whereas

1. A tornado can cause enormous _____ .

2. It was _____ . It had to happen. Nothing could stop it.

3. The damage may _____ last year's damage. In fact, it could be much worse.

4. The amount of destruction was _____ . No one expected it to be so bad.

5. The basement provided _____ from the storm. They were much safer there.

6. Tornadoes start over land; _____ hurricanes begin over water.

Ⓑ COMPREHENSION **Read the quotations. Which of the following people said each one?**

a. Judith Cox   **b.** Lela Hartman   **c.** Joe Hadsall

d. the weather forecaster   **e.** the meteorologist

_____ **1.** "There's going to be rain and strong winds."

_____ **2.** "The air was full of everything."

_____ **3.** "A tornado will strike again."

_____ **4.** "The day started out nice."

_____ **5.** "It only took minutes for people to find out about the tornado."

_____ **6.** "It kept getting darker and darker."

_____ **7.** "There was a great roar."

_____ **8.** "I hope we'll never have another tornado."

Ⓒ DISCUSSION **Work with a partner. Discuss your answers in B. Why did you choose your answers?**

TENSE CHANGES IN INDIRECT SPEECH

Direct Speech			Indirect Speech				
Subject	Reporting Verb	Direct Statement	Subject	Reporting Verb	Noun/ Pronoun	*(that)*	Indirect Statement
He	said,	"I **live** in Indiana."	He	told	Jim		he **lived** in Indiana.
		"I **moved** here in June."			me		he **had moved** there in June.
		"I**'m looking** for an apartment."			you		he **was looking** for an apartment.
		"I**'ve started** a new job."			him		he **had started** a new job.
		"I**'m going to stay** here."			her		he **was going to stay** there.
		"I**'ll invite** you for the holidays."			us		he **would invite** me for the holidays.
		"We **can go** to the park."			them	*(that)*	we **could go** to the park.
		"I **may look** for a roommate."		said			he **might look** for a roommate.
		"I **should get back** to work."					he **should get back** to work.
		"I **have to finish** my report."					he **had to finish** his report.
		"You **must come** to visit."					I **had to come** to visit.
		"We **ought to see** each other more."					we **ought to see** each other more.

GRAMMAR NOTES

1 Change of Verb Tense in Indirect Speech

When the **reporting verb** is in **the simple past**, we often change the verb tense in the indirect speech statement.

DIRECT SPEECH		INDIRECT SPEECH	
simple present	→	simple past	He said, "It's cloudy." *(direct)* He said it **was** cloudy. *(indirect)*
present progressive	→	past progressive	She said, "A tornado **is coming**." *(direct)* She said that a tornado **was coming**. *(indirect)*
simple past	→	past perfect	He said, "Ken **called**." *(direct)* He said that Ken **had called**. *(indirect)*
present perfect	→	past perfect	She told him, "I've heard the news." *(direct)* She told him that she**'d heard** the news. *(indirect)*

Notice that the verb in indirect speech often uses the **past**, but the meaning is **present**.

I just spoke to John. He said it **was** cloudy in Miami.
*(It is cloudy **now** in Miami.)*

2 Modals and Indirect Speech

Modals often change in indirect speech.

DIRECT SPEECH		INDIRECT SPEECH	
will	→	*would*	I said, "The winds **will be** strong." *(direct)* I said the winds **would be** strong. *(indirect)*
can	→	*could*	"You **can stay** with me," he told us. *(direct)* He told us that we **could stay** with him. *(indirect)*
may	→	*might*	He said, "The storm **may cause** damage." *(direct)* He said the storm **might cause** damage. *(indirect)*
must	→	*had to*	"You **must leave**," he told us. *(direct)* He told us that we **had to leave**." *(indirect)*

3 Verbs That Do Not Change in Indirect Speech

Some verbs do not change in indirect speech.

• the modals *could, might, should, ought to,* and *would*	"You **should leave**," he told us. *(direct)* He told us that we **should leave**. *(indirect)*
• past modals *could have, might have, should have, ought to have,* and *would have*	"We **couldn't have known**." *(direct)* They said they **couldn't have known**. *(indirect)*
• verbs in the past perfect	"I **had moved** a week before," he said. *(direct)* He said he **had moved** a week before. *(indirect)*
• present conditional verbs	Jim said, "If I **knew**, I **would tell** you." *(direct)* Jim said if he **knew**, he **would tell** me. *(indirect)*
• past unreal conditional verbs	Ana said, "If I **had known**, I **would have told** you." *(direct)* Ana said if she **had known**, she **would have told** me. *(indirect)*
USAGE NOTE We often do not change the tense when we report something that was **just said**, something that is **still true**, or a **general truth** or **scientific law**.	"Tornadoes **are** worse than a bad storm." She said that tornadoes **are** worse than a bad storm.

4 Time Words in Indirect Speech

Change time words in indirect speech to keep the speaker's **original meaning**. This is especially important when reporting something that was said at a much earlier date.

DIRECT SPEECH		INDIRECT SPEECH	
tomorrow	→	*the next day*	Jim said, "I'll start **tomorrow**." *(June 5)* He said he would start **the next day**. *(Jim's friend reported July 5.)*
yesterday	→	*the day before*	Jim said, "I arrived **yesterday**." *(June 5)* He said he had arrived **the day before**. *(Jim's friend reported July 5.)*
now	→	*then*	"I'll call Mom **now**." She said she'd call Mom **then**.
today	→	*that day*	"**Today** has been terrible." They said **that day** had been terrible.
this week/month	→	*that week/month*	"There has been so much damage **this week**." He said there had been so much damage **that** week.
last week/year	→	*the week/year before*	"They left town **last week**." She said they had left town **the week before**.
next week/year	→	*the following week/year*	"Our electricity won't be restored until **next week**." Luisa reported that their electricity wouldn't be restored until **the following week**.

Change *here* and *this* in indirect speech to keep the speaker's **original meaning**.

DIRECT SPEECH		INDIRECT SPEECH	
here	→	*there*	"I love it **here**. **This** California climate is great." *(Jim is saying this in California.)* Jim said he loved it *there*. He told me *that* California climate was great. *(Jim's friend in Ohio is reporting what Jim said in California.)*
this	→	*that*	

REFERENCE NOTES

For a list of **reporting verbs**, see Appendix 19 on page 462.

For **punctuation rules for direct speech**, see Appendix 28 on page 466.

STEP 3	FOCUSED PRACTICE

EXERCISE 1 DISCOVER THE GRAMMAR

GRAMMAR NOTES 1–5 Read the indirect speech statements. Then choose the direct speech statement that is similar in meaning.

1. The local weather forecaster said that it was going to be a terrible storm.
   - a. "It was going to be a terrible storm."
   - (b.) "It's going to be a terrible storm."
   - c. "It was a terrible storm."

2. She said the winds might exceed 45 miles (28 kilometers) per hour.
   - a. "The winds exceeded 45 miles per hour."
   - b. "The winds would exceed 45 miles per hour."
   - c. "The winds may exceed 45 miles per hour."

3. She said there would be more rain the next day.
   - a. "There will be more rain the next day."
   - b. "There would be more rain tomorrow."
   - c. "There will be more rain tomorrow."

4. She told people that they should try to leave the region.
   - a. "You should try to leave the region."
   - b. "You should have tried to leave the region."
   - c. "You would leave the region."

5. She reported that people were evacuating the city.
   - a. "People are evacuating the city."
   - b. "People were evacuating the city."
   - c. "People evacuated the city."

6. She said that they could expect the damage to be extreme.
   a. "We could expect the damage to be extreme."
   b. "We could have expected the damage to be extreme."
   c. "We can expect the damage to be extreme."

7. She said that the winds were the strongest they had had there.
   a. "The winds are the strongest we have here."
   b. "The winds are the strongest we have had here."
   c. "The winds are the strongest we have had there."

8. She told them that the emergency relief workers had arrived the day before.
   a. "Emergency relief workers arrived the day before."
   b. "Emergency relief workers arrived yesterday."
   c. "Emergency relief workers arrived today."

9. She said that if they hadn't had time to prepare, the damage would have been even greater.
   a. "If we hadn't had time to prepare, the damage would have been even greater."
   b. "If we don't have time to prepare, the damage will be even greater."
   c. "If we didn't have time to prepare, the damage would be even greater."

EXERCISE 2 INDIRECT STATEMENTS AND TENSE CHANGES

GRAMMAR NOTES 1–5 Imagine you heard these statements last week. They were about a storm that happened in another part of the country. Use *They said* to report the statements. Be careful to keep the original meaning of the direct speech.

1. "The storm changed direction last night."

   They said that the storm had changed direction the night before.

2. "It's going to pass north of here."

   They said that the storm is going to pass north of here

3. "The bridge collapsed this afternoon."

   They said that the bridge had collapsed that afternoon

4. "It's not really a tornado. It's just a very big storm."

   They said that it wasn't a tornado but it's just a very big storm
   was

5. "People are leaving town."

   They said people were leaving town

6. "They won't be able to restore the electricity until tomorrow."

   They said they wouldn't be able to restore the electricity until
   the next day

7. "Cars can't use the highway because of the flooding."

   They said that cars couldn't use the highway due to flood

8. "People ought to use bottled water for a few days."

   They said that people ought to use bottled water for a few days
   a few days.

EXERCISE 3 INDIRECT STATEMENTS AND TENSE CHANGES

GRAMMAR NOTES 1–3 Read this interview between radio station WWEA and meteorologist Dr. Andrea Meyers. Then for each statement following the interview, write *That's right* or *That's wrong* and report what Dr. Meyers said about each item. Change the tense when possible.

WWEA: Where do tornadoes occur? Do they only occur in the United States and Canada?

MEYERS: No. Whereas it *is* true that tornadoes are most common in North America, they occur in all seven continents except Antarctica.

WWEA: Is there a time of year when tornadoes are more common?

MEYERS: Yes. They are most common in the spring.

WWEA: What was the largest tornado in history?

MEYERS: The Tri-State Tornado in the United States. And that took place in the spring of 1925.

WWEA: How strong are the winds during a tornado?

MEYERS: Tornado winds can reach a speed between 261 and 318 miles per hour. That's between about 420 and 512 kilometers an hour.

WWEA: And how quickly do they travel across land?

MEYERS: Not as fast. They travel at a speed of 70 miles per hour or less. In kilometers, that's about 112 kilometers or less. However, the Tri-State Tornado reached a traveling speed of 73 miles per hour, or 117.5 kilometers an hour.

WWEA: How long does a tornado typically last?

MEYERS: Usually just a few minutes. The Tri-State, however, lasted three and a half hours.

WWEA: Has North America suffered the most deaths as a result of tornadoes?

MEYERS: No. North America has the *most* tornadoes, but the most deaths have occurred in Bangladesh, in Southeast Asia.

WWEA: One last question. Can tornadoes be prevented?

MEYERS: No. We can't prevent them. They are inevitable. But we can predict tornadoes much better now than in the past. We've made a lot of progress, but we still must improve our ability to predict this force of nature.

1. Tornadoes only occur in North America.

   That's wrong. She said that tornadoes occurred in all seven continents except Antarctica.

2. Tornadoes are most common in the summer.

   That's wrong she said were most common in spring

3. The largest tornado in history was the Tri-State Tornado.

   That's right she said that the largest tornado in history had been

4. Tornado winds can reach a speed of 318 mph (about 512 kph).

   That's right she said that tornado wings could reach 381 mph

5. Tornadoes usually travel at a speed of 70 mph (about 112 kph).

   That's right, she said that tornados ussually traveled

6. The Tri-State Tornado lasted just a few minutes.

   That's wrong. she said that the tri-state had lasted 3 1/2 hrs

7. North America has the most tornadoes.

   That's right, she said that North America had the most tornados

8. Most deaths from tornadoes have occurred in North America.

   That's wrong. she said that the most death had occured Bangladesh

9. We can prevent tornadoes.

   That's wrong she sad that we couldn't prevent tornadoes

10. We still must improve our ability to predict this force of nature.

    That's right she said we still had to improve

EXERCISE 4   DIRECT SPEECH

GRAMMAR NOTES 1–5   Filip and Lena live in Poland. In 2010, there were terrible floods as the result of heavy rainstorms. Read the information and advice that Filip received on the day of the storm. Then write what people said. Use direct speech. Change words to keep the speakers' original meaning.

Filip's mother called. She told him that she was listening to the weather report. She said that she was worried about Filip and Lena. She told him that if they weren't so stubborn, they'd pack up and leave right then.

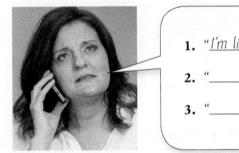

1. "*I'm listening to the weather report.*_____"

2. "_____"

3. "_____"

Filip's father gave him some good advice. He said he'd had some experience with floods. He said Filip and Lena had to put sandbags in front of their doors. He also told Filip that they ought to fill the sinks and the bathtub with clean water. He said they should buy a lot of batteries.

4. "_____"

5. "_____"

6. "_____"

7. "_____"

Filip's brother, Adam, called. He and his wife, Zofia, are worried. Their place is very close to the river. Adam said that they couldn't stay there. He told Filip that they wanted to stay with him and Lena. He said they were leaving that night. Adam told Filip that he and Zofia should have called sooner.

8. "_____"

9. "_____"

10. "_____"

11. "_____"

Filip listened to the storm warning in the afternoon. The forecaster said the storm would hit that night. She warned that the rainfall was going to be very heavy, and she said that the storm might last for several hours.

12. "_____"

13. "_____"

14. "_____"

EXERCISE 5 EDITING

GRAMMAR NOTES 1–5 Read this student's report. There are eleven mistakes in the use of indirect speech. The first mistake is already corrected. Find and correct ten more.

What is it like to live through a flood? For my report, I interviewed the Nemec family, who experienced last month's floods in our city. They reported that ~~we~~ *they* had experienced fear and sadness. On September 14, the family went to a movie. Jerzy, a high school student, said they ~~can't~~ *couldn't* drive the car home because their street was flooded. He said it had happened in only three hours. Mrs. Nemec said that all their belongings ~~are~~ *were* ruined, but that their cat ~~has~~ *had* escaped to an upstairs bedroom. They were sad about losing so many valuable items, but she said she ~~will~~ *would* have been much sadder to lose the family pet. Jerzy's father also said their home had been a complete mess and that the family had worked all ~~this~~ *that* week to clean out the house. Anna, who is in junior high school, wanted to keep her old dollhouse. It had belonged to her mother and her mother's mother. At first, her father ~~said~~ *told* her that she wouldn't be able to keep it because seeing it would just make her sad. Anna replied that she saw memories in this dollhouse—not just broken wood. She said she couldn't bear to throw it away. In the end, they kept it. Mr. Nemec said he and Anna ~~are~~ *were* able to restore the dollhouse a few weeks later. Mrs. Nemec said that Anna had taught them something important ~~today~~ *that day*. She also said that if they had known about the flood in advance, they would ~~had~~ *have* left the city.

EXERCISE 6　LISTENING

25|02 Ⓐ Listen to a couple discuss the weather report about a winter storm. Then read the information. Listen again and check (✓) the correct information.

Schools

1. Today schools:　☑ closed at 10:00　　☐ will close at 1:00
2. Students and teachers:　☐ should stay at school　　☐ should go home immediately
3. Tomorrow schools:　☐ will open　　☐ may stay closed

Roads

4. Road conditions:　☐ are safe　　☐ are dangerous
5. Drivers must:　☐ drive slowly　　☐ pick up passengers
6. Everyone should:　☐ avoid driving　　☐ continue driving

Public Offices

7. Government offices:　☐ will close today　　☐ will remain open tomorrow
8. Libraries:　☐ will stay open　　☐ will close at 1:00
9. Post offices:　☐ will stay open until 5:00　　☐ will be closed tomorrow

Businesses

10. Banks:　☐ will close at noon　　☐ will stay open until 3:00
11. Gas stations:　☐ will close at noon　　☐ will stay open until evening
12. Supermarkets:　☐ are open now　　☐ are closed now

Ⓑ Work with a partner. Compare your answers in A.

EXAMPLE:　A: They said that schools would close at 1:00.
　　　　　B: That's not right. They said that schools had closed at 10:00, not at 1:00.
　　　　　A: Well, let's listen again and check.

EXERCISE 7　WHAT ABOUT YOU?

Ⓐ CONVERSATION Work with a partner. Find out about his or her experience with a weather event.

EXAMPLE:　A: Have you ever experienced an extreme weather event?
　　　　　B: Yes. I was living in Toronto, Canada, and we had several blizzards in one week.
　　　　　A: Did you have to go to a shelter?
　　　　　B: Actually, we couldn't even get out of the house that week because all the roads were blocked. They had to call in the army to clear the roads.
　　　　　A: What did you do? Did you have enough food and water at home?

B Report your conversation to the rest of the class.

EXAMPLE: Peter told me that he had experienced an extreme weather event when he was living in Canada. He said they had several blizzards in one week and that he couldn't leave the house that week. He said...

EXERCISE 8 EXTREME WEATHER

A GROUP PROJECT Work in a group. Choose an extreme weather event from the list in the box. Do an online search to find the answers to the questions below.

1. What is the definition of the extreme weather event?
2. In what parts of the world does it take place?
3. When does it take place?
4. How common is it?
5. What is a historic example of the event?
6. Can the event be predicted?
7. Can the event be prevented?

Drought
Heat Wave
Flood
Wildfire
Blizzard
Winter Storm
Sandstorm
Other: _____

B Report your findings to the rest of the class.

EXAMPLE: A: We researched droughts. A drought is...
B: We looked at the National Weather site. It said that droughts took place mostly in...
C: It said that they happened when...

EXERCISE 9 THAT'S NOT WHAT I HEARD!

GAME Work in a group. Play "Telephone." Student A whispers a statement in the ear of Student B. Student B reports (in a whisper) to Student C what he or she heard. Each student reports to the next student in a whisper and may only say the information once. The last student tells the group what he or she heard. Expect surprises!

EXAMPLE: A: There won't be any class tomorrow.
B: He said that there wouldn't be any class tomorrow.
C: She said that there wouldn't be any gas tomorrow.
D: He said that there wouldn't be any cash tomorrow!

A BEFORE YOU WRITE Work with a partner. Interview your partner about a weather event he or she or someone your partner knows experienced. Answer the questions below.

1. What type of weather event did he or she experience?
2. When and where did it happen?
3. What was it like?
4. How did he or she feel?
5. What did he or she do?
6. What advice would he or she give someone in the same situation?

B WRITE Use your answers to write two paragraphs reporting your partner's (or another person's) experience of a weather event. Use indirect speech. Try to avoid the common mistakes in the chart.

EXAMPLE: Julie told me about a dust storm in Australia several years ago. She said that the sky had gotten very dark and the wind had started to blow hard. Her mother told her they all had to go inside and close the windows. Then . . .

Common Mistakes in Using Indirect Speech with Tense Changes

Change the tense of the verb in indirect speech when the reporting verb is in the simple past and you are reporting something that is no longer true. Do not keep the same tense as in the direct speech.	"It**'s raining** hard." *(said two weeks ago)* He **told** me that it **was raining** hard. NOT He told me that it ~~is raining~~ hard.
Do not change *should, could, might, ought to* in the indirect sentence.	"We **should buy** water." *(said two weeks ago)* He said they **should buy** water. NOT He said that they ~~should have bought~~ water.
Use the correct time and place words in indirect speech to **keep the original meaning** of the direct speech. Do not use the same time or place words in indirect speech if they change the meaning.	"I'll leave **now**." *(said two weeks ago)* She said she would leave **then**. NOT She said she would leave ~~now~~.

C CHECK YOUR WORK Read your paragraphs. Underline all the examples of indirect speech. Circle all the verbs and time and place words in the indirect speech. Use the Editing Checklist to check your work.

Editing Checklist

Did you use . . . ?

☐ the correct verb tenses

☐ time and place words to keep the speaker's original meaning

D REVISE YOUR WORK Read your paragraphs again. Can you improve your writing? Make changes if necessary. Give your paragraphs a title.

UNIT 25 REVIEW

Test yourself on the grammar or the unit.

Ⓐ Circle the correct words to complete the indirect speech sentences.

Direct Speech	Indirect Speech
"It's cloudy."	She said it <u>was / were</u> cloudy. **1.**
"You should take a coat."	He told me <u>she / I</u> should <u>take / have taken</u> a coat. **2.** **3.**
"The temperature may drop."	She said the temperature <u>must / might</u> drop. **4.**
"Tomorrow will be nice."	Yesterday, you said that <u>tomorrow / today</u> <u>will / would</u> be nice. **5.** **6.**
"We can expect a lot of damage here in Florida."	She said they <u>can / could</u> expect a lot of damage <u>here / there</u> **7.** **8.** in Florida. *(reported a week later in Texas)*

Ⓑ Rewrite each direct statement as an indirect statement. Keep the original meaning.
(The direct statement was said to you two months ago.)

Direct Speech	Indirect Speech
1. "It's going to rain."	She said _____.
2. "It could be the worst storm this year."	He said _____.
3. "It's going to start soon."	She said _____.
4. "We should buy water."	He said _____.
5. "We must leave right now."	He told me _____.
6. "I'll call you tomorrow."	She said _____.

Ⓒ Find and correct six mistakes.

What a storm! They said it is going to be bad, but it was terrible. They said it will last two days, but it lasted four. On the first day of the storm, my mother called and told me that we should have left the house right now. (I still can hear her exact words: "You should leave the house *right now*!") We should have listened to her! We just didn't believe it was going to be so serious. I told her last night that if we had known, we would had left right away. We're lucky we survived. I just listened to the weather forecast. Good news! They said tomorrow should have been sunny.

Now check your answers on page 482.

Indirect Instructions, Commands, Advice, Requests, Invitations

HEALTH ISSUES

OUTCOMES
• Report other people's instructions, commands, advice, requests, and invitations, using indirect speech
• Identify specific information in an interview transcript
• Identify medical advice reported in a conversation
• Discuss health issues and possible home remedies
• Report how someone followed instructions
• Write about a health problem one had and about the health advice one received

---

STEP 1   GRAMMAR IN CONTEXT

BEFORE YOU READ

Look at the photo. Discuss the questions.

1. What time is it? Where is the woman?

2. How does the woman feel? Why does she feel that way?

READ

▶ 26|01   Read this transcript of a radio interview with the director of a sleep clinic.

Here's to Your Health

SUNG: Good morning! This is Connie Sung, bringing you "Here's to Your Health," a program about today's health issues. This morning, we've invited Dr. William Ray, director of the Sleep Disorders[1] Clinic, to talk to us about insomnia. As you probably know, insomnia is a problem with getting to sleep or staying asleep. Welcome to the show, Doctor!

RAY: Thanks, Connie. It's great to be here.

SUNG: Your book *Night Shift*[2] will be coming out soon. In it, you tell people to pay more attention to sleep disorders. But why is losing a little sleep such a big problem?

RAY: Good question. I always tell people to think of the worst industrial disaster[3] they've ever heard about. Usually, it was caused at least in part by fatigue due to sleep

---

1 *disorders:* physical or mental problems that can affect health for a long period of time
2 *shift:* a work period, especially in a factory (the night shift is often midnight to 8:00 a.m.)
3 *industrial disaster:* an accident in a factory that causes a great deal of damage and loss of life

deprivation.[4] Then I ask them to think about what can happen if they drive when they're tired. Every year, more than 100,000 automobile accidents in this country are caused by sleepy drivers.

SUNG: A hundred thousand! That's astonishing!

RAY: And costly, too. Recently, a large study of workers' fatigue reported that the problem costs U.S. employers around $136.4 billion a year in lost work time.

SUNG: So, how can people deal with this problem? If I came to your clinic, for example, what would you advise me to do?

RAY: First, I would find out about some of your habits. If you drank coffee or cola late in the day, I would tell you to stop. The caffeine in these drinks interferes with sleep.

SUNG: What about old-fashioned remedies like warm milk?

RAY: Actually, a lot of home remedies make sense. We tell patients to have a snack before they go to bed. High-carbohydrate[5] foods like bananas are good. Warm milk helps, too. But I'd advise you not to eat a heavy meal before bed.

SUNG: My doctor told me to get more exercise, but when I run at night, I have a hard time getting to sleep.

RAY: It's true that if you exercise regularly, you'll sleep better. But we always tell patients not to exercise too close to bedtime.

SUNG: Suppose I try these remedies and they don't help?

RAY: If the problem persists, we often ask patients to come and spend a night at our sleep clinic. Our equipment monitors the patient through the night. In fact, if you're really interested, we can invite you to come to the clinic for a night.

SUNG: Maybe I should do that.

---

4 *deprivation:* not having something that you need or want
5 *high-carbohydrate:* containing a great deal of sugar or starch (for example fruit, potatoes, and rice)

AFTER YOU READ

A VOCABULARY **Choose the word or phrase that best completes each sentence.**

1. An **astonishing** fact is very _____.
   a. frightening   b. surprising   c. uninteresting

2. **Fatigue** is a feeling of extreme _____.
   a. excitement   b. pain   c. tiredness

3. Something that **interferes** with your sleep _____ it.
   a. helps   b. prevents   c. causes

4. Marta **monitors** the amount of carbohydrates she eats by taking _____ every day.
   a. notes   b. pills   c. sugar

5. My grandparents use traditional **remedies**. Those old _____ fascinate me.
   a. recipes   b. stories   c. treatments

6. After Ethan took pain medication, his headache **persisted**. It _____ for days.
   a. stopped   b. continued   c. improved

B COMPREHENSION   Check (✓) the things Dr. Ray advises people with insomnia to do.

☐ **1.** Stop drinking coffee and cola late in the day.

☐ **2.** Eat a heavy meal before bed.

☐ **3.** Get more exercise.

☐ **4.** Exercise right before bedtime.

☐ **5.** Have a banana before bed.

☐ **6.** Spend the night at a sleep clinic.

C DISCUSSION   Work with a partner. Compare your answers to the questions in B. Why did you or didn't you check each item?

STEP 2   GRAMMAR PRESENTATION

INDIRECT INSTRUCTIONS, COMMANDS, ADVICE, REQUESTS, INVITATIONS

Direct Speech

Subject	Reporting Verb	Direct Speech
He	said,	"**Drink** warm milk." "**Don't drink** coffee." "Can you **turn out** the light, please?" "Why don't you **visit** the clinic?"

Indirect Speech

Subject	Reporting Verb	Noun/ Pronoun	Indirect Speech
He	told advised asked	Connie her	**to drink** warm milk. **not to drink** coffee. **to turn out** the light.
	said		
	invited	her	**to visit** the clinic.

GRAMMAR NOTES

In **indirect speech**, use an **infinitive** (*to* + **base form of the verb**) for instructions, commands, advice, requests, and invitations.

• **instructions**	"**Come** early," said the doctor. *(direct)* The doctor said **to come** early. *(indirect)*
• **commands**	The doctor told her, "**Lie down**." *(direct)* The doctor told her **to lie down**. *(indirect)*
• **advice**	She said, "**Drink** more water." *(direct)* She advised her **to drink** more water. *(indirect)*
• **requests**	"Could you please **arrive** by 8:00?" *(direct)* He asked her **to arrive** by 8:00. *(indirect)*
• **invitations**	"Will you **join** me for lunch?" *(direct)* He invited us **to join** him for lunch. *(indirect)*

In **indirect speech**, use a **negative infinitive** (*not* + **infinitive**) for negative instructions, commands, advice, and requests.

• **negative instructions**	"**Don't eat** after 9:00 p.m.," he said. *(direct)* He said **not to eat** after 9:00 p.m. *(indirect)*
• **negative commands**	Ms. Tan told me, "**Don't wake** Lee." *(direct)* Ms. Tan told me **not to wake** Lee. *(indirect)*
• **negative advice**	"**Don't eat** so much sugar," he said. *(direct)* He advised me **not to eat** so much sugar. *(indirect)*
• **negative requests**	Jan said, "Please **don't set** the alarm." *(direct)* Jan asked me **not to set** the alarm. *(indirect)*

REFERENCE NOTES

For general information on **direct and indirect speech**, see Unit 24 on page 378.

For a list of **reporting verbs**, see Appendix 19 on page 462.

For **punctuation rules for direct speech**, see Appendix 28 on page 466.

EXERCISE 1 DISCOVER THE GRAMMAR

Ⓐ GRAMMAR NOTES 1–2 Connie Sung decided to write an article about her recent visit to Dr. Ray's clinic. Read her notes for the article. Underline the indirect instructions, commands, advice, requests, and invitations. Circle the reporting verbs that introduce them.

● ● ●

A Dream Job

2/18 **11:00 a.m.** The clinic called and (asked) me to arrive at 8:30 tonight. They told me to bring my pajamas and toothbrush. They told me people also like to bring their own pillow.

8:30 p.m. I arrived on schedule. My room was small but cozy. Only the video camera and cable told me I was in a sleep clinic. Juan Estrada, the technician for the night shift, told me to relax and watch TV for an hour. Then he left me alone in the room.

9:30 p.m. Juan came back and got me ready for the test. He pasted twelve small metal disks to my face, legs, and stomach. I asked him to explain, and he told me that the disks, called electrodes, would be connected to a machine that records electrical activity in the brain.

11:30 p.m. Juan came back and asked me to get into bed. After he hooked me up to the machine, he instructed me not to leave the bed that night. I fell asleep easily.

2/19 **7:00 a.m.** Juan came to awaken me and to disconnect the wires. I told him that I didn't think insomnia was my problem—those electrodes hadn't interfered with my sleep at all! He invited me to join him in the next room, where he had spent the whole night monitoring the equipment. I looked at the pages of graphs and asked myself aloud whether Juan and Dr. Ray would be able to read my weird dream of the night before. Juan laughed and told me not to worry. "Those just show electrical impulses," he assured me.

8:00 a.m. Dr. Ray reviewed my data with me. He told me I had healthy sleep patterns, except for some leg movements. He told me to get more exercise, and I promised I would.

Ⓑ Look at the underlined words in A. Then check (✓) the clinic's and Juan's exact words.

✓ **1.** "Arrive at 8:30 tonight."

☐ **2.** "Bring your pajamas and toothbrush."

☐ **3.** "Relax."

☐ **4.** "Don't watch TV."

☐ **5.** "Don't get into bed."

☐ **6.** "Don't leave the bed."

☐ **7.** "Join him in the next room."

☐ **8.** "Get more exercise."

EXERCISE 2 INDIRECT INSTRUCTIONS

GRAMMAR NOTES 1-2 Helen is a nurse who people call for health advice. Read each question for Helen and report her instructions (affirmative and negative), using the verbs in parentheses.

MIKE: Do you have a remedy for insomnia? I suffer from constant fatigue.

HELEN: Try exercising regularly, early in the day. And don't drink anything with caffeine after 2:00 p.m.

1. (say) _She said to try exercising regularly, early in the day._

2. (tell) _She told him not to drink anything with caffeine after 2:00 p.m._

ANNE: What can I do to soothe a sore throat? I never take medicine unless I have to.

HELEN: One remedy is to drink hot herbal tea with honey. But don't drink black tea. It will make your throat dry.

3. (say) _She say to try to drink hot herbal tea with honey._

4. (tell) _she told her not to drink black tea I will make your throat dry._

LOU: I get leg cramps at night. They wake me up, and I can't get back to sleep.

HELEN: The next time you feel a cramp, do this: Pinch the place between your upper lip and your nose. The cramp should stop right away. Sounds simple, but it's astonishing how well this works.

5. (say) _She said pinch the place betwen your upper lip and yournose_

PETE: Do you know of an inexpensive way to remove stains on teeth?

HELEN: Make a toothpaste of one tablespoon of baking soda and a little water. Brush as usual.

6. (tell) _She told him to make a toothpaste of one soda_

7. (say) _he said to brush as usual._

MARLA: What can I do to ease an itchy poison ivy rash?

HELEN: Spread cool, cooked oatmeal over the rash. Also, try soaking the rash in a cool bath with a quarter cup of baking soda. Don't scratch the rash. That will make it worse.

8. (tell) _She said spread cool cooked oatmeal over the rash_

9. (say) _She say d try to soa ras in cool bath_

10. (tell) _She told Don't scratch the rash_

LISA: Help! Bugs love me. They bite me all the time. Is there anything I can do to stop them?

HELEN: There are a few things you can do to keep bugs away. Eat onions or garlic every day. Your skin will have a slight odor that bugs hate. Or ask your doctor about a vitamin B supplement.

11. (say) _she said eat onion or garlic every day_

12. (tell) _She told her to ask your doctor about vitamin B_

EXERCISE 3 DIRECT AND INDIRECT SPEECH

A GRAMMAR NOTES 1–2 Connie had a dream at the sleep clinic. She wrote about it in her journal. Read her account of the dream and underline the indirect instructions, commands, advice, requests, and invitations.

● ● ●

I dreamed that an extraterrestrial came into my room. He told me to get up. Then he said to follow him. There was a spaceship outside the clinic. It was an astonishing sight! The creature from outer space invited me to come aboard. I asked him to lead the way! Juan, the lab technician, was on the ship. Suddenly, Juan told me to pilot the ship. He ordered me not to leave the controls. Then he went to sleep. Next, Dr. Ray was at my side giving me instructions. He told me to slow down. Then he said to point the ship toward the Earth. There was a loud knocking noise as we hit the ground, and I told everyone not to panic. Then I heard Juan tell me to wake up. I opened my eyes and saw him walking into my room at the sleep clinic.

B Complete the comic strip by writing what each character said.

EXERCISE 4 EDITING

GRAMMAR NOTES 1–2 Read this entry in a student's journal. There are eight mistakes in the use of indirect instructions and advice. The first mistake is already corrected. Find and correct seven more. Don't forget to check punctuation. Mistakes with quotation marks count as one mistake for the sentence.

● ● ●

MY POSTS

I am SO tired! I hardly got any sleep at all last night. That makes three sleepless nights in a

row, so I decided to call one of those health lines that gives you advice. The nurse I spoke

to told me ~~to~~ exercise every day. But, and this is important, she also said ~~no~~ *not* to exercise late in

the day. That can interfere with sleep. I'll try that. She asked me about what I eat and drink.

When she heard about all the coffee I drink, she told me ~~to~~ *not to* drink any in the evening.

No coffee! I need coffee to stay awake! She said ~~having~~ *to have* milk at night instead because there

is a chemical in milk that can make you sleepy. She had some other good tips for me, too.

She told ~~me to~~ keep the bedroom cool. People sleep better when the room isn't warm. Oh, and

she said ~~that~~ not to look at a computer, e-book, or cell phone screen for an hour before

bedtime. The "blue" light from these screens also interferes with sleep. I didn't know that!

And I told her what my mother used to say. Mom always told me ✗to *get*ting up and scrub

the floor when I couldn't sleep.✗ The

nurse agreed that sometimes works.

She advised one of her patients ~~to~~

balance his checkbook. He went right

to sleep just to escape from the task!

By the way, look at this funny cartoon

about insomnia!

"I couldn't sleep."

Anyhow, the nurse was very helpful and all her ideas sound good. In fact, I want to try them

out right away. The only problem is, I'm so excited about them, I'm not sure I'll be able to

fall asleep tonight!

EXERCISE 5 LISTENING

▶26|02 **A** Marta is telling a friend about her experience at a headache clinic. Listen to their conversation. Read the list. Then listen again and check (✓) the correct column to show what the doctors at the clinic told Marta to do, what they told her not to do, and what they didn't mention.

	Do	Don't Do	Not Mentioned
1. Monitor the headaches.	✓	☐	☐
2. Get regular exercise.	☐	☐	☐
3. Get eight hours of sleep.	☐	☐	☐
4. Take painkillers.	☐	☐	☐
5. Use an ice pack.	☐	☐	☐
6. Massage around the eyes.	☐	☐	☐
7. Eat three big meals a day.	☐	☐	☐
8. Eat chocolate.	☐	☐	☐
9. Avoid cheese.	☐	☐	☐

▶26|02 **B** Work with a partner. Listen again. Discuss your answers in A. Why did you choose each answer?

EXAMPLE: A: For number 1, the answer is "Do." They told her to monitor her headaches.
B: That's right. They told her to write down when she got a headache.
A: They also told her to write down what she was doing before she got the headache. What about number 2?

EXERCISE 6 HOME REMEDIES

PROBLEM SOLVING Work with a partner. What advice have you heard for the following problems? Discuss what to do and what not to do for them.

EXAMPLE: A: My mother always told me to hold a burn under cold water.
B: They say not to put butter on a burn.

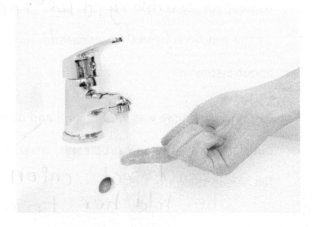

- minor burns
- insomnia
- insect bites
- headaches
- snoring
- hiccups
- a cold
- blisters
- poison ivy
- a sore throat
- a toothache
- Other: _____

EXERCISE 7 HOME ALONE

PICTURE DISCUSSION Jeff's parents went out for the evening and left a list of instructions for him. Work in pairs. Read the list and look at the picture. Talk about which instructions Jeff followed and which ones he didn't follow. Use indirect instructions.

EXAMPLE: A: His parents told him not to stay up after 10:00, but it's 11:30 now and he's not in bed—he's asleep on the couch and having a nightmare.
  B: They also said to . . .

Dear Jeff,
We'll be home late. Here are a few things to remember:

- Don't stay up after 10:00. You need to get more sleep.

- Don't drink any cola — all that sugar keeps you awake. Drink some milk instead.

- Have some cake, but please save some for us!

- Please take the garbage out. Also, wash the dishes and put them away.

- And please don't let the cat in — You know that you're allergic to cats!

- Keep the back door closed.

- Do your homework.

- Don't watch any horror movies. (They give you nightmares — remember?)

- Don't invite your friends over tonight.

Love,
Mom and Dad

A BEFORE YOU WRITE Think about a health problem you (or someone you know) had. Answer the questions.

What was the problem? _____

Who did you (or the person) ask for advice? _____

What advice did you (or the person) receive? Use direct speech with quotation marks.

Things to do	**Things not to do**
_____	_____
_____	_____
_____	_____

Did the advice work? _____

B WRITE Use your answers in A to write one or two paragraphs about the advice you or someone you know received. Use indirect speech to report the advice. Try to avoid the common mistakes in the chart below.

EXAMPLE: Four years ago, I got a bad rash from poison ivy. It really itched, and I felt miserable. My friend had had a lot of experience with this annoying health problem, so I asked him for advice. He told me to put some cucumber slices on the rash. But, most importantly, he told me not to scratch. That advice was easier said than done! My friend also advised me to . . .

Common Mistakes in Using Indirect Instructions and Advice

Use an **infinitive** to report indirect instructions and advice. Do not leave out *to*.	He told me **to drink** a lot of water. NOT He told me ~~drink~~ a lot of water.
Use *not* + **infinitive** to report indirect negative instructions and advice. Do not use *don't*.	He told me *not* **to scratch** the rash. NOT He told me ~~don't scratch~~ the rash.

C CHECK YOUR WORK Read your paragraph(s). Underline all the examples of indirect instructions and advice. Circle *not*. Use the Editing Checklist to check your work.

Editing Checklist

Did you use . . . ?

☐ infinitives to report indirect instructions and advice

☐ negative infinitives to report indirect negative instructions and advice

D REVISE YOUR WORK Read your paragraph(s) again. Can you improve your writing? Make changes if necessary. Give your paragraph(s) a title.

UNIT 26 REVIEW

Test yourself on the grammar of the unit.

A Circle the correct punctuation mark or words to complete the sentences.

1. I arrived at 8:00 because the doctor asked me to come early . / ?

2. The assistant asked me to give / gave her my health insurance card.

3. The doctor said, "To lie down." / "Please lie down."

4. She advised me don't / not to drink so much coffee.

5. Some experts say / tell to eat a snack before bedtime.

6. At the sleep clinic, the technician told / said me to relax and watch TV.

7. The doctor invited / advised me not to have a late dinner.

B Rewrite the direct speech as an indirect instruction, command, request, invitation, or as advice. Use an appropriate reporting verb (*tell*, *ask*, *invite*, or *advise*). Use pronouns.

1. Officer David Zhu to Anita: "Please show me your license."

   _____

2. Doctor Sue Rodriguez to Sam: "You ought to get more exercise."

   _____

3. Ms. Carson to her students: "Please come to the English Department party."

   _____

4. Robert to Nina: "Could you turn on the light, please?"

   _____

5. Lisa to Nina and Paulo: "Why don't you hang out at my house?"

   _____

C Find and correct eight mistakes. Remember to check punctuation.

Too much stress is bad for your health. So, I asked my doctor give me some tips on how to reduce everyday stress. First of all, she told me exercising every day. She also told me to don't work too long without taking a break. She advised me doing things to relax. For example, she said that to listen to music. She also said me to sit with my eyes closed and to concentrate on my breathing. That helps lower blood pressure. She also advised me no drink too many beverages with caffeine. Finally, she said to "get enough sleep"—at least seven hours a night!

Now check your answers on page 482.

Indirect Questions

JOB INTERVIEWS

OUTCOMES
• Report other people's questions, using indirect speech
• Identify specific information in a business article
• Identify and discuss details in a conversation
• Role-play and discuss a job interview
• Complete a questionnaire about work values, discuss the answers, and report conversations
• Write a report on a job interview

STEP 1 GRAMMAR IN CONTEXT

BEFORE YOU READ

Look at the photo and at the title of the article. Discuss the questions.

1. What are the people doing?
2. Are the man's questions typical in this situation? What is the woman's reaction?
3. What do you think a *stress interview* is?

READ

▶27|01 Read this article about job interviews.

The Stress Interview

A few weeks ago, Melissa Morrow had an unusual job interview. First, the interviewer asked why she couldn't work under pressure. Before she could answer, he asked if she had cleaned out her car recently. Right after that, he wanted to know who had written her application letter for her. Melissa was shocked, but she handled herself well. She asked the interviewer whether he was going to ask her any serious questions. Then she politely ended the interview.

Melissa had had a *stress interview*, a type of job interview that asks tough, tricky questions, with long silences and negative evaluations of the job candidate. To the

Why can't you work under pressure?
Have you cleaned out your car recently?
Who wrote your application letter for you?

Do I really want this job?

unhappy candidate, this may seem unnecessarily nasty on the interviewer's part. However, some positions require an ability to handle just this kind of pressure. If there is an accident in an oil well near the coast, for example, the oil company's public relations officer[1] must remain calm when hostile[2] reporters ask how the accident could have occurred.

The uncomfortable atmosphere[3] of a stress interview gives the potential employer a chance to watch a candidate react to pressure. In one case, the interviewer ended each interview by saying, "We're really not sure that you're the right person for this job." One excellent candidate asked the interviewer angrily if he was sure he knew how to conduct an interview. She clearly could not handle the pressure she would encounter as a TV news reporter—the job she was interviewing for.

Stress interviews may be appropriate for some jobs, but they can also work against a company. Some excellent candidates may refuse the job after a hostile interview. Melissa Morrow handled her interview extremely well, but she later asked herself if she really wanted to work for that company. Her answer was *no*.

A word of warning to job candidates: Not all tough questioning is legitimate.[4] In some countries, certain questions are illegal unless the answers are directly related to the job. If an interviewer asks how old you are, whether you are married, or how much money you owe, you can refuse to answer. If you think a question isn't appropriate, then ask the interviewer how the answer specifically relates to that job. If you don't get a satisfactory explanation, you don't have to answer the question. And remember: Whatever happens, don't lose your cool.[5] The interview will be over before you know it!

---

1 *public relations officer:* someone hired by a company to explain to the public what the company does so that the public will understand it and approve of it
2 *hostile:* angry and unfriendly
3 *atmosphere:* the feeling that you get from a situation or a place
4 *legitimate:* proper and allowable
5 *lose your cool:* get excited and angry

AFTER YOU READ

A VOCABULARY **Choose the word or phrase that best completes each sentence.**

1. A job **evaluation** gives a worker _____.
   a. more money   b. more vacation time   c. comments on his or her work

2. A bad way to **handle** an interview is to _____.
   a. say the right things   b. get angry   c. ask good questions

3. A **candidate** for a job promotion _____ get a better position.
   a. may   b. will   c. can't

4. A job with a lot of **pressure** _____.
   a. pays well   b. is easy   c. is difficult

5. Sara's behavior was **appropriate**. She did the _____ thing.
   a. right   b. wrong   c. easiest

6. A **potential** problem is one that _____.
   a. is very serious   b. may happen   c. has an easy solution

B COMPREHENSION Read the statements. Check (✓) *True* or *False*.

	True	False
1. Melissa told the interviewer she couldn't work under pressure.	☐	☐
2. Melissa asked, "Are you going to ask me any serious questions?"	☐	☐
3. One candidate asked if the interviewer knew how to interview.	☐	☐
4. Melissa asked herself how long she wanted to work for the company.	☐	☐
5. You should always answer the interview question, "Are you married?"	☐	☐
6. It's OK to ask an interviewer, "How does the answer relate to this job?"	☐	☐

C DISCUSSION Work with a partner. Compare your answers in B. Why did you check *True* or *False*?

STEP 2   GRAMMAR PRESENTATION

INDIRECT QUESTIONS

Direct Speech: *Yes/No* Questions

Subject	Reporting Verb	Direct Question
He	asked,	"**Do you have** any experience?" "**Can you create** spreadsheets?" "**Will you stay** for a year?"

Indirect Speech: *Yes/No* Questions

Subject	Reporting Verb	(Noun/ Pronoun)	Indirect Question	
He	asked	(Melissa) (her)	*if* *whether (or not)*	**she had** any experience. **she could create** spreadsheets. **she would stay** for a year.

Direct Speech: *Wh-* Questions About the Subject

Subject	Reporting Verb	Direct Question
He	asked,	"*Who* **told** you about the job?" "*What* **happened** on your last job?" "*Which company* **hired** you?"

Indirect Speech: *Wh-* Questions About the Subject

Subject	Reporting Verb	(Noun/ Pronoun)	Indirect Question	
He	asked	(Bob) (him)	*who*	**had told** him about the job.
			what	**had happened** on his last job.
			which company	**had hired** him.

Direct Speech: *Wh-* Questions About the Object

Subject	Reporting Verb	Direct Question
He	asked,	"*Who* **do you work** for?" "*What* **do you do** there?" "*Which job* **did you accept**?"

Indirect Speech: *Wh-* Questions About the Object

Subject	Reporting Verb	(Noun/ Pronoun)	Indirect Question	
He	asked	(Melissa) (her)	*who*	**she worked** for.
			what	**she did** there.
			which job	**she had accepted**.

Direct Speech: *Wh-* Questions with *When*, *Where*, *Why*, and *How*

Subject	Reporting Verb	Direct Question
He	asked,	"*When* **did you start** your new job?" "*Where* **do you work** now?" "*Why* **have you changed** jobs?" "*How much* **did you earn** there?"

Indirect Speech: *Wh-* Questions with *When*, *Where*, *Why*, and *How*

Subject	Reporting Verb	(Noun/ Pronoun)	Indirect Question	
He	asked	(Melissa) (her)	*when*	**she had started** her new job.
			where	**she worked** now.
			why	**she had changed** jobs.
			how much	**she had earned** there.

GRAMMAR NOTES

1 Indirect Questions

We often use indirect speech to **report questions**.

The most common **reporting verb** for both direct and indirect questions is *ask*.	"Did you find a new job?" she *asked*. *(direct)* She *asked* **if I had found a new job.** *(indirect)*

As in indirect statements, when the reporting verb is in the **simple past**, the **verb tense in the indirect question often changes**. For example:

• simple present becomes simple past	"**Do** you **like** your new job?" he asked. *(direct)* He *asked* me if I **liked** my new job. *(indirect)*
• simple past becomes past perfect	"**Did** you **find** it online?" he wanted to know. *(direct)* He *asked* if I **had found** it online. *(indirect)*
• present perfect becomes past perfect	"How long **have** you **been** there?" he asked. *(direct)* He *asked* me how long I **had been** there. *(indirect)*

BE CAREFUL! When the reporting verb is in the **simple present**, the verb tense in the indirect question **does not change**.	He asked me, "Where **do** you **work**?" *(direct)* He always *asks* me where I **work**. *(indirect)* NOT He always asks me where I ~~worked~~.
Remember to make **pronoun changes** and other changes to keep the speaker's original meaning.	He asked, "Why do **you** want to work **here**?" *(direct)* He asked me why **I** wanted to work **there**. *(indirect)*
IN WRITING Do not end an indirect question with a question mark. End it with a period.	She asked me where I had worked before. NOT She asked me where I had worked before~~?~~

2 Indirect *Yes/No* Questions

Use *if* or **whether** in indirect *yes/no* questions.

	She asked, "Can you type?" *(direct)*
• *if*	She asked me *if* **I could type.** *(indirect)*
• *whether*	She asked me *whether* **I could type.** *(indirect)*
USAGE NOTE *Whether* is more formal than *if*.	My boss wants to know *whether* **the report is ready.**
We can also use *whether or not* to report *yes/no* questions.	He wants to know *whether or not* **the report is ready.**

3 Indirect *Wh-* Questions

Use **question words** in indirect *wh-* questions.

You can use any question word in an indirect question. For example:

• *where*	"*Where* is your office?" *(direct)* I asked *where* **his office was.** *(indirect)*
• *how much*	"*How much* is the salary?" *(direct)* I asked *how much* **the salary was.** *(indirect)*

Use **statement word order (subject + verb)**, not question word order, for all **indirect questions**. Do not use the auxiliaries *do*, *does*, or *did*.

The word order in the indirect question is the same word order as in a **statement**.	SUBJECT + VERB **Samantha is** sure.
• indirect *yes/no* questions	"**Is Samantha** sure?" *(direct)* He asked me **if Samantha is** sure. *(indirect)* "**Did he hire** Li?" *(direct)* I asked **if he had hired** Li. *(indirect)*
• indirect *wh-* questions about the **subject**	"**Who is** late?" *(direct)* She asked **who was** late. *(indirect)* "**Who hired** Li?" *(direct)* I asked **who had hired** Li. *(indirect)*
• indirect *wh-* questions about the **object**	"Who **did he hire**?" *(direct)* I asked who **he had hired**. *(indirect)*
• indirect *wh-* questions with *when*, *where*, *why* and *how* or *how much/many*	"Why **did they hire** Li?" *(direct)* I asked why **they had hired** Li. *(indirect)*
BE CAREFUL! Do not use question word order or the auxiliaries *do*, *does*, *did* in indirect questions.	"Where **do you live**?" *(direct)* She asked me where **I lived**. *(indirect)* NOT She asked me ~~where do you live~~.
BE CAREFUL! If a direct question about the subject has the form **question word + *be* + noun**, then the indirect question has the form **question word + noun + *be*.**	"**Who *is* the boss**?" *(direct)* I asked them **who the boss *was*.** *(indirect)* NOT I asked them ~~who was the boss~~.

REFERENCE NOTES

For more information about **indirect speech**, see Unit 24 on page 378 and Unit 25 on page 395.

For a list of **reporting verbs in questions**, see Appendix 19 on page 462.

For **punctuation rules for direct speech**, see Appendix 28 on page 466.

EXERCISE 1   DISCOVER THE GRAMMAR

Ⓐ GRAMMAR NOTES 1–4   Bruno Lopez is telling a friend about his job interview. Underline the indirect questions in the conversation.

ANDREA: So, how did the interview go?

BRUNO: It went well! The interviewer, Mr. Chen, asked me a lot of good questions.

ANDREA: Great. Tell me about it.

BRUNO: Well, first, he asked me <u>how much experience I'd had</u>, and I told him I'd been a sales manager for ten years. Let's see.... He also asked what I would change about my current job. I thought that was a good question.

ANDREA: It was. What did you say?

BRUNO: Well, I didn't want to say anything negative, so I told him that I was ready to take on a lot more responsibility.

ANDREA: Good answer! What else did he ask?

BRUNO: Oh, you know, the usual things. He asked what my greatest success had been, and how much I was making at my current job. He also asked me how I handled on-the-job stress.

ANDREA: Did you tell him you have no problems handling stress?

BRUNO: Of course! Then he asked me what my goals were. Oh, and he asked me if *I* had any questions for *him*.

ANDREA: Did you?

BRUNO: Yes. I had researched the company online and had several questions. Mr. Chen seemed pleased with them.

ANDREA: So, do you think you'll get a job offer?

BRUNO: I already did! At the end of the interview, he asked me when I could start!

Ⓑ Check (✓) the direct questions that the interviewer asked Bruno in A.

☑ **1.** "How much experience have you had?"

☐ **2.** "What would I change about my current job?"

☐ **3.** "What was your greatest success?"

☐ **4.** "How much are you making at your current job?"

☐ **5.** "How have you handled on-the-job stress?"

☐ **6.** "What were your goals?"

☐ **7.** "Do you have any questions for me?"

☐ **8.** "When can you start?"

EXERCISE 2 WORD ORDER

GRAMMAR NOTES 1–4 Jason has an interview next week. His neighbor, Claire, wants to know all about it. Report Claire's questions. Put the words in parentheses in the correct order.

1. CLAIRE: I heard you're going on an interview next week. What kind of job is it?
   JASON: It's for an accounts-assistant job.

   She asked what kind of job it was.
   (asked / kind of job / what / was / it / she)

2. CLAIRE: Oh, really? When is the interview?
   JASON: It's on Tuesday at 9:00.

   _____
   (the interview / she / was / when / asked)

3. CLAIRE: Where's the company?
   JASON: It's downtown on the west side.

   _____
   (was / where / she / the company / asked)

4. CLAIRE: Do you need directions?
   JASON: No, I know the way.

   _____
   (asked / needed / she / if / he / directions)

5. CLAIRE: How long does it take to get there?
   JASON: About half an hour.

   _____
   (asked / to get there / it / she / takes / how long)

6. CLAIRE: Are you going to drive?
   JASON: I think so. It's probably the fastest way.

   _____
   (was going to / asked / if / he / drive / she)

7. CLAIRE: Who's going to interview you?
   JASON: Um. I'm not sure. Probably the manager of the department.

   _____
   (she / was going to / him / who / interview / asked)

8. CLAIRE: Well, good luck. When will they let you know?
   JASON: It will take a while. They have a lot of candidates.

   _____
   (him / they / would / asked / she / when / let / know)

EXERCISE 3 INDIRECT QUESTIONS WITH NO TENSE CHANGES

GRAMMAR NOTES 1–4 Read the information in the box. Write sentences about questions employers cannot ask during an interview in many countries. Use indirect questions, and do not change the tense in the indirect questions.

You Can't Ask That!

• •

In some countries, employers must hire only on the basis of skills and experience. In Canada, most countries in Europe, and in the United States, for example, an interviewer cannot ask an applicant certain questions unless the information is related to the job. Here are some questions an interviewer may *not* ask:

- How old are you?
- Have you ever been arrested?
- What is your religion?
- How many children do you have?
- Are you married?
- How tall are you?
- What does your husband (or wife) do?
- Where were you born?

1. _They can't ask how old you are._

2. _____

3. _____

4. _____

5. _____

6. _____

7. _____

8. _____

EXERCISE 4
INDIRECT QUESTIONS WITH VERB AND PRONOUN CHANGES

GRAMMAR NOTES 1–4 Read the questions that were asked during Jason's interview. Jason asked some of the questions, and the manager, Ms. Suarez, asked others. Decide who asked each question. Then rewrite each question as indirect speech. Make verb and pronoun changes if necessary.

1. "What type of training is available for the job?"

   Jason asked Ms. Suarez what type of training was available for the job.

2. "What kind of experience do you have?"

   Ms. Suarez... aske (Jason) what kind of experience he had?

3. "Is there opportunity for promotion?"

   He asked if there was an opportunity for promotion

4. "Why did you apply for this position?"

   Ms Suarez asked Jason whie he had applied for the position

5. "Are you interviewing with other companies?"

   Ms Suarez asked if he was ntervied with other companies

6. "Did you get along well with your last employer?"

   Ms suarez asked if had gotten along with his last employer

7. "How is job performance rewarded?"

   He asked how was the job performance was rewarded.

8. "What was your salary at your last job?"

   Ms Suarez asked what his salary had been at job last job

9. "What will my responsibilities be?"

   Jason asked what his responsabilities would be.

10. "When does the job start?"

    Jason when the job started. job.

EXERCISE 5 EDITING

GRAMMAR NOTES 1–4 Read this memo an interviewer wrote after an interview. There are seven mistakes in the use of indirect questions. The first mistake is already corrected. Find and correct six more. Don't forget to check punctuation. Mistakes with quotation marks count as one mistake for the sentence.

May 15, 2017

TO: Francesca Giuffrida
FROM: Ken Marley
SUBJECT: Interview with Alex Kaminski

This morning I interviewed Alex Kaminski for the administrative assistant position.

Since this job requires a lot of contact with the public, I thought it was appropriate to

do some stress questioning. I asked Mr. Lopez why ~~couldn't he~~ *he couldn't* work under pressure.

I also ~~told~~ *asked* him, "Why does your supervisor dislike you?" Finally, I inquired when he

would quit the job with our company~~?~~,

Mr. Kaminski remained calm throughout the interview. He answered all my questions,

and he had some excellent questions of his own. He asked ~~"~~if we expected changes

in the job~~."~~ He also asked how often ~~do we perform~~ *performed* employee evaluations. I was

quite impressed when he asked why ~~did~~ I decide to join this company.

Mr. Kaminski is an excellent candidate for the job, and I believe he will handle the

responsibilities well. At the end of the interview, Mr. Kaminski inquired when we

could let him know our decision. I asked him ~~if~~ *whether* or not he was considering another job,

and he said he was. I think we should act quickly in order not to lose this excellent

potential employee.

EXERCISE 6 LISTENING

▶ 27|02   **A** You are going to hear a conversation about a job interview that took place in Canada. Read the checklist. Then listen to the conversation. Listen again and check (✓) the topics that the interviewer asked about.

POSSIBLE JOB INTERVIEW TOPICS	
OK to Ask	**Not OK to Ask**
☐ Name	☑ Age
☐ Address	☐ Race
☐ Work experience	☐ Sex
☑ Reason for leaving job	☐ Religion
☐ Reason for seeking position	☐ National origin
☐ Salary	☐ Height or weight
☐ Education	☐ Marital status
☐ Professional affiliations	☐ Information about spouse
☐ Convictions¹ for crimes	☐ Arrest record
☐ Skills	☐ Physical disabilities
☐ Job performance	☐ Children
☐ Permission to work in Canada	☐ Citizenship
	☐ English language skill
	☐ Financial situation

1 *convictions:* a court's decisions that a person is guilty of a crime

▶ 27|02   **B** Work with a partner. Listen again and discuss the seven illegal questions the interviewer asks.

EXAMPLE: A: He asked her how old she was.

B: That's right. In Canada, you can't ask about age. It's illegal.

How old are you?

EXERCISE 7 A JOB INTERVIEW

A ROLE PLAY You are going to role-play a job interview. Before you role-play, work with a partner. Student A is the interviewer. Student B is the job candidate. Read the résumé and the job-listings advertisement. Write at least three questions to ask each other.

EXAMPLE: Questions to ask the candidate: *Why did you leave your job at Union Hospital?*

Questions to ask the interviewer: *How many doctors work here?*

Pat Rogers

215 West Hill Drive
Baltimore, MD 21233
Telephone: (410) 555-7777
progers@email.com

EDUCATION

Taylor Community College
Associate's degree (Business) 2015

Middlesex High School
High school diploma, 2013

EXPERIENCE

2015–Present   **Medical receptionist**
Patients Plus, Baltimore, MD
Responsibilities: Greet patients, make appointments, answer telephones, update computer records

2013–2015   **Admitting clerk, hospital admissions office**
Union Hospital, Baltimore, MD
Responsibilities: Interviewed patients for admission, input information in computer, answered telephones

JOB LISTINGS

MEDICAL RECEPTIONIST

For busy doctor's office. Mature individual needed to answer phones, greet patients, make appointments. Some filing and billing. Similar experience preferred. Computer skills necessary.

B Work in a group. With your partner in A, use your questions to role-play your interview for the group.

EXAMPLE: A: Why did you leave your job at Union Hospital?
B: I liked my job, but I wanted more responsibility.

C Discuss each role-play interview with your group. Use the questions below to guide your discussion. Support your ideas by reporting questions that were asked during the interview.

1. Was it a stress interview? Why or why not?

   EXAMPLE: A: I think it was a stress interview because the interviewer asked him why he couldn't find a new job.
   B: Yes. And he also asked him why he didn't have good computer skills. . . .

2. Did the interviewer ask any illegal questions? Which ones were illegal?

3. Which of the candidate's questions were the most useful in evaluating the job? Why do you think so?

4. Which of the interviewer's questions gave the clearest picture of the candidate? Why do you think so?

5. If you were the interviewer, would you hire this candidate? Why or why not?

6. If you were the candidate, would you want to work for this company? Why or why not?

EXERCISE 8 WHAT ABOUT YOU?

CONVERSATION Work in a group. Talk about a personal experience with a school or job interview. (If you do not have a personal experience, use the experience of someone you know.) Answer the questions below.

1. What did the interviewer ask?

   EXAMPLE: A: The interviewer asked me if I was married.
   B: That isn't legal, is it?
   A: I don't think so.
   C: What did you say?
   A: I asked him . . .

2. What was the most difficult question to answer? Why?

3. Were there any questions that you didn't think were appropriate? What did you say?

4. What did you ask the interviewer?

EXERCISE 9 WORK VALUES

A DISCUSSION You are going to have a discussion about values. Your values are the things that are most important to you. Before your discussion, complete this work values questionnaire on your own. (If none of the answers match your values, add your own.)

Work Values Questionnaire

1. Why do you want to work?
- ○ To make a lot of money.
- ○ To help people.
- ○ To become well known.
- ○ Other: _____

2. Where do you prefer to work?
- ○ I'd like to travel.
- ○ In an office.
- ○ At home.
- ○ Other: _____

3. When do you want to work?
- ○ 9–5 every day.
- ○ On a changing schedule.
- ○ On my own schedule.
- ○ Other: _____

4. What kind of routine do you like?
- ○ The same type of task all day.
- ○ A variety of tasks every day.
- ○ Tasks that change often.
- ○ Other: _____

5. How much job pressure can you handle?
- ○ I like a high-pressure job.
- ○ I can handle some, but not a lot.
- ○ Just enough to keep me awake.
- ○ Other: _____

6. Who would you like to work with?
- ○ I work best with a team.
- ○ I like to work by myself.
- ○ I enjoy working with the public.
- ○ Other: _____

B Work with a partner. Ask your partner three of the questions in the questionnaire in A and discuss your answers. Then answer the other questions and discuss your answers.

EXAMPLE: A: So, why do you want to work?
B: I like working. I find it interesting. What about you? Why do you want to work?
A: Well, I need to make money to . . .

C Work with another pair and report your conversations in B.

EXAMPLE: A: I asked Sami why he wanted to work. He told me . . .
B: I asked Lisa why she wanted to work. She said that . . .

A BEFORE YOU WRITE Before you look for work, it's a good idea to talk to people who are already working in jobs that might interest you. In these kinds of "informational interviews," you can ask what the tasks in that job are, why people like or dislike the work, or how much you can expect to be paid. Write a list of questions to ask in an informational job interview. Then interview a classmate and write his or her answers.

Questions	Answers
_____	_____
_____	_____
_____	_____

B WRITE Use your questions and answers in A to write a report on an informational interview. Use indirect questions and answers. Try to avoid the common mistakes in the chart.

EXAMPLE: I interviewed Pete Ortiz, who is an assistant in the computer lab. I wanted to talk to him because I'm interested in applying for a job there. I asked Pete if he liked working there, and he told me he liked it most of the time. I also asked him how long . . .

Common Mistakes in Using Indirect Questions

Use *if* or **whether** in an indirect *yes/no* question. Do not use the auxiliaries *do*, *does*, or *did*.	She asked me *if* I like my present job. **NOT** She asked me ~~do~~ I like my present job.
Use **statement word** order in indirect questions. Do not use question word order. Do not use the auxiliaries *do*, *does*, or *did*.	She asked me **how fast** I typed. **NOT** She asked me how fast ~~do I type~~.
Use a **period** at the end of an indirect question. Do not use a question mark.	He asked me where I lived. **NOT** He asked me where I lived~~?~~

C CHECK YOUR WORK Read your report. Underline the indirect *yes/no* questions once. Underline the indirect *wh-* questions twice. Use the Editing Checklist to check your work.

Editing Checklist

Did you use . . . ?

☐ *if* or *whether* in indirect *yes/no* questions

☐ question words in indirect *wh-* questions

☐ statement word order for all indirect questions

☐ a period at the end of indirect questions

D REVISE YOUR WORK Read your report again. Can you improve your writing? Make changes if necessary. Give your report a title.

UNIT 27 **REVIEW**

Test yourself on the grammar or the unit.

A Circle the correct punctuation mark or words to complete the sentences.

1. She asked what my name was . / ?

2. He asked me if / do I had work experience.

3. I asked them where was their office / their office was.

4. They asked where I lived / did I live.

5. They asked me why had I / I had left my last job.

B Rewrite the direct questions in parentheses as indirect questions. (The direct questions were asked last year.)

1. They asked _____
   (Who did the company hire?)

2. He asked me _____
   (Did you take the job?)

3. She asked _____
   (Do you like your job?)

4. He asked me _____
   (How long have you worked there?)

5. I asked _____
   (How many employees work here?)

6. They asked _____
   (Why do you want to work for us?)

7. I asked _____
   (What's the starting salary?)

8. They asked _____
   (Can you start soon?)

C Find and correct seven mistakes. Remember to check punctuation.

They asked me so many questions! They asked me where did I work. They asked who was my boss. They asked why I did want to change jobs. They asked how much money I made. They ask me who I have voted for in the last election. They even asked me what my favorite color was? Finally, I asked myself whether or no I really wanted that job!

Now check your answers on page 482.

28

Embedded Questions
TIPPING AROUND THE WORLD

OUTCOMES
- Ask for information or express something you don't know, using embedded questions
- Extract key information from an interview transcript
- Identify and discuss details in a call-in radio show
- Discuss tipping around the world, giving opinions
- Discuss problems one had during a first-time experience
- Role-play a conversation between a hotel clerk and a guest asking for information
- Write about a confusing or surprising situation

STEP 1 GRAMMAR IN CONTEXT

BEFORE YOU READ

Look at the cartoon. Discuss the questions.

1. What is unusual about the vending machine?
2. What is the man worried about?

READ

▶28|01 Read this interview about tipping from *World Travel (WT)* magazine.

The Tip:
Who? When? and How much?

In China, it used to be illegal. In New Zealand, it's uncommon. In Germany, it's included in the restaurant bill. In the United States and Canada, it's common, but it isn't logical: You tip the person who delivers flowers, but not the person who delivers a package.

Do *you* often wonder what to do about tipping? *We* do, so to help us through the tipping maze[1] we interviewed author Irene Frankel. Her book, *Tips on Tipping: The Ultimate Guide to Who, When, and How Much to Tip*, answers all your questions about this complicated practice.

WT: Tell me why you decided to write a book about tipping.

IF: I began writing it for people from

"I wonder how much we should give."

---

1 *maze:* something that is complicated and hard to understand

cultures where tipping isn't a custom. But when I started researching, I found that Americans were also unsure how to tip, so *Tips* became a book to clarify tipping practices for people traveling to the United States *and* for people living here.

WT: Does your book explain who to tip?

IF: Oh, absolutely. It tells you who to tip, how much to tip, and when to tip. And equally important, it tells you when not to tip.

WT: That *is* important. Suppose[2] I don't know whether to tip someone, and I left your book at home. Is it OK to ask?

IF: Sure. If you don't know whether to leave a tip, the best thing to do is ask. People usually won't tell you what to do, but they *will* tell you what most customers do.

WT: I always wonder what to do when I get bad service. Should I still tip?

IF: Don't tip the ordinary amount, but tip *something* so that the service person doesn't think that you just forgot to leave a tip.

WT: That makes sense. Here's another thing I've always wondered about. Is there any reason why we tip a restaurant server but we don't a flight attendant?

IF: Not that I know. The rules for tipping in the United States aren't very logical, and there are often contradictions in who we tip.

WT: Another thing—I've never really understood why a restaurant tip depends on the amount of the bill rather than on the amount of work involved in serving the meal. After all, bringing out a $20 dish of food involves the same amount of work as carrying out a $5 plate.

IF: You're right. It makes no sense. That's just the way it is.

WT: One last question. Suppose I'm planning a trip to Egypt. Tell me how I can learn about tipping customs in that country.

IF: There are a number of Internet sites where you can learn what the rules are for tipping in each country. The *World Travel* site is always reliable. You can also find that information in travel books for the country you're planning to visit.

WT: Well, thanks for all the good tips! I know our readers will find them very helpful. *I* certainly did.

IF: Thank *you*.

---

2 *suppose:* imagine that something is true and its possible results; a way to ask "What if . . . ?"

AFTER YOU READ

A VOCABULARY Match the words with their definitions.

_____ 1. clarify	**a.** not unusual
_____ 2. custom	**b.** reasonable and sensible
_____ 3. ultimate	**c.** a traditional way of doing something
_____ 4. logical	**d.** to make clear
_____ 5. ordinary	**e.** to be affected by
_____ 6. depend on	**f.** best

COMPREHENSION Check (✓) the questions that the interviewer *(WT)* wants the author *(IF)* to answer.

☐ **1.** When did you decide to write a book about tipping?

☐ **2.** Who do I tip?

☐ **3.** Is it OK to ask someone whether I should leave a tip?

☐ **4.** How much should I tip if I get bad service?

☐ **5.** What Internet sites should I use to find out more?

☐ **6.** How can I learn about tipping customs in other countries?

C **DISCUSSION** Work with a partner. Compare your answers in B. Why did you or didn't you check each item?

STEP 2   GRAMMAR PRESENTATION

EMBEDDED QUESTIONS

Direct *Yes/No* Question
Did I leave the right tip?
Was five dollars enough?
Should we leave a tip?

Main Clause	Embedded *Yes/No* Question
I don't know	*if* **I left** the right tip.
Can you tell me	*if* **I left** the right tip?
I wonder	*whether (or not)* **five dollars was** enough.
Do you know	*whether (or not)* **five dollars was** enough?
We're not sure	*whether (or not)* **to leave** a tip.

Direct *Wh-* Question
Who **is our server?**
Why **didn't he leave** a tip?
How much **should we give?**

Main Clause	Embedded *Wh-* Question
I don't know	*who* **our server is.**
Can you tell me	*who* **our server is?**
I wonder	*why* **he didn't leave** a tip.
Do you know	*why* **he didn't leave** a tip?
We're not sure	*how much* **to give.**

GRAMMAR NOTES

1 Embedded Questions

Embedded questions are **questions** that are **inside another sentence**.

• inside a **statement**	I don't know **who our server is.**
• inside **another question**	Do you remember **who our server is?**

IN WRITING If the embedded question is inside a **statement**, use a **period** at the end of the sentence.	I wonder **if that's our server.** **NOT** I wonder if that's our server?
If the embedded question is inside a **question**, use a **question mark** at the end of the sentence.	Do you know **if that's our server?**

2 Use of Sentences with Embedded Questions

Sentences with embedded questions have **two main uses**:

• to **express** something you **do not know**	***I don't know** if the tip is included.* (statement)
• to **ask for information**	***Do you know** if the tip is included?* (question)

The **phrase introducing the embedded question** (for example, *I don't know* or *Do you know*) shows if the sentence expresses something you do not know or asks for information.

USAGE NOTE We use **sentences with embedded questions** instead of direct questions to be **more polite**, especially when we speak to people we don't know well.	Where should I leave the tip?
	   (less polite)
	 ***Can you tell me** where I should leave the tip?*
	   (more polite)

3 Common Phrases That Introduce Embedded Questions

Embedded questions always **follow certain phrases**.

Use these phrases in **statements**:

I don't know . . .	*I'm not sure . . .*	***I don't know** what the name of the café is.*
I don't understand . . .	*I wonder . . .*	***I wonder** what time the restaurant closes.*
I'd like to know . . .	*Let's ask . . .*	***Let's ask** what today's specials are.*

Use these phrases in **questions**:

Do you know . . . ?	*Can you tell me . . . ?*	***Do you know** how much the shrimp is?*
Can you remember . . . ?	*Could you explain . . . ?*	***Could you explain** what that sign means?*

4 Embedded *Yes/No* Questions

A direct *yes/no* **question** can be embedded in a statement or question.	**Do they sell pizza?** *(direct question)* I wonder *if they sell pizza.* *(embedded question in a statement)* Do you know *if they sell pizza?* *(embedded question in a question)*
Begin embedded *yes/no* **questions** with *if*, *whether*, or *whether or not*.	Do you know *if they ordered it?*
USAGE NOTE *Whether* is more **formal** than *if*.	Do you know *whether they ordered it?* Do you know *whether or not they ordered it?*

5 Embedded *Wh-* Questions

A direct *wh-* **question** can be embedded in a statement or question.	**Who delivered it?** *(direct question)* I wonder *who delivered it.* *(embedded question in a statement)* Do you know *who delivered it?* *(embedded question in a question)*
Begin embedded *wh-* **questions** with a *wh-* **word** (*who, what, which, whose, when, where, why, how, how much, how many*).	I wonder *who our server is.* Do you know *when the restaurant closes?* People wonder *how much they should tip.*

6 Word Order in Embedded Questions

Use **statement word order** (**subject + verb**), not question word order, for all **embedded questions**.

The word order in the embedded question is the same word order as in a **statement**.	SUBJECT + VERB **Eva ordered** pizza.
• embedded *yes/no* questions	Did Eva order pizza? *(direct)* Do you know *if Eva ordered* pizza? *(embedded)*
• embedded *wh-* questions about the **subject**	Who ordered pizza? *(direct)* I can't remember *who ordered* pizza. *(embedded)*
• embedded *wh-* questions about the **object**	What does it cost? *(direct)* Can you tell me *what it costs*? *(embedded)*
• embedded *wh-* questions with *when, where, why, how, how much,* or *how many*	When do they open? *(direct)* Do you know *when they open*? *(embedded)*

CONTINUED ▶

BE CAREFUL! Do not use question word order and the auxiliaries *do*, *does*, or *did* in embedded questions. Also, do not leave out *if* or *whether* in embedded *yes/no* questions.	I wonder ***why* they ordered** pizza. NOT I wonder why ~~did they order~~ pizza. I don't know ***if* they ordered** pizza. NOT I don't know ~~did they order~~ pizza.
BE CAREFUL! If a direct question about the subject has the form *be* + **noun**, then the embedded question has the form **noun** + *be*.	Who *is* **our server**? *(direct)* Do you know who **our server** *is*? *(embedded)* NOT Do you know who ~~is our server~~? ***Is* our order** ready? *(direct)* Do you know if **our order** *is* ready? *(embedded)* NOT Do you know ~~is our order~~ ready?

7 Infinitives in Embedded Questions

In embedded questions, you can also use **infinitives** after a **question word or** *whether*.	
• **question word + infinitive**	Let's ask ***where* to leave** the tip. *(Let's ask where we should leave the tip.)*
• *whether* **+ infinitive**	Can you tell me ***whether* to leave** a tip? *(Can you tell me whether I should leave a tip?)*
BE CAREFUL! Do not use the infinitive after *if* or *why*.	I don't understand ***why* I should tip**. NOT I don't understand why ~~to tip~~.

REFERENCE NOTE

For a list of **phrases introducing embedded questions**, see Appendix 21 on page 463.

EXERCISE 1 DISCOVER THE GRAMMAR

GRAMMAR NOTES 1–7 Read this advertisement for *Tips on Tipping*. Underline the embedded questions.

TIPS ON TIPPING

This book is for you if...

- you've ever avoided a situation just because you didn't know how much to tip.

- you've ever realized (too late) that you were supposed to offer a tip.

- you've ever given a huge tip and then wondered if a tip was necessary at all.

- you've ever needed to know how to calculate the right tip instantly.

- you're new to the United States and you're not sure who you should tip here.

- you'd like to learn how tipping properly can get you the best service for your money.

What readers are saying...

"Essential, reliable information—I can't imagine how I got along without it."

—Chris Sarton, Minneapolis, Minnesota

"Take *Tips* along if you want a stress-free vacation."

—Midori Otaka, Osaka, Japan

"I took my fiancée to dinner at Deux Saisons and knew exactly how to tip everyone!"

—S. Prasad, San Francisco, California

"You need this book—whether you stay in hostels or five-star hotels."

—Cuno Pumpin, Bern, Switzerland

Do you want to learn who to tip, when to tip, and how much to tip? Get the ultimate guide to tipping and get all the answers to your tipping questions!

EXERCISE 2 EMBEDDED QUESTIONS

GRAMMAR NOTES 1–6 Complete this travel column about tipping customs around the world. Change the direct questions in parentheses to embedded questions. Use correct punctuation.

Tipping customs vary, so travelers should find out who, where, and how much to tip. Here are some frequently asked questions.

Q: Can you tell me whether *I should tip in Canada?*
                                     1. (Should I tip in Canada?)
A: Yes. Tipping practices in Canada are similar to those in the United States.

Q: I know that most restaurants and cafés in France include a service charge. I don't understand *how I can tell if the tip is included in the bill.*
                         2. (How can I tell if the tip is included in the bill?)
A: Look for the phrase *service compris* (service included) on the bill.

Q: I'm going to China next month. I understand that tipping used to be illegal there. Do you know
_____
                         3. (Will restaurant servers accept tips now?)
A: It depends on where you are. In large cities with a lot of tourists, you can leave a small tip in a restaurant if there isn't already a service charge on the check. In small cities, your tip may not be accepted.

Q: On a recent trip to Iceland, I found that most service people refused tips. I don't know
_____
                         4. (Why did this happen?)
A: In Iceland, people often feel insulted by tips. Just say thank you—that's enough.

Q: I'll be in Dubai on business next month, and I'll be taking a lot of taxis. Can you tell me
_____
                         5. (Should I tip the driver?)
A: You don't really have to, but many people leave a small tip of 5 to 10 AED (Arab Emirate Dirhams). Or you can round the fare up to the nearest paper bill.

Q: My husband and I are planning a trip to several cities in Australia and New Zealand. Please tell us
_____
                         6. (Who expects a tip and who doesn't?)
A: Restaurant servers expect a tip of 10 percent, but you don't need to tip taxi drivers.

Q: I'm moving to Japan, and I have a lot of luggage. I'm finding some contradictions on travel websites. One says not to tip in Japan, but another says to tip airport porters. Could you tell me
_____
                         7. (Is it the custom to tip airport and train porters?)
A: There's a fixed fee[1] per bag for airport porters, not a tip. Most train stations don't have porters. We recommend shipping your luggage from the airport. I hope that clarifies things!

---

1 *fixed fee:* a price that does not change

EXERCISE 3 EMBEDDED QUESTIONS

GRAMMAR NOTES 1–6 **Two foreign exchange students are visiting Rome, Italy. Complete their conversations. Choose the appropriate questions from the list and change them to embedded questions. Use correct punctuation.**

- ~~How much are we supposed to tip the driver?~~
- Could we rent a car and drive there?
- Do they have tour buses that go there?
- How much does the subway cost?
- How far are you going?
- How are we going to choose?
- How much does a bus tour cost?
- What did they put in the sauce?
- Where is the Forum?
- ~~Where is it?~~

Rome: The Forum

Conversation 1

DRIVER: Where do you want to go? The airport?

MARTINA: The Hotel Forte. Do you know <u>where it is?</u>
1.

DRIVER: Sure. Get in and I'll take you there.

MARTINA: *(whispering)* I wonder <u>how much we're supposed to tip the driver.</u>
2.

MIUKI: According to the book, the custom is to leave 10 to 15 percent. I've got it.

Conversation 2

MARTINA: There's so much to see in Rome. I don't know _____
3.

MIUKI: We could take a bus tour of the city first, and then decide.

MARTINA: Does the guidebook say _____
4.

MIUKI: Yeah. About $15 per person, plus tips for the guide and the driver.

Conversation 3

MARTINA: That was delicious.

MIUKI: Let's try to find out _____
5.

MARTINA: It tasted like it had a lot of garlic and basil. I'll ask the server.

Conversation 4

MARTINA: Excuse me. Can you tell me _____
6.

OFFICER: Sure. Just turn right and go straight.

Conversation 5

MIUKI: Let's take the subway. Do you know _____
                                                                                                                      7.

MARTINA: It's not expensive. I don't think it depends on _____
                                                                                                                     8.

Conversation 6

MARTINA: I'd like to visit Ostia Antica. It's supposed to be like the ruins at Pompeii.

MIUKI: I wonder _____
                                                                                                  9.

MARTINA: I really don't want to go with a big group of people. What about you? Do you know

_____
                                                                                    10.

MIUKI: Sure! It would be nice to drive around and see some of the countryside, too.

EXERCISE 4 QUESTION WORD + INFINITIVE

GRAMMAR NOTE 7 **Complete the conversation between Martina and Miuki. Use a question word and the infinitive form of the verbs from the box.**

figure out	get	go	invite	leave	~~wear~~

MARTINA: I can't decide _____*what to wear*_____ Friday night.
                                                                       1.

MIUKI: Your red dress. You always look great in it. By the way, where are you going?

MARTINA: Trattoria da Luigi. It's Janek's birthday, so I wanted to take him someplace special—not just

the ordinary places we usually go to. We're meeting there at 8:00.

MIUKI: Great! You know _____ there, don't you?
                                                          2.

MARTINA: Yes, but I'm not sure _____.
                                                             3.

MIUKI: Leave at 7:30. That'll give you enough time.

MARTINA: I'd like to take Janek someplace for dessert afterward. He loves desserts, but I don't know

_____.
                                    4.

MIUKI: The desserts at da Luigi's are supposed to be pretty good.

MARTINA: Oh. By the way, since it's Janek's birthday, I'm paying. But I'm still not quite sure

_____ the tip.
                                    5.

MIUKI: Service is usually included in Italy. The menu should tell you. So, who else is going?

MARTINA: Well, I thought about asking a few people to join us, but I really didn't know

_____.
                                    6.

MIUKI: Don't worry. I'm sure it will be fine with just the two of you.

EXERCISE 5 EDITING

GRAMMAR NOTES 1–7 Read this post to a travelers' website. There are ten mistakes in the use of embedded questions. The first mistake is already corrected. Find and correct nine more. Don't forget to check punctuation.

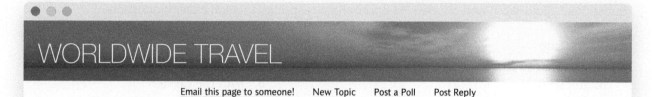

Email this page to someone!   New Topic   Post a Poll   Post Reply

Subject: **Tipping at the Hair Salon in Italy**

Posted April 10 by Jenna Thompson

if or whether

I wonder ⌃ you can help clarify some tipping situations for me. I never know what doing at the

hair salon. I don't know if I should tip the person who washes my hair? What about the person

who cuts it, and the person who colors it? And what happens if the person is the owner.

Do you know do I still need to tip him or her? That doesn't seem logical. (And often I'm not

even sure who is the owner!) Then I never know how much to tip or where should I leave

the tip? Do I leave it on the counter or in the person's hands? What if somebody's hands are

wet or have hair color on them? Can I just put the tip in his or her pocket? It all seems so

complicated! I can't imagine how do customers figure all this out? What's the custom? I really

need to find out what to do—and FAST! My hair is getting very long and dirty.

Please help!

I wonder
how much
I should tip.

EXERCISE 6 LISTENING

28|02 **A** A call-in radio show is taking questions from callers about tipping. Listen to the callers' questions. Listen again and choose the appropriate response to each caller's question.

1. **Caller One**
   a. between 15 and 20 percent of the bill
   b. the server

2. **Caller Two**
   a. about 15 percent of the fare
   b. only if you are happy with the ride

3. **Caller Three**
   a. before you leave
   b. on the table

4. **Caller Four**
   a. the manager
   b. don't leave a tip

5. **Caller Five**
   a. one dollar
   b. with the cashier

6. **Caller Six**
   a. look it up on the Internet
   b. It's included in the bill.

7. **Caller Seven**
   a. at least three dollars
   b. the person who delivers your food

28|02 **B** Work with a partner. Listen to each conversation again. Discuss your answers. Why did you, or didn't you, choose each response? Do you agree with the advice in each response?

EXAMPLE: A: Caller number one wants to know how much to tip in a restaurant. She asked how much to tip—she didn't ask *who* to tip.

B: Right. So, the answer is "a"—between 15 and 20% of the bill.

A: Do you agree with that advice?

B: I don't know. I think it depends on how good the service is.

EXERCISE 7 TO TIP OR NOT TO TIP?

DISCUSSION Work in a group. Discuss these questions.

1. Do you think tipping is a good system? Why or why not?

   EXAMPLE: A: I'm not sure whether tipping is good or not. I think people should get paid enough so that they don't have to count on tips to live.

   B: I wonder if you would still get good service if the tip were included.

   C: Sure you would. A service charge is included in a lot of countries, and the service is still good.

2. Were you ever in a situation where you didn't know what to do about a tip? What did you do?

3. How do people tip in your country and in other countries you know?

EXERCISE 8 WHAT ABOUT YOU?

CONVERSATION Think about the first time you did something. Use one of the situations below or an idea of your own. Then work with a partner. Talk about what problems you had.

EXAMPLE: A: I remember the first
          time I went to Italy.
          I was at a restaurant
          and I didn't know how
          to get the server's
          attention.
       B: When I was in Austria,
          I didn't know whether
          to tip or not.

• traveled to a foreign country

• went on a job interview

• drove a car

• became a parent

• Other: _____

EXERCISE 9 INFORMATION PLEASE!

ROLE PLAY Work with a partner. Student A is a desk clerk at a hotel. Student B is a guest at the hotel. The guest asks the clerk for information about some of the things in the list below. Use embedded questions.

EXAMPLE: A: Can I help you?
       B: Yes. Could you tell me where to find a good, inexpensive restaurant around here?
       A: There are some nice restaurants around the university.

• restaurants

• interesting sights

• transportation

• entertainment

• banks

• shopping

• tipping

• laundry

A BEFORE YOUR WRITE Think about a situation that confused or surprised you such as a new job or being in a new country. Answer the questions.

Where were you? _____

What confused or surprised you? _____

What questions did you ask yourself? (Use direct questions, for example: *Should I leave a tip?*)

_____

_____

B WRITE Use your answers to write a paragraph about the situation that surprised you. Use embedded questions. Try to avoid some of the common mistakes in the chart.

EXAMPLE: When I was an exchange student in China, my Chinese friends always wanted to know how old I was. I couldn't understand why . . . I wasn't sure whether . . .

Common Mistakes in Using Embedded Questions

Use **statement word order** for embedded questions. Do not use question word order.	Do you know **what** I should do? **NOT** Do you know what ~~should I do~~?
You can use **an infinitive** after a **question word** or *whether*. Do not use an infinitive after *why* or *if*.	Can you tell me **how** to do it? **NOT** Can you tell me ~~why to do~~ it? I'm not sure **whether** to go. **NOT** I'm not sure ~~if to go~~.
Use a **period** at the end of a **statement** with an embedded question. Do not use a question mark.	I don't know **who** I can ask. **NOT** I don't know who I can ask~~?~~
Use a **question mark** at the end of a **question** with an embedded question. Do not use a period.	Do you know **where** to leave the tip? **NOT** Do you know where to leave the tip~~.~~

C CHECK YOUR WORK Read your paragraph. Underline the embedded questions. Circle the question words, *whether*, or *if*. Use the Editing Checklist to check your work.

Editing Checklist

Did you use . . . ?

☐ *if, whether (or not)*, or a *wh-* word to begin an embedded question

☐ an infinitive after a question word or *whether*

☐ statement word order (subject + verb) for embedded questions

☐ a period at the end of statements with embedded questions

☐ a question mark at the end of questions with embedded questions

D REVISE YOUR WORK Read your paragraph again. Can you improve your writing? Make changes if necessary. Give your paragraph a title.

UNIT 28 REVIEW

Test yourself on the grammar of the unit.

Ⓐ Circle the correct words and punctuation marks to complete the sentences.

1. I wonder whether <u>should we / we should</u> tip the driver.

2. Do you remember who <u>is our server / our server is?</u>

3. I don't know why she ordered pizza <u>? / .</u>

4. Let's ask how <u>can we / to</u> get to the museum.

5. I wonder if <u>to / I should</u> take a taxi.

6. Can you tell me whether I need to tip the owner of a hair salon <u>? / .</u>

7. I'm not sure <u>whether / did</u> they read the book on tipping.

Ⓑ Rewrite the questions in parentheses to complete the embedded questions. Use correct punctuation.

1. Can you remember _____
   (Where is the restaurant?)

2. I don't know _____
   (Does the subway go to the museum?)

3. We're not sure _____
   (Should we tip the porter?)

4. I can't imagine _____
   (Why didn't we buy the book on tipping?)

5. Let's ask _____
   (How much should we tip the tour guide?)

6. I'd like to know _____
   (Do you have any travel books?)

7. Could you explain _____
   (What does this sign say?)

Ⓒ Find and correct six mistakes. Remember to check punctuation.

A: Hi. Is this a good time to call? I wasn't sure what time you have dinner?

B: This is fine. I didn't know were you back from your trip.

A: We got back two days ago. I can't remember if I email you some photographs.

B: Yes. They were great. Can you tell me where took you that picture of the lake? I want to go!

A: Hmm. I'm not sure which one was that. We saw a lot of lakes in Switzerland.

B: I'll show it to you. I'd really like to find out where is it.

Now check your answers on page 483.

Appendices

1 Irregular Verbs

When two forms are listed, the more common form is listed first.

BASE FORM	SIMPLE PAST	PAST PARTICIPLE
arise	arose	arisen
awake	awoke	awoken
be	was or were	been
beat	beat	beaten/beat
become	became	become
begin	began	begun
bend	bent	bent
bet	bet	bet
bite	bit	bitten
bleed	bled	bled
blow	blew	blown
break	broke	broken
bring	brought	brought
build	built	built
burn	burned/burnt	burnt/burned
burst	burst	burst
buy	bought	bought
catch	caught	caught
choose	chose	chosen
cling	clung	clung
come	came	come
cost	cost	cost
creep	crept	crept
cut	cut	cut
deal	dealt	dealt
dig	dug	dug
dive	dove/dived	dived
do	did	done
draw	drew	drawn
dream	dreamed/dreamt	dreamed/dreamt
drink	drank	drunk
drive	drove	driven
eat	ate	eaten
fall	fell	fallen
feed	fed	fed
feel	felt	felt
fight	fought	fought
find	found	found
fit	fit/fitted	fit
flee	fled	fled
fling	flung	flung
fly	flew	flown
forbid	forbid/forbade	forbidden
forget	forgot	forgotten
forgive	forgave	forgiven
freeze	froze	frozen
get	got	gotten/got
give	gave	given

BASE FORM	SIMPLE PAST	PAST PARTICIPLE
go	went	gone
grind	ground	ground
grow	grew	grown
hang	hung*/hanged**	hung*/hanged**
have	had	had
hear	heard	heard
hide	hid	hidden
hit	hit	hit
hold	held	held
hurt	hurt	hurt
keep	kept	kept
kneel	knelt/kneeled	knelt/kneeled
knit	knit/knitted	knit/knitted
know	knew	known
lay	laid	laid
lead	led	led
leap	leaped/leapt	leaped/leapt
leave	left	left
lend	lent	lent
let	let	let
lie (lie down)	lay	lain
light	lit/lighted	lit/lighted
lose	lost	lost
make	made	made
mean	meant	meant
meet	met	met
pay	paid	paid
prove	proved	proven/proved
put	put	put
quit	quit	quit
read /rid/	read /rɛd/	read /rɛd/
ride	rode	ridden
ring	rang	rung
rise	rose	risen
run	ran	run
say	said	said
see	saw	seen
seek	sought	sought
sell	sold	sold
send	sent	sent
set	set	set
sew	sewed	sewn/sewed
shake	shook	shaken
shave	shaved	shaved/shaven
shine (intransitive)	shone/shined	shone/shined
shoot	shot	shot
show	showed	shown
shrink	shrank/shrunk	shrunk/shrunken

* hung = *hung an object such as a painting*
** hanged = *executed by hanging*

BASE FORM	SIMPLE PAST	PAST PARTICIPLE	BASE FORM	SIMPLE PAST	PAST PARTICIPLE
shut	shut	shut	swear	swore	sworn
sing	sang	sung	sweep	swept	swept
sink	sank/sunk	sunk	swim	swam	swum
sit	sat	sat	swing	swung	swung
sleep	slept	slept	take	took	taken
slide	slid	slid	teach	taught	taught
speak	spoke	spoken	tear	tore	torn
speed	sped/speeded	sped/speeded	tell	told	told
spend	spent	spent	think	thought	thought
spill	spilled/spilt	spilled/spilt	throw	threw	thrown
spin	spun	spun	understand	understood	understood
spit	spit/spat	spat	upset	upset	upset
split	split	split	wake	woke	woken
spread	spread	spread	wear	wore	worn
spring	sprang	sprung	weave	wove/weaved	woven/weaved
stand	stood	stood	weep	wept	wept
steal	stole	stolen	win	won	won
stick	stuck	stuck	wind	wound	wound
sting	stung	stung	withdraw	withdrew	withdrawn
stink	stank/stunk	stunk	wring	wrung	wrung
strike	struck	struck/stricken	write	wrote	written

2 Non-Action Verbs

APPEARANCE
appear
be
look *(seem)*
represent
resemble
seem
signify

VALUE
cost
equal
weigh

EMOTIONS
admire
adore
appreciate
care
detest
dislike
doubt
envy
fear
forgive
hate
like
love
miss
regret
respect
trust

MENTAL STATES
agree
assume
believe
consider
disagree
disbelieve
estimate
expect
feel *(believe)*
find *(believe)*
forget
guess
hesitate
hope

imagine
know
mean
mind
presume
realize
recognize
remember
see *(understand)*
suppose
suspect
think *(believe)*
understand
wonder

POSSESSION AND RELATIONSHIP
belong
come from *(origin)*
contain
have
own
possess

SENSES AND PERCEPTIONS
feel
hear
hurt
notice
observe
perceive
recognize
see
seem
smell
sound
taste

WANTS AND PREFERENCES
desire
hope
need
prefer
want
wish

3 Verbs and Expressions Used Reflexively

allow yourself
amuse yourself
ask yourself
avail yourself of
be hard on yourself
be pleased with yourself
be proud of yourself
be yourself

behave yourself
believe in yourself
blame yourself
buy yourself
cut yourself
deprive yourself of
dry yourself
enjoy yourself

feel proud of yourself
feel sorry for yourself
forgive yourself
help yourself
hurt yourself
imagine yourself
introduce yourself
keep yourself (busy)

kill yourself
look after yourself
look at yourself
prepare yourself
pride yourself on
push yourself
remind yourself

see yourself
take care of yourself
talk to yourself
teach yourself
tell yourself
treat yourself
wash yourself

(s.o. = someone   s.t. = something)

Separable phrasal verbs show the object between the verb and the particle: **call** s.o. **up**.
Verbs that must be separated have an asterisk (*): **do** s.t. **over***.
Inseparable phrasal verbs show the object after the particle: **carry on** s.t.
Phrasal verbs that can have a **gerund as object** are followed by *doing*: **put off** doing s.t.

PHRASAL VERB	MEANING
ask s.o. **over***	*invite to one's home*
block s.t. **out**	*stop from passing through (light/noise)*
blow s.t. **out**	*stop burning by blowing air on it*
blow s.t. **up**	*make explode*
bring s.t. **about**	*make happen*
bring s.o. or s.t. **back**	*return*
bring s.o. **down***	*depress*
bring s.t. **out**	*introduce (a new product/book)*
bring s.o. **up**	*raise (a child)*
bring s.t. **up**	*bring attention to*
build s.t. **up**	*increase*
burn s.t. **down**	*burn completely*
call s.o. **back***	*return a phone call*
call s.o. **in**	*ask for help with a problem*
call s.t. **off**	*cancel*
call s.o. **up**	*contact by phone*
calm s.o. **down**	*make less excited*
carry on s.t.	*continue*
carry s.t. **out**	*complete (a plan)*
cash in on s.t.	*profit from*
charge s.t. **up**	*charge with electricity*
check s.t. **out**	*examine*
cheer s.o. **up**	*cause to feel happier*
clean s.o. or s.t. **up**	*clean completely*
clear s.t. **up**	*explain*
close s.t. **down**	*close by force*
come from s.o. or s.t.	*have been born in a particular family or place*
come off s.t.	*become unattached*
come up with s.t.	*invent*
count on s.t. or s.o.	*depend on*
cover s.o. or s.t. **up**	*cover completely*
cross s.t. **out**	*draw a line through*
cut s.t. **down**	*1. bring down by cutting (a tree)* *2. reduce*
cut s.t. **off**	*1. stop the supply of* *2. remove by cutting*
cut s.t. **out**	*remove by cutting*
cut s.t. **up**	*cut into small pieces*
deal with s.t.	*handle*
do s.t. **over***	*do again*
do s.o. or s.t. **up**	*make more beautiful*
draw s.t. **together**	*unite*
dream s.t. **up**	*invent*
drink s.t. **up**	*drink completely*
drop s.o. or s.t. **off**	*take someplace in a car and leave there*
drop out of s.t.	*quit*
empty s.t. **out**	*empty completely*
end up doing s.t.	*do something you didn't plan to do*
end up with s.t.	*have an unexpected result*
fall for s.o.	*feel romantic love for*

PHRASAL VERB	MEANING
fall for s.t.	*be tricked by, believe*
figure s.o. **out**	*understand (the behavior)*
figure s.t. **out**	*solve, understand after thinking about it*
fill s.t. **in**	*complete with information*
fill s.t. **out**	*complete (a form)*
fill s.t. **up**	*fill completely*
find s.t. **out**	*learn information*
fix s.t. **up**	*redecorate (home)*
follow through with s.t.	*complete*
get s.t. **across**	*get people to understand an idea*
get off s.t.	*leave (a bus/train)*
get on s.t.	*board (a bus/train)*
get out of s.t.	*leave (a car/taxi)*
get s.t. **out of** s.t.*	*benefit from*
get over s.t.	*recover from*
get through with s.t.	*finish*
get to s.o. or s.t.	*1. reach s.o. or s.t.* *2. upset s.o.*
get together with s.o.	*meet*
give s.t. **away**	*give without charging money*
give s.t. **back**	*return*
give s.t. **out**	*distribute*
give s.t. **up**	*quit, abandon*
give up doing s.t.	*quit, stop*
go after s.o. or s.t.	*try to get or win, pursue*
go along with s.t.	*support*
go on doing s.t.	*continue*
go over s.t.	*review*
hand s.t. **in**	*give work (to a boss/teacher), submit*
hand s.t. **out**	*distribute*
hand s.t. **over**	*give*
hang s.t. **up**	*put on a hook or hanger*
help s.o. **out**	*assist*
hold s.t. **on**	*keep attached*
keep s.o. or s.t. **away**	*cause to stay at a distance*
keep s.t. **on***	*not remove (a piece of clothing/ jewelry)*
keep on doing s.t.	*continue*
keep s.o. or s.t. **out**	*not allow to enter*
keep up with s.o. or s.t.	*go as fast as*
lay s.o. **off**	*end employment*
lay s.t. **out**	*1. arrange according to plan* *2. spend money*
leave s.t. **on**	*1. not turn off (a light/radio)* *2. not remove (a piece of clothing/ jewelry)*
leave s.t. **out**	*not include, omit*
let s.o. **down**	*disappoint*
let s.o. or s.t. **in**	*allow to enter*
let s.o. **off**	*1. allow to leave (from a bus/car)* *2. not punish*

PHRASAL VERB	MEANING	PHRASAL VERB	MEANING
light s.t. **up**	*illuminate*	**stick with/to** s.o. or s.t.	*not quit, not leave, persevere*
look after s.o. or s.t.	*take care of*	**straighten** s.o. **out**	*change bad behavior*
look for s.o. or s.t.	*try to find*	**straighten** s.t. **up**	*make neat*
look into s.t.	*research*	**switch** s.t. **on**	*start (a machine/light)*
look s.o. or s.t. **over**	*examine*	**take** s.t. **away**	*remove*
look s.t. **up**	*try to find (in a book/on the Internet)*	**take** s.o. or s.t. **back**	*return*
make s.t. **up**	*create*	**take** s.t. **down**	*remove*
miss out on s.t.	*lose the chance for something good*	**take** s.t. **in**	1. *notice, understand, and remember*
move s.t. **around***	*change the location*		2. *earn (money)*
pass s.t. **on**	*give to others*	**take** s.t. **off/out**	*remove*
pass s.t. **out**	*distribute*	**take** s.o. **on**	*hire*
pass s.o. or s.t. **over**	*decide not to use*	**take** s.t. **on**	*agree to do*
pass s.o. or s.t. **up**	*decide not to use, reject*	**take over** s.t.	*get control of*
pay s.o. or s.t. **back**	*repay*	**take** s.t. **up**	*begin a job or activity*
pick s.o. or s.t. **out**	1. *choose*	**talk** s.o. **into***	*persuade*
	2. *identify*	**talk** s.t. **over**	*discuss*
pick s.o. or s.t. **up**	1. *lift*	**team up with** s.o.	*start to work with*
	2. *go get someone or something*	**tear** s.t. **down**	*destroy*
pick s.t. **up**	1. *buy, purchase*	**tear** s.t. **off**	*remove by tearing*
	2. *get (an idea/a new book)*	**tear** s.t. **up**	*tear into small pieces*
	3. *answer the phone*	**think about** doing s.t.	*consider*
point s.o. or s.t. **out**	*indicate*	**think back on** s.t.	*remember*
put s.t. **away**	*put in an appropriate place*	**think** s.t. **over**	*consider*
put s.t. **back**	*return to its original place*	**think** s.t. **up**	*invent*
put s.o. or s.t. **down**	*stop holding*	**throw** s.t. **away/out**	*put in the trash, discard*
put s.o. **off**	*discourage*	**touch** s.t. **up**	*improve by making small changes*
put s.t. **off**	*delay*	**try** s.t. **on**	*put clothing on to see if it fits*
put off doing s.t.	*delay*	**try** s.t. **out**	*use to see if it works*
put s.t. **on**	*cover the body (with clothes/lotion)*	**turn** s.t. **around***	*make it work well*
put s.t. **together**	*assemble*	**turn** s.o. or s.t. **down**	*reject*
put s.t. **up**	*erect*	**turn** s.t. **down**	*lower the volume (a TV/radio)*
run into s.o.	*meet accidentally*	**turn** s.t. **in**	*give work (to a boss/teacher), submit*
see s.t. **through***	*complete*	**turn** s.o. or s.t. **into***	*change from one form to another*
send s.t. **back**	*return*	**turn** s.o. **off***	*[slang] destroy interest in*
send s.t. **out**	*mail*	**turn** s.t. **off**	*stop (a machine/light), extinguish*
set s.t. **up**	1. *prepare for use*	**turn** s.t. **on**	*start (a machine/light)*
	2. *establish (a business/ an organization)*	**turn** s.t. **over**	*turn so the top side is at the bottom*
settle on s.t.	*choose after thinking about many possibilities*	**turn** s.t. **up**	*make louder (a TV/radio)*
		use s.t. **up**	*use completely, consume*
show s.o. or s.t. **off**	*display the best qualities*	**wake** s.o. **up**	*awaken*
show up on s.t.	*appear*	**watch out for** s.o. or s.t.	*be careful about*
shut s.t. **off**	*stop (a machine/light)*	**work** s.t. **off**	*remove by work or activity*
sign s.o. **up (for** s.t.**)**	*register*	**work** s.t. **out**	*solve, find a solution to a problem*
start s.t. **over***	*start again*	**write** s.t. **down**	*write on a piece of paper*
		write s.t. **up**	*write in a finished form*

PHRASAL VERB	MEANING
act up	cause problems
blow up	explode
break down	stop working (a machine)
break out	happen suddenly
burn down	burn completely
call back	return a phone call
calm down	become less excited
catch on	1. begin to understand
	2. become popular
cheer up	make happier
clean up	clean completely
clear up	become clear
close down	stop operating
come about	happen
come along	come with, accompany
come around	happen
come back	1. return
	2. become fashionable again
come by	visit
come down	become less (prices)
come in	enter
come off	become unattached
come on	1. do as I say
	2. let's go
come out	appear
come up	arise
dress up	wear special clothes
drop in	visit by surprise
drop out	quit
eat out	eat in a restaurant
empty out	empty completely
end up	reach a final place or condition
fall off	become detached
find out	learn information
fit in	be accepted in a group
follow through	complete
fool around	act playful
get ahead	make progress, succeed
get along	have a good relationship
get away	go on vacation
get back	return
get by	survive
get through	1. finish
	2. succeed in reaching s.o. by phone
get together	meet
get up	1. get out of bed
	2. stand

PHRASAL VERB	MEANING
give up	quit
go ahead	begin or continue to do something
go away	leave
go back	return
go down	become less (price, number), decrease
go off	explode (a gun/fireworks)
go on	continue
go out	leave
go over	succeed with an audience
go up	1. be built
	2. become more (price, number), increase
grow up	become an adult
hang up	end a phone call
help out	assist
hold on	1. wait
	2. not hang up the phone
keep away	stay at a distance
keep out	not enter
keep up	go as fast
lie down	recline
light up	illuminate
look out	be careful
make up	end a disagreement, reconcile
miss out	lose the chance for something good
pass away	die
pay off	be worthwhile
pick up	improve
play around	have fun
run out	not have enough
set out	begin an activity or a project
show up	appear
sign up	register
sit down	take a seat
slip up	make a mistake
stand up	rise
start over	start again
stay up	remain awake
straighten up	make neat
take off	depart (a plane)
tune in	1. watch or listen to (a show)
	2. pay attention
turn up	appear
wake up	stop sleeping
watch out	be careful
work out	1. be resolved
	2. exercise
	3. understand

6 Irregular Plural Nouns

SINGULAR	PLURAL	SINGULAR	PLURAL	SINGULAR	PLURAL	SINGULAR	PLURAL
analysis	analyses	half	halves	man	men	deer	deer
basis	bases	knife	knives	woman	women	fish	fish
crisis	crises	leaf	leaves	child	children	sheep	sheep
hypothesis	hypotheses	life	lives	foot	feet		
		loaf	loaves	tooth	teeth		
		shelf	shelves	goose	geese		
		wife	wives	mouse	mice		
				person	people		

7 Adjectives That Form the Comparative and Superlative in Two Ways

The more common form of the comparative and the superlative is listed first.

ADJECTIVE	COMPARATIVE	SUPERLATIVE
common	more common/commoner	most common/commonest
cruel	crueler/more cruel	cruelest/most cruel
deadly	deadlier/more deadly	deadliest/most deadly
friendly	more friendly/friendlier	most friendly/friendliest
handsome	more handsome/handsomer	most handsome/handsomest
happy	happier/more happy	happiest/most happy
lively	livelier/more lively	liveliest/most lively
lonely	lonelier/more lonely	loneliest/most lonely
lovely	lovelier/more lovely	loveliest/most lovely
narrow	narrower/more narrow	narrowest/most narrow
pleasant	more pleasant/pleasanter	most pleasant/pleasantest
polite	more polite/politer	most polite/politest
quiet	quieter/more quiet	quietest/most quiet
shallow	shallower/more shallow	shallowest/most shallow
simple	simpler/more simple	simplest/most simple
sincere	more sincere/sincerer	most sincere/sincerest
stupid	stupider/more stupid	stupidest/most stupid
true	truer/more true	truest/most true

8 Irregular Comparisons of Adjectives, Adverbs, and Quantifiers

ADJECTIVE	ADVERB	COMPARATIVE	SUPERLATIVE
bad	badly	worse	the worst
far	far	farther/further	the farthest/furthest
good	well	better	the best
little	little	less	the least
many/a lot of	—	more	the most
much*/a lot of	much*/a lot	more	the most

* *Much* is usually only used in questions and negative statements.

9 Participial Adjectives

-ED	-ING	-ED	-ING	-ED	-ING
alarmed	alarming	disturbed	disturbing	moved	moving
amazed	amazing	embarrassed	embarrassing	paralyzed	paralyzing
amused	amusing	entertained	entertaining	pleased	pleasing
annoyed	annoying	excited	exciting	relaxed	relaxing
astonished	astonishing	exhausted	exhausting	satisfied	satisfying
bored	boring	fascinated	fascinating	shocked	shocking
confused	confusing	frightened	frightening	surprised	surprising
depressed	depressing	horrified	horrifying	terrified	terrifying
disappointed	disappointing	inspired	inspiring	tired	tiring
disgusted	disgusting	interested	interesting	touched	touching
distressed	distressing	irritated	irritating	troubled	troubling

10 Verbs Followed by Gerunds (Base Form of Verb + -ing)

acknowledge	delay	escape	imagine	postpone	report
admit	deny	excuse	justify	practice	resent
advise	detest	explain	keep *(continue)*	prevent	resist
allow	discontinue	feel like	keep on*	prohibit	risk
appreciate	discuss	finish	limit	propose	suggest
avoid	dislike	forgive	mention	put off*	support
ban	end up*	give up*	mind *(object to)*	quit	think about* *(consider)*
can't help	endure	go	miss	recall	tolerate
celebrate	enjoy	go on*	permit	recommend	understand
consider					

*These phrasal verbs can be followed by a gerund.

11 Verbs Followed by Infinitives (*To* + Base Form of Verb)

afford	can't wait	grow	mean *(intend)*	pretend	threaten
agree	claim	help*	need	promise	volunteer
aim	choose	hesitate	neglect	refuse	wait
appear	consent	hope	offer	rush	want
arrange	decide	hurry	pay	seem	wish
ask	deserve	intend	plan	struggle	would like
attempt	expect	learn	prepare	swear	yearn
can('t) afford	fail	manage			

* *Help* is often followed by the base form of the verb (example: *I helped paint the kitchen*).

12 Verbs Followed by Gerunds or Infinitives

begin	forget*	like	prefer	regret*	stop*
can't stand	hate	love	remember*	start	try
continue					

*These verbs can be followed by either a gerund or an infinitive, but there is a big difference in meaning *(see Unit 9)*.

13 Verbs Followed by Object + Infinitive

advise	choose*	get	order	promise*	tell
allow	convince	help**	pay*	remind	urge
ask*	encourage	hire	permit	request	want*
beg*	expect*	instruct	persuade	require	warn
cause	forbid	invite	prefer*	teach	would like*
challenge	force	need*			

*These verbs can also be followed by an infinitive without an object (example: *ask to leave* or *ask someone to leave*).

** *Help* is often followed by the base form of the verb, with or without an object (example: *I helped (her) paint the kitchen*).

14 Adjectives Followed by Infinitives

afraid	delighted	eager	happy	ready	sorry
alarmed	depressed	easy	hesitant	relieved	surprised
amazed	determined	embarrassed	likely	reluctant	touched
angry	difficult	encouraged	lucky	right	upset
anxious	disappointed	excited	pleased	sad	willing
ashamed	distressed	fortunate	prepared	shocked	wrong
curious	disturbed	glad	proud		

15 Nouns Followed by Infinitives

attempt	desire	offer	plan	reason	time
chance	dream	opportunity	price	request	trouble
choice	failure	permission	promise	right	way
decision	need				

16 Adjective + Preposition Combinations

accustomed to	bored with/by	disappointed with	happy about	responsible for	sorry for/about
afraid of	capable of	excited about	known for	sad about	surprised at/
amazed at/by	careful of	famous for	interested in	safe from	about/by
angry at	certain about	fed up with	nervous about	satisfied with	terrible at
ashamed of	concerned about	fond of	opposed to	shocked at/by	tired of
aware of	content with	glad about	pleased about	sick of	used to
awful at	curious about	good at	ready for	slow at/in	worried about
bad at	different from				

17 Verb + Preposition Combinations

admit to	believe in	dream about/of	pay for	succeed in	think about
advise against	choose between	feel about	plan on	talk about	wonder about
apologize for	complain about	insist on	rely on	thank someone for	worry about
approve of	decide on	object to	resort to		

1 SOCIAL MODALS AND EXPRESSIONS

FUNCTION	MODAL OR EXPRESSION	TIME	EXAMPLES
Ability	can can't	Present	Sam **can swim**. He **can't skate**.
	could couldn't	Past	We **could swim** last year. We **couldn't skate**.
	be able to* not be able to*	All verb forms	Lea **is able to run** fast. She **wasn't able to run** fast last year.
Possibility	can can't	Present or future	I **can help** you now. I **can't help** you tomorrow.
Permission	can can't could may may not	Present or future	**Can** I **sit** here? **Can** I **call** tomorrow? Yes, you **can**. No, you **can't**. Sorry. **Could** he **leave** now? **May** I **borrow** your pen? Yes, you **may**. No, you **may not**. Sorry.
Requests	can can't could will would	Present or future	**Can** you **close** the door, please? Sure, I **can**. Sorry, I **can't**. **Could** you please **answer** the phone? **Will** you **wash** the dishes, please? **Would** you please **mail** this letter?
Advice	should shouldn't ought to had better** had better not**	Present or future	You **should study** more. You **shouldn't miss** class. We **ought to leave**. We**'d better go**. We**'d better not stay**.
Advisability in the Past and Regret or Criticism	should have shouldn't have ought to have could have might have	Past	I **should have become** a doctor. I **shouldn't have wasted** time. He **ought to have told** me. She **could have gone** to college. You **might have called**. I waited for hours.
Necessity	have to* not have to*	All verb forms	He **has to go** now. I **had to go** yesterday. I **will have to go** soon. He **doesn't have to go** yet.
	have got to* must	Present or future	He**'s got to leave**! You **must use** a pen for the test.
Prohibition	must not can't	Present or future	You **must not drive** without a license. You **can't drive** without a license.

*The meaning of this expression is similar to the meaning of a modal. Unlike a modal, the verb changes for present tense third-person singular.

**The meaning of this expression is similar to the meaning of a modal. Like a modal, it has no -*s* for third-person singular.

FUNCTION	MODAL OR EXPRESSION	TIME	EXAMPLES
Conclusions and Possibility	must must not have to* have got to*	Present	This **must be** her house. Her name is on the door. She **must not be** home. I don't see her car. She **has to know** him. They went to school together. He**'s got to be** guilty. We saw him do it.
	may may not might might not could	Present or future	She **may be** home now. It **may not rain** tomorrow. Lee **might be sick** today. He **might not come** to class. They **could be** at the library. It **could rain** tomorrow.
	may have may not have might have might not have could have	Past	They **may have left** already. I don't see them. They **may not have arrived** yet. He **might have called**. I'll check my phone messages. He **might not have left** a message. She **could have forgotten** to mail the letter.
Impossibility	can't	Present or future	That **can't be** Ana. She left for France yesterday. It **can't snow** tomorrow. It's going to be too warm.
	couldn't	Present or future	He **couldn't be** guilty. He wasn't in town when the crime occurred. The teacher **couldn't give** the test tomorrow. Tomorrow's Saturday.
	couldn't have	Past	You **couldn't have failed**. You studied too hard.

*The meaning of this expression is similar to the meaning of a modal. Unlike a modal, the verb changes for present tense third-person singular.

19 Reporting Verbs

STATEMENTS

acknowledge	claim	explain	remark	state
add	comment	indicate	repeat	suggest
admit	complain	maintain	reply	tell
announce	conclude	mean	report	warn
answer	confess	note	respond	whisper
argue	declare	observe	say	write
assert	deny	promise	shout	yell
believe	exclaim			

INSTRUCTIONS, COMMANDS, ADVICE, REQUESTS, INVITATIONS

advise	invite
ask	order
caution	say
command	tell
demand	urge
instruct	warn

QUESTIONS

ask
inquire
question

20 Time Word Changes in Indirect Speech

DIRECT SPEECH		INDIRECT SPEECH
now	→	then
today	→	that day
tomorrow	→	the next day or the following day or the day after
yesterday	→	the day before or the previous day
this week/month/year	→	that week/month/year
last week/month/year	→	the week/month/year before
next week/month/year	→	the following week/month/year

21 Phrases Introducing Embedded Questions

I don't know ...	I'd like to know ...	Do you know ...?
I don't understand ...	I need to know ...	Do you understand ...?
I wonder ...	I want to know ...	Can you tell me ...?
I'm not sure ...	I want to understand ...	Could you explain ...?
I can't remember ...	I'd like to find out ...	Can you remember ...?
I can't imagine ...	We need to find out ...	Would you show me ...?
It doesn't say ...	Let's ask ...	Who knows ...?

22 Spelling Rules for the Simple Present: Third-Person Singular (*He*, *She*, *It*)

1 Add *-s* for most verbs.

work	work**s**
buy	buy**s**
ride	ride**s**
return	return**s**

2 Add *-es* for verbs that end in *-ch*, *-s*, *-sh*, *-x*, or *-z*.

watch	watch**es**
pass	pass**es**
rush	rush**es**
relax	relax**es**
buzz	buzz**es**

3 Change the *y* to *i* and add *-es* when the base form ends in **consonant + y**.

study	stud**ies**
hurry	hurr**ies**
dry	dr**ies**

4 Do not change the *y* when the base form ends in **vowel + y**. Add *-s*.

play	play**s**
enjoy	enjoy**s**

5 A few verbs have **irregular forms**.

be	**is**
do	**does**
go	**goes**
have	**has**

23 Spelling Rules for Base Form of Verb + *-ing* (Progressive and Gerund)

1 Add *-ing* to the base form of the verb.

read	read**ing**
stand	stand**ing**

2 If the verb ends in a **silent -e**, drop the final *-e* and add *-ing*.

leave	leav**ing**
take	tak**ing**

3 In **one-syllable** verbs, if the last three letters are a consonant-vowel-consonant combination (CVC), double the last consonant and add *-ing*.

```
C V C
↓ ↓ ↓
s i t        sit**ting**
```

```
C V C
↓ ↓ ↓
p l a n      plan**ning**
```

EXCEPTION: Do not double the last consonant in verbs that end in *-w*, *-x*, or *-y*.

sew	sew**ing**
fix	fix**ing**
play	play**ing**

4 In verbs of **two or more syllables** that end in a consonant-vowel-consonant combination, double the last consonant only if the last syllable is stressed.

admít	admit**ting**	*(The last syllable is stressed, so double the -**t**.)*
whísper	whisper**ing**	*(The last syllable is not stressed, so don't double the -**r**.)*

5 If the verb ends in *-ie*, change the *ie* to *y* before adding *-ing*.

die	d**ying**
lie	l**ying**

Stress
´ shows main stress.

24 Spelling Rules for Base Form of Verb + -ed (Simple Past and Past Participle of Regular Verbs)

1 If the verb ends in a **consonant**, add **-ed**.

return	return**ed**
help	help**ed**

2 If the verb ends in **-e**, add **-d**.

live	live**d**
create	create**d**
die	die**d**

3 In **one-syllable** verbs, if the last three letters are a consonant-vowel-consonant combination (CVC), double the last consonant and add **-ed**.

```
C V C
↓ ↓ ↓
h o p          hop**ped**
```

```
C V C
↓ ↓ ↓
g r a b        grab**bed**
```

EXCEPTION: Do not double the last consonant in **one-syllable** verbs that end in **-w**, **-x**, or **-y**.

bow	bow**ed**
mix	mix**ed**
play	play**ed**

4 In verbs of **two or more syllables** that end in a consonant-vowel-consonant combination, double the last consonant only if the last syllable is stressed.

prefér	prefer**red**	*(The last syllable is stressed, so double the -r.)*
vísit	visit**ed**	*(The last syllable is not stressed, so don't double the -t.)*

5 If the verb ends in **consonant + y**, change the **y** to **i** and add **-ed**.

worry	worr**ied**
carry	carr**ied**

6 If the verb ends in **vowel + y**, add **-ed**. (Do not change the **y** to **i**.)

play	play**ed**
annoy	annoy**ed**

EXCEPTIONS:

lay	la**id**
pay	pa**id**
say	sa**id**

Stress
ˊ shows main stress.

25 Spelling Rules for the Comparative (-er) and Superlative (-est) of Adjectives

1 With **one-syllable** adjectives, add **-er** to form the comparative. Add **-est** to form the superlative.

cheap	cheap**er**	cheap**est**
bright	bright**er**	bright**est**

2 If the adjective ends in **-e**, add **-r** or **-st**.

nice	nice**r**	nice**st**

3 If the adjective ends in **consonant + y**, change **y** to **i** before you add **-er** or **-est**.

pretty	prett**ier**	prett**iest**

EXCEPTION:

shy	shy**er**	shy**est**

4 In **one-syllable** adjectives, if the last three letters are a consonant-vowel-consonant combination (CVC), double the last consonant before adding **-er** or **-est**.

```
C V C
↓ ↓ ↓
b i g          big**ger**        big**gest**
```

EXCEPTION: Do not double the last consonant in adjectives that end in **-w** or **-y**.

slow	slow**er**	slow**est**
gray	gray**er**	gray**est**

26 Spelling Rules for Adverbs Ending in *-ly*

1 Add *-ly* to the corresponding adjective.

nice	nice**ly**
quiet	quiet**ly**
beautiful	beautiful**ly**

EXCEPTION:

true	tru**ly**

2 If the adjective ends in **consonant + *y***, change the *y* to *i* before adding *-ly*.

easy	eas**ily**

3 If the adjective ends in *-le*, drop the *e* and add *-y*.

possible	possib**ly**

4 If the adjective ends in *-ic*, add *-ally*.

basic	basic**ally**
fantastic	fantastic**ally**

27 Capitalization and Punctuation Rules

	USE FOR . . .	EXAMPLES
capital letter	• the first-person pronoun *I*	Tomorrow **I** will be here at 2:00.
	• proper nouns	His name is **Karl**. He lives in **Germany**.
	• the first word of a sentence	**When** does the train leave? **At** 2:00.
apostrophe (')	• possessive nouns	Is that **Marta's** coat?
	• contractions	**That's** not hers. **It's** mine.
comma (,)	• after items in a list	He bought **apples, pears, oranges,** and **bananas**.
	• before sentence connectors *and*, *but*, *or*, and *so*	They watched TV**, and** she played video games. She's tired**, so** she's going to bed now.
	• after the first part of a sentence that begins with *because*	***Because*** it's raining**,** we're not walking to the office.
	• after the first part of a sentence that begins with a preposition	***Across from*** the post office**,** there's a good restaurant.
	• after the first part of a sentence that begins with a time clause or an *if*-clause	***After*** he arrived**,** we ate dinner. ***If*** it rains**,** we won't go.
	• before and after a nonidentifying adjective clause in the middle of a sentence	Tony**, who lives in Paris,** emails me every day.
	• before a nonidentifying adjective clause at the end of a sentence	I get emails every day from Tony**, who lives in Paris**.
exclamation point (!)	• at the end of a sentence to show surprise or a strong feeling	You're here! That's great! Stop! A car is coming!
period (.)	• at the end of a statement	Today is Wednesday**.**
question mark (?)	• at the end of a question	What day is today**?**

28 Direct Speech Punctuation Rules

Direct speech can either come **after or before** the reporting verb.

1 When direct speech comes **after** the reporting verb:

EXAMPLES: He said, **"I had a good time."**
She asked, **"Where's the party?"**
They shouted, **"Be careful!"**

a. Put a comma after the reporting verb.

b. Use opening quotation marks (**"**) before the first word of the direct speech.

c. Begin the quotation with a capital letter.

d. Use the appropriate end punctuation for the direct speech:
If the direct speech is a statement, use a period (**.**).
If the direct speech is a question, use a question mark (**?**).
If the direct speech is an exclamation, use an exclamation point (**!**).

e. Put closing quotation marks (**"**) after the end punctuation of the quotation.

2 When direct speech comes **before** the reporting verb:

EXAMPLES: **"I had a good time,"** he said.
"Where's the party?" she asked.
"Be careful!" they shouted.

a. Begin the sentence with opening quotation marks (**"**).

b. Use the appropriate end punctuation for the direct speech:
If the direct speech is a statement, use a comma (**,**).
If the direct speech is a question, use a question mark (**?**).
If the direct speech is an exclamation, use an exclamation point (**!**).

c. Use closing quotation marks after the end punctuation for the direct speech (**"**).

d. Begin the reporting clause with a lowercase letter.

e. Use a period at the end of the main sentence (**.**).

29 Pronunciation Table

▶ A|01   These are the pronunciation symbols used in this text. Listen to the pronunciation of the key words.

VOWELS				CONSONANTS			
SYMBOL	KEY WORD	SYMBOL	KEY WORD	SYMBOL	KEY WORD	SYMBOL	KEY WORD
i	beat, feed	ə	banana, among	p	pack, happy	z	zip, please, goes
ɪ	bit, did	ɚ	shirt, murder	b	back, rubber	ʃ	ship, machine, station,
eɪ	date, paid	aɪ	bite, cry, buy, eye	t	tie		special, discussion
ɛ	bet, bed	aʊ	about, how	d	die	ʒ	measure, vision
æ	bat, bad	ɔɪ	voice, boy	k	came, key, quick	h	hot, who
ɑ	box, odd, father	ɪr	beer	g	game, guest	m	men
ɔ	bought, dog	ɛr	bare	tʃ	church, nature, watch	n	sun, know, pneumonia
oʊ	boat, road	ɑr	bar	ʤ	judge, general, major	ŋ	sung, ringing
ʊ	book, good	ɔr	door	f	fan, photograph	w	wet, white
u	boot, food, student	ʊr	tour	v	van	l	light, long
ʌ	but, mud, mother			θ	thing, breath	r	right, wrong
				ð	then, breathe	y	yes, use, music
				s	sip, city, psychology	ţ	butter, bottle

30 Pronunciation Rules for the Simple Present: Third-Person Singular (*He, She, It*)

1 The third-person singular in the simple present always ends in the letter *-s*. There are, however, three different pronunciations for the final sound of the third-person singular.

/s/	/z/	/ɪz/
talk**s**	lov**es**	danc**es**

2 The final sound is pronounced /s/ after the voiceless sounds /p/, /t/, /k/, and /f/.

top	to**ps**	take	ta**kes**
get	ge**ts**	laugh	lau**ghs**

3 The final sound is pronounced /z/ after the voiced sounds /b/, /d/, /g/, /v/, /m/, /n/, /ŋ/, /l/, /r/, and /ð/.

describe	descri**bes**	remain	remai**ns**
spend	spen**ds**	sing	sin**gs**
hug	hu**gs**	tell	tel**ls**
live	li**ves**	lower	lowe**rs**
seem	see**ms**	bathe	ba**thes**

4 The final sound is pronounced /z/ after all **vowel sounds**.

agree	agr**ees**	stay	sta**ys**
try	tr**ies**	know	kn**ows**

5 The final sound is pronounced /ɪz/ after the sounds /s/, /z/, /ʃ/, /ʒ/, /tʃ/, and /dʒ/. /ɪz/ adds a syllable to the verb.

miss	mi**sses**	massage	massa**ges**
freeze	free**zes**	watch	wat**ches**
rush	ru**shes**	judge	ju**dges**

6 *Do* and *say* have a change in vowel sound.

do /du/	does /dʌz/
say /seɪ/	says /sɛz/

31 Pronunciation Rules for the Simple Past and Past Participle of Regular Verbs

1 The regular simple past and past participle always end in the letter *-d*. There are three different pronunciations for the final sound of the regular simple past and past participle.

/t/	/d/	/ɪd/
race**d**	live**d**	attend**ed**

2 The final sound is pronounced /t/ after the voiceless sounds /p/, /k/, /f/, /s/, /ʃ/, and /tʃ/.

hop	ho**pped**	address	addre**ssed**
work	wor**ked**	publish	publi**shed**
laugh	lau**ghed**	watch	wat**ched**

3 The final sound is pronounced /d/ after the voiced sounds /b/, /g/, /v/, /z/, /ʒ/, /dʒ/, /m/, /n/, /ŋ/, /l/, /r/, and /ð/.

rub	ru**bbed**	rhyme	rhy**med**
hug	hu**gged**	return	retur**ned**
live	li**ved**	bang	ban**ged**
surprise	surpri**sed**	enroll	enro**lled**
massage	massa**ged**	appear	appea**red**
change	chan**ged**	bathe	ba**thed**

4 The final sound is pronounced /d/ after all **vowel sounds**.

agree	agr**eed**	enjoy	enj**oyed**
die	d**ied**	snow	sn**owed**
play	pl**ayed**		

5 The final sound is pronounced /ɪd/ after /t/ and /d/. /ɪd/ adds a syllable to the verb.

start	star**ted**	decide	deci**ded**

Glossary of Grammar Terms

action verb A verb that describes an action.

> Alicia **ran** home.

active sentence A sentence that focuses on the agent (the person or thing doing the action).

> **Ari kicked** the ball.

addition A clause or a short sentence that follows a statement and expresses similarity or contrast with the information in the statement.

> Pedro is tall, **and so is Alex.**
> Trish doesn't like sports. **Neither does her sister.**

adjective A word that describes a noun or pronoun.

> It's a **good** plan, and it's not **difficult.**

adjective clause A clause that identifies or gives additional information about a noun.

> The woman **who called you** didn't leave her name.
> Samir, **who you met yesterday,** works in the lab.

adverb A word that describes a verb, an adjective, or another adverb.

> She drives **carefully.**
> She's a **very** good driver.
> She drives **really** well.

affirmative A statement without a negative, or an answer meaning *Yes.*

> He **works.** *(affirmative statement)*
> **Yes**, he **does.** *(affirmative short answer)*

agent The person or thing doing the action in a sentence. In passive sentences, the word *by* is used before the agent.

> This article was written **by my teacher.**

article A word that goes before a noun.
The indefinite articles are *a* and *an.*

> I ate **a** sandwich and **an** apple.

The definite article is *the.*

> I didn't like **the** sandwich. **The** apple was good.

auxiliary verb (also called **helping verb**) A verb used with a main verb. *Be, do,* and *have* are often auxiliary verbs. Modals (*can, should, may, must . . .*) are also auxiliary verbs.

> I **am** exercising right now.
> **Do** you like to exercise?
> I **should** exercise every day.

base form The simple form of a verb without any endings (*-s, -ed, -ing*) or other changes.

> **be, have, go, drive**

clause A group of words that has a subject and a verb. A sentence can have one or more clauses.

> **We are leaving now.** *(one clause)*
> **If it rains, we won't go.** *(two clauses)*

common noun A word for a person, place, or thing (but not the name of the person, place, or thing).

> Teresa lives in a **house** near the **beach.**

comparative The form of an adjective or adverb that shows the difference between two people, places, or things.

> Alain is **shorter** than Brendan. *(adjective)*
> Brendan runs **faster** than Alain. *(adverb)*

conditional sentence A sentence that describes a condition and its result. The sentence can be about the past, the present, or the future. The condition and result can be real or unreal.

> If it **rains,** I **won't go.** *(future real)*
> If it **had rained,** I **wouldn't have gone.** *(past unreal)*

continuous See **progressive.**

contraction A short form of a word or words. An apostrophe (') replaces the missing letter or letters.

> **she's** = she is
> **can't** = cannot

count noun A noun that you can count. It has a singular and a plural form.

> one **book**, two **books**

definite article *the*

This article goes before a noun that refers to a specific person, place, or thing.

Please bring me **the book** on **the table**.

dependent clause (also called **subordinate clause**) A clause that needs a main clause for its meaning.

When it's hot out, I go to the beach.

direct object A noun or pronoun that receives the action of a verb.

Marta kicked **the ball**. Ian caught **it**.

direct speech (also called **quoted speech**) Language that gives the exact words a speaker used. In writing, quotation marks come before and after the speaker's words.

"I saw Bob yesterday," she said.
"Was he in school?" he asked.

embedded question A question that is inside another sentence.

I don't know **where the restaurant is**.
Do you know **if it's on Tenth Street**?

formal Language used in business situations or with adults you do not know.

Good afternoon, Mr. Rivera. Please have a seat.

gerund A noun formed with verb + *-ing* that can be used as a subject or an object.

Swimming is great exercise.
I enjoy **swimming**.

helping verb See **auxiliary verb**.

identifying adjective clause (also called **restrictive adjective clause**) A clause that identifies which member of a group the sentence is about.

There are ten students in the class. The student **who sits in front of me** is from Russia.

if-**clause** The clause that states the condition in a conditional sentence.

If I had known you were here, I would have called you.

imperative A sentence that gives a command or instructions.

Hurry!
Turn left on Main Street.

indefinite article *a* or *an*

These articles go before a noun that does not refer to a specific person, place, or thing.

Can you bring me **a book**? I'm looking for something to read.

indefinite pronoun A pronoun such as *someone, something, anyone, anything, anywhere, no one, nothing, nowhere, everyone,* and *everything*. An indefinite pronoun does not refer to a specific person, place, or thing.

Someone called you last night.
Did **anything** happen?

indirect object A noun or pronoun (often a person) that receives something as the result of the action of the verb.

I told **John** the story.
He gave **me** some good advice.

indirect question Language that reports what a speaker asked without using the exact words.

He asked **what my name was**.
He asked **if he had met me before**.

indirect speech (also called **reported speech**) Language that reports what a speaker said without using the exact words.

Ann said **she had seen Bob the day before**.
She asked **if he was in school**.

infinitive *to* + base form of the verb

I want **to leave** now.

infinitive of purpose *(in order) to* + base form

This form gives the reason for an action.

I go to school **(in order) to learn** English.

informal Language used with family, friends, and children.

Hi, Pete. Sit down.

information question See *wh-* **question**.

inseparable phrasal verb A phrasal verb whose parts must stay together.

We **ran into** Tomás at the supermarket.
NOT We ~~ran Tomás into~~ . . .

intransitive verb A verb that does not have an object.

> She **paints**.
> We **fell**.

irregular A word that does not change its form in the usual way.

> good → well
> bad → worse
> go → went

main clause A clause that can stand alone as a sentence.

> **I called my friend Tom**, who lives in Chicago.

main verb A verb that describes an action or state. It is often used with an auxiliary verb.

> Jared is **calling**.
> Does he **call** every day?
> Paulo is **studying** in Barcelona this semester.
> Do you **know** him?

modal A type of auxiliary verb. It goes before a main verb or stands alone as a short answer. It expresses ideas such as ability, advice, permission, and possibility. *Can, could, will, would, may, might, should,* and *must* are modals.

> **Can** you swim?
> Yes, I **can**.
> You really **should** learn to swim.

negative A statement or answer meaning *No.*

> He **doesn't** work. *(negative statement)*
> **No**, he **doesn't**. *(negative short answer)*

non-action verb (also called **stative verb**) A verb that does not describe an action. It describes such things as thoughts, feelings, and senses.

> I **remember** that word.
> Chris **loves** ice cream.
> It **tastes** great.

non-count noun A noun you usually do not count (*air, water, rice, love . . .*). It has only a singular form.

> The **rice** is delicious.

nonidentifying adjective clause (also called **nonrestrictive adjective clause**) A clause that gives additional information about the noun it refers to. The information is not necessary to identify the noun. It is separated from the rest of the sentence by commas.

> My sister Diana, **who usually hates sports,** recently started tennis lessons.

nonrestrictive adjective clause See **nonidentifying adjective clause**.

noun A word for a person, place, or thing.

> My **sister**, **Anne**, works in an **office**.
> She uses a **computer**.

object A noun or a pronoun that receives the action of a verb. Sometimes a verb has two objects.

> Layla threw **the ball**.
> She threw **it** to **Tom**.
> She threw **him the ball**.

object pronoun A pronoun (*me, you, him, her, it, us, them*) that receives the action of the verb.

> I gave **her** a book.
> I gave **it** to **her**.

object relative pronoun A relative pronoun that is an object in an adjective clause.

> I'm reading a book **that** I really like.

paragraph A group of sentences, usually about one topic.

particle A word that looks like a preposition and combines with a main verb to form a phrasal verb. It often changes the meaning of the main verb.

> He looked the word **up**.
> *(He looked for the meaning of the word in the dictionary.)*

passive causative A sentence formed with *have* or *get* + object + past participle. It is used to talk about services that you arrange for someone to do for you.

> She **had the car checked** at the service station.
> He's going to **get his hair cut** by André.

passive sentence A sentence that focuses on the object (the person or thing receiving the action). The passive is formed with *be* + past participle.

> **The ball was kicked** by Ari.

past participle A verb form (verb + -ed). It can also be irregular. It is used to form the present perfect, past perfect, and future perfect. It can also be an adjective.

> We've **lived** here since April.
> They had **spoken** before.
> She's **interested** in math.

phrasal verb (also called *two-word verb*) A verb that has two parts (verb + particle). The meaning is often different from the meaning of its separate parts.

> He **grew up** in Texas. *(became an adult)*
> His parents **brought** him **up** to be honest. *(raised)*

phrase A group of words that form a unit without a main verb. Many phrases give information about time or place.

> **Last year**, we were living **in Canada**.

plural A form that means *two or more*.

> There **are** three **people** in the restaurant.
> **They are** eating dinner.
> **We** saw **them**.

possessive Nouns, pronouns, or adjectives that show a relationship or show that someone owns something.

> Zach is **Megan's** brother. *(possessive noun)*
> Is that car **his**? *(possessive pronoun)*
> That's **his** car. *(possessive adjective)*

predicate The part of a sentence that has the main verb. It tells what the subject is doing or describes the subject.

> My sister **works for a travel agency**.

preposition A word or phrase that goes before a noun or a pronoun to show time, place, or direction.

> Amy and I went **to** the cafeteria **on** Friday. She sits **next to** me **in** class.

progressive (also called **continuous**) The verb form *be* + verb + *-ing*. It focuses on the continuation (not the completion) of an action.

> She**'s reading** the paper.
> We **were watching** TV when you called.

pronoun A word used in place of a noun.

> That's my brother. You met **him** at my party.

proper noun A noun that is the name of a person, place, or thing. It begins with a capital letter.

> **Maria** goes to **Central High School**.
> It's on **High Street**.

punctuation Marks used in writing (period, comma, . . .) that make the meaning clear. For example, a period (**.**) shows the end of a sentence and that the sentence is a statement, not a question.

> "Come in," she said**.**

quantifier A word or phrase that shows an amount (but not an exact amount). It often comes before a noun.

> Josh bought **a lot of** books last year.
> He doesn't have **much** money.

question See *yes/no* question, *wh-* question, **tag question**, **indirect question**, and **embedded question**.

question word See *wh-* **word**.

quoted speech See **direct speech**.

real conditional sentence A sentence that talks about general truths, habits, or things that happen again and again if a condition occurs. It can also talk about things that will happen in the future under certain circumstances.

> If it rains, he takes the bus.
> If it rains tomorrow, we'll take the bus with him.

regular A word that changes its form in the usual way.

> play   →   played
> fast   →   faster
> quick →   quickly

relative pronoun A word that connects an adjective clause to a noun in the main clause.

> He's the man **who** lives next door.
> I'm reading a book **that** I really like.

reported speech See **indirect speech**.

reporting verb A verb such as *said*, *told*, or *asked*. It introduces direct and indirect speech. It can also come after the quotation in direct speech.

> Li **said**, "I'm going to be late." or "I'm going to be late," Li **said**. or "I'm going to be late," **said** Li.
> She **told** me that she was going to be late.

restrictive adjective clause See **identifying adjective clause**.

result clause The clause in a conditional sentence that talks about what happens if the condition occurs.

> If it rains, **I'll stay home**.
> If I had a million dollars, **I would travel**.
> If I had had your phone number, **I would have called you**.

sentence A group of words that has a subject and a main verb.

> **Computers are** very useful.

separable phrasal verb A phrasal verb whose parts can separate.

> Tom **looked** the word **up** in a dictionary.
> He **looked** it **up**.

short answer An answer to a *yes/no* question.

> A: Did you call me last night?
> B: **No, I didn't.** or **No.**

singular A form that means *one*.

> They have **a sister**.
> **She works** in a hospital.

statement A sentence that gives information. In writing, it ends in a period.

> Today is Monday.

stative verb See **non-action verb**.

subject The person, place, or thing that the sentence is about.

> **Ms. Chen** teaches English.
> **Her class** is interesting.

subject pronoun A pronoun that shows the person (*I, you, he, she, it, we, they*) that the sentence is about.

> **I** read a lot.
> **She** reads a lot, too.

subject relative pronoun A relative pronoun that is the subject of an adjective clause.

> He's the man **who** lives next door.

subordinate clause See **dependent clause**.

superlative The form of an adjective or adverb that is used to compare a person, place, or thing to a group of people, places, or things.

> Cindi is **the oldest** dancer in the group. *(adjective)*
> She dances **the most gracefully**. *(adverb)*

tag question A statement + tag. The **tag** is a short question at the end of the statement. Tag questions check information or comment on a situation.

> You're Jack Thompson, **aren't you?**
> It's a nice day, **isn't it?**

tense The form of a verb that shows the time of the action.

> **simple present:** Fabio **talks** to his friend every day.
> **simple past:** Fabio **talked** to his teacher yesterday.

third-person singular The pronouns *he, she*, and *it* or a singular noun. In the simple present, the third-person-singular verb ends in *-s*.

> Tomás **works** in an office. *(Tomás = he)*

three-word verb A phrasal verb + preposition.

> Slow down! I can't **keep up with** you.

time clause A clause that begins with a time word such as *when, before, after, while,* or *as soon as*.

> I'll call you **when I get home**.

transitive verb A verb that has an object.

> She **likes** apples.

two-word verb See **phrasal verb**.

unreal conditional sentence A sentence that talks about unreal conditions and their unreal results. The condition and its result can be untrue, imagined, or impossible.

> If I were a bird, I would fly around the world.
> If you had called, I would have invited you to the party.

verb A word that describes what the subject of the sentence does, thinks, feels, senses, or owns.

> They **run** two miles every day.
> She **loved** that movie.
> He **has** a new camera.

wh- question (also called **information question**) A question that begins with a *wh-* word. You answer a *wh-* question with information.

> A: **Where** are you going?
> B: To the store.

wh- word (also called **question word**) A word such as *who, what, when, where, which, why, how,* and *how much.* It can begin a *wh-* question or an embedded question.

> **Who** is that?
> **What** did you see?
> **When** does the movie usually start?
> I don't know **how much** it costs.

yes/no question A question that begins with a form of *be* or an auxiliary verb. You can answer a *yes/no* question with *yes* or *no.*

> A: **Are** you a student?
> B: **Yes,** I am. **or No,** I'm not.
> A: **Do** you come here often?
> B: **Yes,** I do. **or No,** I don't.

Unit Review Answer Key

Note: In this answer key, where a short or contracted form is given, the full or long form is also correct (unless the purpose of the exercise is to practice the short or contracted forms).

UNIT 1

A 1. studies
2. are coming
3. do
4. understand
5. use

B 1. 'm looking for
2. think
3. 's not **or** isn't carrying
4. need
5. see
6. 's standing
7. 's waiting
8. sounds
9. don't believe
10. wants

C Hi Leda,

How ~~do you do~~ *are you doing* these days? We're all fine. I'm writing to tell you that ~~we~~ *we're* not living in California anymore. We just moved to Oregon. Also, ~~we expect~~ *we're expecting* a baby!

We're looking for an interesting name for our new daughter. Do you have any ideas? Right now, we're thinking about *Gabriella* because ~~it's having~~ *it has* good nicknames. For example, *Gabby*, *Bree*, and *Ella* all seem good to us. How ~~are~~ *do* those nicknames sound to you?

We hope you'll write soon and tell us your news.

Love,
Samantha

UNIT 2

A 1. met
2. was working
3. saw
4. had
5. When
6. was thinking
7. gave

B 1. were…doing
2. met
3. were waiting
4. met
5. were studying
6. noticed
7. entered

C It was 2005. I ~~studied~~ *was studying* French in Paris ~~while~~ *when* I met Paul. Like me, Paul was from California. We were both taking the same 9:00 a.m. conversation class. After class, we always ~~were going~~ *went* to a café with some of our classmates. One day, while we ~~was~~ *were* drinking café au lait, Paul ~~was asking~~ *asked* me to go to a movie with him. After that, we started to spend most of our free time together. We really got to know each other well, and we discovered that we had a lot of similar interests. When the course was over, we left Paris and ~~were going~~ *went* back to California together. The next year, we got married!

UNIT 3

A 1. has been
2. took
3. has been reading
4. started
5. has gone
6. for
7. have become

B 1. has been working **or** has worked
2. discovered
3. didn't know
4. found out
5. got
6. has been going **or** has gone
7. hasn't found
8. has been having **or** has had

C A: How long ~~did~~ *have* you been doing adventure sports?
B: ~~I've gotten~~ *I got* interested five years ago, and I haven't stopped since then.
A: You're lucky to live here in Colorado. It's a great place for adventure sports. ~~Did you live~~ *Have you lived* **or** *Have you been living* here long?
B: No, not long. ~~I've~~ *I* moved here last year. I used to live in Alaska.
A: I haven't ~~go~~ *gone* there yet, but I've heard it's great.
B: It *is* great. When you go, be sure to visit Denali National Park.

UNIT 4

A 1. had gotten
2. had been studying
3. had graduated
4. moved
5. hadn't given

B 1. had…been playing
2. joined
3. 'd decided
4. 'd been practicing
5. 'd taught
6. Had…come
7. 'd…moved
8. 'd…been living
9. hadn't been expecting

C When five-year-old Sarah Chang enrolled in
the Juilliard School, she ~~has~~ *had* already been playing
the violin for more than a year. Her parents, both
musicians, had ~~been moving~~ *moved* from Korea to further
their careers. They had ~~gave~~ *given* their daughter a violin
as a fourth birthday present, and Sarah had been
~~practiced~~ *practicing* hard since then. By seven, she ^ already
performed with several local orchestras. A child
prodigy, Sarah became the youngest person to receive
the Hollywood Bowl's Hall of Fame Award. She
had already ~~been receiving~~ *received* several awards including
the Nan Pa Award—South Korea's highest prize for
musical talent.

UNIT 5

A 1. turn
2. Are
3. doing
4. is
5. is going to
6. you're
7. finishes

B 1. will…be doing or are…going to be doing
2. 'll be leaving
3. 'll…be going
4. won't be coming or 're not going to be coming
5. Is…going to cause or Will…cause
6. No…it isn't. or No…it won't.
7. 'll be or 's going to be
8. 'll see

C A: How long are you going to ~~staying~~ *stay or be staying* in Beijing?

B: I'm not sure. I'll let you know as soon as ~~I'll~~ find
out, OK?

A: OK. It's going to be a long flight. What will you
~~doing~~ *do or be doing* to pass the time?

B: I'll ~~be work~~ *work or be working* a lot of the time. And I'm going to try
to sleep.

A: Good idea. Have fun, and ~~I'm emailing~~ *I'll email* you all the
office news. I promise.

UNIT 6

A 1. have been selling
2. we get
3. have been exercising
4. I'll have read
5. By

B 1. 'll have been living
2. 'll have been studying
3. 'll have graduated
4. graduate
5. 'll have found
6. 'll have made
7. 'll have earned

C I'm so excited about your news! By the time you
read this, you'll already have ~~moving~~ *moved* into your new
house! And I have some good news, too. By the end
of this month, I'll have ~~save~~ *saved* $5,000. That's enough
for me to buy a used car! And that means that by this
time next year, ~~I drive~~ *I'll have driven* to California to visit you! I have
more news, too. By the time I ~~will~~ graduate, I will
have ~~been~~ started my new part-time job. I hope that
by this time next year, I'll also ~~had~~ *have* finished working
on my latest invention—a solar-powered flashlight.

It's hard to believe that in June, we will have been
~~being~~ friends for ten years. Time sure flies! And we'll
have ~~been stayed~~ *stayed or been staying* in touch even though we are 3,000
miles apart. Isn't technology a great thing?

UNIT 7

A 1. isn't
2. Didn't
3. You've
4. it
5. has
6. she
7. Shouldn't

B 1. have
2. No, I haven't
3. Aren't
4. No, I'm not
5. are
6. won't
7. Yes, you will

C A: Ken hasn't come back from Korea yet, has ~~Ken~~ *he*?

B: ~~No~~ *Yes*, he has. He got back last week. Didn't he call
you when he got back?

A: No, he didn't. He's probably busy. There are a lot

of things to do when you move, ~~isn't~~ there? *(aren't)*

B: Definitely. And I guess his family ~~wanted~~ to spend a *(will want)*

lot of time with him, won't they?

A: I'm sure they will. You know, I think I'll just call

him. You have his phone number, ~~have~~ you? *(don't)*

B: Yes, I do. Could you wait while I get it off my

phone? You're not in a hurry, ~~aren't~~ you? *(are)*

UNIT 8

A **1.** does   **5.** doesn't
     2. So   **6.** too
     3. hasn't either   **7.** either
     4. but

B **1.** I speak Spanish, and so does my brother.
     or …my brother does too.
     2. I can't speak Russian, and neither can my brother.
     or …my brother can't either.
     3. Jaime lives in Chicago, but his brother doesn't.
     4. Chen doesn't play tennis, but his sister does.
     5. Diego doesn't eat meat, and neither does Lila.
     or …Lila doesn't either.

C   My friend Alicia and I have a lot in common. She

comes from Los Angeles, and so ~~I do~~. She speaks *(do I)*

Spanish. I ~~speak~~ too. Her parents are both teachers, *(do)*

and mine ~~do~~ too. She doesn't have any brothers or *(are)*

sisters. ~~Either~~ do I. There are some differences, too. *(Neither)*

Alicia is very reserved, but ~~I am~~. I like to talk about *(I'm not)*

my feelings and say what's on my mind. Alicia doesn't

like sports, but I ~~don't~~. I'm on several school teams, *(do)*

~~and~~ she isn't. I think our differences make things more *(but)*

interesting, and so ~~do~~ Alicia! *(does)*

UNIT 9

A **1.** to use
     2. (in order) to save
     3. ordering
     4. to relax
     5. (to) study
     6. preparing
     7. Stopping
     8. to eat
     9. not to have or not having
     10. Cooking

B **1.** doesn't or didn't remember going
     2. wants or wanted Al to take
     3. wonders or wondered about Chu's or Chu eating
     4. didn't stop to have
     5. forgot to mail

C A: I was happy to hear that the cafeteria is serving

salads now. I'm eager ~~trying~~ them. *(to try)*

B: Me too. Someone recommended ~~to eat~~ more salads *(eating)*

to lose weight.

A: It was that TV doctor, right? He's always urging ~~we~~ *(us)*

to exercise more, too.

B: That's the one. He's actually convinced me to stop
~~to eat~~ meat. *(eating)*

A: Interesting! That would be a hard decision for us
~~making~~, though. We love to barbecue. *(to make)*

UNIT 10

A **1.** helped   **4.** let
     2. had   **5.** got
     3. made

B **1.** didn't or wouldn't let me have
     2. got them to buy
     3. made me walk
     4. had me feed
     5. didn't or wouldn't help me take
     6. got him to give
     7. let them have

C   Lately, I've been thinking a lot about all the people

who helped me ~~adjusting~~ to moving here when I was *(adjust or to adjust)*

a kid. My parents got me ~~join~~ some school clubs, so *(to join)*

I met other kids. Then my dad helped me ~~improved~~ *(improve or to improve)*

my soccer game so that I could join the team. And my

mom never let me ~~to stay~~ home. She made me ~~to get~~ *(stay)* *(get)*

out and do things. My parents also spoke to my new

teacher and had ~~she~~ call on me a lot, so the other kids *(her)*

got to know me quickly. Our next-door neighbors

helped, too. They got ~~I~~ to walk their dog Red, and *(me)*

Red introduced me to all her human friends! The fact

that so many people wanted to help me made me

~~to realize~~ that I was not alone. Before long, I felt part *(realize)*

of my new school, my new neighborhood, and my

new life.

A **1.** f   **3.** a   **5.** b   **7.** g
   2. e   **4.** c   **6.** d

B **1.** get through with my work
   2. pick it up
   3. count on her
   4. call me back
   5. got off the phone
   6. put my pajamas on
   7. turned the lights off

C   I'm so tired of telemarketers ~~calling up me~~ *calling me up* as
soon as I get back from work or just when I sit ~~up~~ *down*
for a relaxing dinner! It's gotten to the point that I've
stopped picking *up* the phone when it rings between
6:00 and 8:00 p.m. ~~up~~. I know I can count on it
being a telemarketer who will try to talk me into
spending money on something I don't want. But it's
still annoying to hear the phone ring, so sometimes
I ~~turn off it~~ *turn it off*. Then, of course, I worry that it may
be someone important. So I end up checking caller
ID to find out. I think the Do Not Call list is a great
idea. Who ~~thought up it~~ *thought it up*? I'm going to ~~sign for it up~~ *sign up for it*
tomorrow!

A **1.** are   **4.** which
   2. whose   **5.** that
   3. thinks   **6.** who

B **1.** who or that behave   **5.** that or which hurt
   2. who uses   **6.** which…upset
   3. which…convince   **7.** whose…is
   4. who or that…speaks

C   It's true that we are often attracted to people
who or that
~~which~~ are very different from ourselves. An extrovert,
whose
~~which~~ personality is very outgoing, will often connect
is
with a romantic partner who ~~are~~ an introvert. They
has
are both attracted to someone that ~~have~~ different
strengths. My cousin Valerie, who is an extreme
extrovert, recently married Bill, whose idea of a party
is a Scrabble game on the Internet. Can this marriage
which
succeed? Will Bill learn the salsa, ~~that~~ is Valerie's

favorite dance? Will Valerie start collecting unusual
who
words? Their friends, ~~that~~ care about both of them,
are hoping for the best.

A **1.** whose   **4.** who
   2. that   **5.** when
   3. where   **6.** who

B **1.** where   **5.** whose
   2. that or which   **6.** who(m)
   3. that or which   **7.** when or that
   4. who(m) or that

C
that or which or no relative pronoun
I grew up in an apartment building ~~who~~ my
grandparents owned. There was a small dining room
where   *which*
~~when~~ we had family meals and a kitchen in ~~that~~ I ate
whose
my breakfast. My aunt, uncle, and cousin, in ~~who~~
home I spent a lot of my time, lived in an identical
apartment on the fourth floor. I remember the time
that my parents gave me a toy phone set that we
used ~~it~~ so I could talk to my cousin. There weren't
many children in the building, but I often visited
whose
the building manager, ~~who's~~ son I liked. I enjoyed
when or that or no relative pronoun
living in the apartment, but for me the day ~~where~~
we moved into our own house was the best day of
my childhood.

A **1.** get   **6.** to post
   2. may   **7.** must not
   3. 've got   **8.** be able to
   4. can't   **9.** might be
   5. help

B **1.** 'd better not give or shouldn't give or ought not
        to give
   2. must register or 'd better register or 've got
        to register
   3. must not be
   4. must get or has to get or has got to get
   5. can't eat or must not eat
   6. may come or might come or could come

C **1.** Could that ~~being~~ *be* Amelie in this photograph?
   2. With this site, I ~~must not~~ *don't have to* call to keep in touch with
        friends. It's just not necessary.

3. I don't know this person. I guess I'd ~~not better~~ *better not* accept him as a friend on my Facebook page.

4. That doesn't look anything like Anton. It ~~doesn't have to~~ *can't* be him.

5. Were you able ~~remove~~ *to remove* that embarrassing photo?

UNIT 15

A **1.** have
2. ought
3. could
4. given
5. shouldn't
6. should I

B **1.** I should've studied for the math test.
2. You could have shown me your class notes.
3. I shouldn't have stayed up so late the night before the test.
4. He ought to have called you.
5. You might've invited me to join the study group.

C I shouldn't have ~~stay~~ *stayed* up so late. I overslept and missed my bus. I ~~ought have~~ *ought to have* asked Erik for a ride. I got to the office late, and my boss said, "You might ~~had~~ *have* called." She was right. I ~~shouldn't have~~ *should've* called. At lunch, my co-workers went out together. They really could ~~of~~ *have* invited me to join them. Should ~~have I~~ *I have* said something to them? Then, after lunch, my mother called. She said, "Yesterday was Aunt Em's birthday. You could've ~~sending~~ *sent* her a card!" I really think my mother might ~~has~~ *have* reminded me. Not a good day! I ~~shouldn't have~~ *should've* just stayed in bed.

UNIT 16

A **1.** must
2. might not have
3. have
4. taken
5. may
6. have
7. couldn't

B **1.** might not have gotten my message **or** may not have gotten my message
2. must not have studied
3. couldn't have forgotten our date **or** can't have forgotten our date
4. may have been at the movies **or** might have been at the movies **or** could have been at the movies
5. must have forgotten
6. must not have seen me

C Why did the Aztecs build their capital city in the middle of a lake? Could they ~~had~~ *have* wanted the protection of the water? They might have ~~been~~. Or the location may ~~has~~ *have* helped them to control nearby societies. At first, it must have ~~being~~ *been* an awful place, full of mosquitoes and fog. But it must ~~no~~ *not* have been a bad idea—the island city became the center of a very powerful empire. To succeed, the Aztecs had to have ~~became~~ *become* fantastic engineers quite quickly. When the Spanish arrived, they couldn't have ~~expect~~ *expected* the amazing palaces, floating gardens, and well-built canals. They must have been astounded.

UNIT 17

A **1.** Spanish is spoken in Bolivia.
2. They play soccer in Bolivia.
3. Reza Deghati took the photo.
4. The articles were translated into Spanish.
5. Quinoa is grown in the mountains.
6. They named the main street El Prado.

B **1.** was discovered
2. is spoken
3. is grown
4. is exported
5. are employed **or** have been employed
6. was made
7. has been performed
8. is attended

C Photojournalist Alexandra Avakian was born and ~~raise~~ *raised* in New York. Since she began her career, she has covered many of the world's most important stories. Her work ~~have~~ *has* been published in many newspapers and magazines including *National Geographic*, and her photographs have ~~being~~ *been* exhibited around the world. Avakian has also written a book, *Window of the Soul: My Journey in the Muslim World*, which was ~~been~~ published in 2008. It has not yet been translated ~~by translators~~ into other languages, but the chapter titles appear in both English and Arabic. Avakian's book ~~have be~~ *has been* discussed on international TV, radio, and numerous websites.

UNIT 18

A
1. done
2. be replaced
3. could
4. had
5. be
6. won't
7. has
8. handled

B
1. should be trained
2. have to be given
3. must be tested
4. can be experienced
5. will be provided
6. may be sent
7. could…be developed

C
    The new spacesuits are going to be ~~testing~~ *tested* underwater today. They've got to ~~been~~ *be* improved before they can be used on the Moon or Mars. Two astronauts are going to be wearing them while they're working, and they'll *be* ^ watched by the engineers. This morning, communication was lost with the Earth's surface, and all decisions had to be ~~make~~ *made* by the astronauts themselves. It was a very realistic situation. This crew ~~will got~~ *will have* **or** *has got* to be very well prepared for space travel. They're going to the Moon in a few years.

UNIT 19

A
1. have it cut
2. done
3. get
4. your house painted
5. by

B
1. get it repaired
2. have them cleaned
3. have them shortened
4. get it colored
5. get it fixed
6. had it removed
7. get it renewed
8. 'll have it checked **or** 'm going to have it checked **or** 'm having it checked

C
    I'm going on vacation next week. I'd like to have ~~done some work~~ *some work done* in my office, and this seems like a good time for it. Please have my carpet ~~clean~~ *cleaned* while I'm gone. And could you have my computer and printer looked at? It's been quite a while since they've been serviced. Ted wants to have my office painted ~~by a painter~~ while I'm gone. Please tell him any color is fine except pink! Last week, I ~~had designed some new brochures~~ *had some new brochures designed* by Perfect Print. Please call the printer and have them delivered directly to the sales reps. And could you also ~~get made up more business cards~~ *get more business cards made up*? When I get back, it'll be time to plan the holiday party. I think we should have it catered this year ~~from~~ *by* a professional. While I'm gone, why don't you call around and get some estimates from caterers? ~~Has~~ *Have* the estimates sent to Ted. Thanks.

UNIT 20

A
1. do…do
2. are
3. is
4. shop
5. happens
6. doesn't stay
7. closes
8. go
9. feel
10. think

B
1. When **or** If it's 7:00 a.m. in Honolulu, what time is it in Mumbai?
2. If you love jewelry, you should visit an international jewelry show.
3. A tourist may have more fun if she tries bargaining.
4. If **or** When you're shopping at an outdoor market, you can always bargain for a good price.
5. But don't try to bargain if **or** when you're shopping in a big department store.

C
1. If I don't like something I bought online, then I ~~returned~~ *return* it.
2. Don't buy from an online site~~,~~ if you don't know anything about the company.
3. When ~~he'll~~ *he* shops online, Frank always saves a lot of time.
4. I always ~~fell~~ *fall* asleep if I fly at night. It happens every time.
5. Isabel always has a wonderful time~~,~~ when she visits Istanbul.

UNIT 21

A
1. d
2. f
3. a
4. c
5. b
6. e

B
1. a. take
   b. 'll be **or** 'm going to be
2. a. will…do **or** are…going to do
   b. don't get
   c. 'll stay **or** 'm going to stay
   d. get

480   Unit Review Answer Key

3. a. pass
b. 'll celebrate *or* 'm going to celebrate

C It's been a hard week, and I'm looking forward to the weekend. If the weather ~~will be~~ *is* nice tomorrow, Marco and I are going to go to the beach. The ocean is usually too cold for swimming at this time of year, so I probably ~~don't~~ *won't* go in the water unless it's really hot outside. But I love walking along the beach and breathing in the fresh sea air.

If Marco has time, he might ~~makes~~ *make* some sandwiches to bring along. Otherwise, we'll just get some pizza. I hope it'll be a nice day. I just listened to the weather report, and there may be some rain in the afternoon. ~~Unless~~ *If* it rains, ~~we~~ *we'll* probably go to the movies instead. That's our Plan B. But I really want to go to the beach, so I'm keeping my fingers crossed!

UNIT 22

A **1.** I'd feel   **5.** could
2. were   **6.** weren't
3. could   **7.** I'd
4. you found

B **1.** would…do   **5.** would become
2. found   **6.** put
3. Would…take   **7.** made
4. knew   **8.** would learn

C **1.** Pablo wishes he ~~can~~ *could* speak German.
2. If he had the time, ~~he'll~~ *he'd* study in Germany. But he doesn't have the time right now.
3. He could get a promotion ~~when~~ *if* he spoke another language.
4. His company ~~may~~ *might* pay the tuition if he took a course.
5. What would you do if you ~~are~~ *were* in Pablo's situation?

UNIT 23

A **1.** hadn't told   **4.** If
2. had   **5.** gone
3. would have been

B **1. a.** would've been
b. hadn't missed
c. had been
d. wouldn't have discovered
2. a. hadn't accepted
b. had taken
c. wouldn't have met
3. a. hadn't seen
b. wouldn't have believed

C Tonight, we watched the movie *Back to the Future* starring Michael J. Fox. I might never ~~had~~ *have* seen it if I hadn't read his autobiography, *Lucky Man*. His book was so good that I wanted to see his most famous movie. Now, I wish I ~~saw~~ *had seen* it in the theater when it first came out, but I hadn't even been born yet! It would have been better if we ~~would have~~ *had* watched it on a big screen. Fox was great. He looked really young—just like a teenager. But I would have recognized him even ~~when~~ *if* I hadn't known he was in the film.

In real life, when Fox was a teenager, he was too small to become a professional hockey player. But if he hadn't looked so young, he ~~can't~~ *couldn't or wouldn't* have gotten his role in the TV hit series *Family Ties*. In Hollywood, he had to sell his furniture to pay his bills, but he kept trying to find an acting job. If he ~~would have~~ *had* given up, he might never have become a star.

UNIT 24

A **1.** says   **5.** she'd cooked
2. "I'd love to."   **6.** told
3. planned   **7.** had been
4. he   **8.** his

B **1.** (that) she always gets up early **or** she always got up early.
2. (that) water boils at 100 degrees Celsius **or** water boiled at 100 degrees Celsius.
3. (that) he liked my haircut **or** he likes my haircut.
4. (that) she loved the pasta **or** she had loved the pasta.
5. (that) it was his own recipe **or** it is his own recipe.
6. (that) she mailed him the check **or** she had mailed him the check.
7. (that) his boss had liked his work **or** his boss liked his work.

C 1. A psychologist I know often tells me ˣthat people today tell hundreds of lies every day.ˣ

2. Yesterday, Mia's boyfriend ~~said~~ *told* her that he liked her new dress.

3. When she heard that, Mia said she didn't really believe ~~you~~ *him*.

4. I didn't think that was so bad. I said that her boyfriend ~~tells~~ *told or had told* her a little white lie.

5. But Mia hates lying. She said that to ~~me~~ *her*, all lies were wrong.

UNIT 25

A 1. was   5. today
2. I   6. would
3. take   7. could
4. might   8. there

B 1. (that) it was going to rain
2. (that) it could be the worst storm this year
3. (that) it was going to start soon
4. (that) they should buy water
5. (that) they had to leave right then
6. (that) she would call me the next day

C What a storm! They said it ~~is~~ *was* going to be bad, but it was terrible. They said it ~~will~~ *would* last two days, but it lasted four. On the first day of the storm, my mother called and told me that we should ~~have left~~ *leave* the house right ~~now~~ *then*. (I still can hear her exact words: "You should leave the house *right now!*") We should have listened to her! We just didn't believe it was going to be so serious. I told her last night that if we had known, we would ~~had~~ *have* left right away. We're lucky we survived. I just listened to the weather forecast. Good news! They said tomorrow should ~~have been~~ *be* sunny.

UNIT 26

A 1. . (period)   5. say
2. give   6. told
3. "Please lie down."   7. advised
4. not to

B 1. He told or asked her to show him her license.
2. She advised or told him to get more exercise.

3. She invited or asked them to come to the English Department party.
4. He asked her to turn on the light.
5. She invited or asked them to hang out at her house.

C Too much stress is bad for your health. So, I asked my doctor ˄*to* give me some tips on how to reduce everyday stress. First of all, she told me ~~exercising~~ *to exercise* every day. She also told me ~~to don't~~ *not to* work too long without taking a break. She advised me ~~doing~~ *to do* things to relax. For example, she said ~~that~~ to listen to music. She also ~~said~~ *told* me to sit with my eyes closed and to concentrate on my breathing. That helps lower blood pressure. She also advised me ~~no~~ *not to* drink too many beverages with caffeine. Finally, she said to ˣget enough sleepˣ—at least seven hours a night!

UNIT 27

A 1. . (period)   4. I lived
2. if   5. I had
3. their office was

B 1. who the company had hired.
2. if or whether or whether or not I had taken the job.
3. if or whether or whether or not I liked my job.
4. how long I had worked there.
5. how many employees worked there.
6. why I wanted to work for them.
7. what the starting salary was.
8. if or whether or whether or not I could start soon.

C They asked me so many questions! They asked me where ~~did I work~~ *I worked*. They asked me who ~~was my boss~~ *my boss was*. They asked why I ~~did want~~ *wanted* to change jobs. They asked how much money I made. They ~~ask~~ *asked* me who I ~~have~~ *had* voted for in the last election. They even asked me what my favorite color was? Finally, I asked myself whether or ~~no~~ *not* I really wanted that job!

UNIT 28

A 1. we should   5. I should
2. our server is   6. ? (question mark)
3. . (period)   7. whether
4. to

B 1. where the restaurant is?
2. if ~~or~~ whether the subway goes to the museum.
3. if ~~or~~ whether we should tip the porter.
4. why we didn't buy the book on tipping.
5. how much we should tip the tour guide.
6. if ~~or~~ whether you have any travel books.
7. what this sign says?

C A: Hi. Is this a good time to call? I wasn't sure what
time you have dinner?

B: This is fine. I didn't know _{^ *if or whether you were*} ~~were you~~ back from
your trip.

A: We got back two days ago. I can't remember if I
emailed
~~email~~ you some photographs.

B: Yes. They were great. Can you tell me where ^{*you took*} ~~took~~
~~you~~ that picture of the lake? I want to go!

A: Hmm. I'm not sure which one ^{*that was*} ~~was that~~. We saw a
lot of lakes in Switzerland.

B: I'll show it to you. I'd really like to find out where
it is
~~is it~~.

Information Gaps, Student B

EXERCISE 10 DR. EON'S CALENDAR

A INFORMATION GAP Work with a partner. Student B will follow the instructions below. Student A will follow the instructions on page 83.

STUDENT B

- Complete Dr. Eon's calendar. Get information from Student A. Ask questions and fill in the calendar. Answer Student A's questions.

EXAMPLE: A: What will Dr. Eon be doing on Sunday the first?
B: She'll be flying to Tokyo. What about on the second? Will she be taking the day off?
A: No, she'll be meeting with Dr. Kato.

FEBRUARY 2077

SUNDAY	MONDAY	TUESDAY	WEDNESDAY	THURSDAY	FRIDAY	SATURDAY
1 fly to Tokyo	2 meet with Dr. Kato	3 attend World Future Conference →	4	5	6	7 →
8	9	10 →	11 →	12 fly to Denver	13 visit Mom and Dad →	14 →
15	16 give speech at Harvard University	17 meet with Dr. Rover	18 →	19	20 →	21
22 relax!	23 work at home →	24	25	26	27 →	28

B Now compare calendars with your partner. Are they the same?

EXERCISE 11 LONDON AND VANCOUVER

INFORMATION GAP Work with a partner. Student B will follow the instructions below.
Student A will follow the instructions on page 115.

STUDENT B

- Read about London and answer Student A's questions.

  EXAMPLE: A: London is the largest city in the United Kingdom, isn't it?
  B: Yes, it is.

LONDON

London is the capital and largest city of the
United Kingdom. It is also one of the oldest
and largest cities in the world. Located in
southeastern England, the city lies on the River
Thames, which links it to shipping routes
throughout the world. Because of its size, the
city is divided into thirty-two "boroughs" or
parts. With its many museums, palaces, parks,
and theaters, tourism is a major industry. In
fact, millions of tourists visit the city every
year to take advantage of its many cultural and
historical offerings. Unfortunately, like many
great urban centers, London has problems such
as traffic congestion, crime, and homelessness.

- Now look at the questions below. What do you know about Vancouver? Complete the
  questions by circling the correct words and writing the tags.

  1. Vancouver is / (isn't) the largest city in Canada, _is it_____?

  2. It lies / doesn't lie on the Atlantic Coast, _____?

  3. It has / doesn't have a very large port, _____?

  4. It is / isn't a very beautiful city, _____?

  5. Many / Not many tourists visit the city, _____?

  6. You can / can't hear many different languages there, _____?

  7. Movie production is / isn't an important industry in Vancouver, _____?

- Ask Student A the questions. Student A will read a paragraph about Vancouver and tell
  you if your information is correct or not.

  EXAMPLE: B: Vancouver isn't the largest city in Canada, is it?
  A: No, it isn't. It's the third largest city.

EXERCISE 10 THE PHILIPPINES

A INFORMATION GAP Work with a partner. Student B will follow the instructions below. Student A will follow the instructions on page 283.

STUDENT B

- The Philippines consists of many islands and has many natural resources. Look at the map of Mindanao and complete the chart. Write *Y* for *Yes* if Mindanao has a particular resource and *N* for *No* if it does not.

- Student A has the map of Luzon. Ask Student A questions about Luzon and complete the chart for Luzon.

  EXAMPLE: **B:** Is tobacco grown in Luzon?
  A: Yes, it is. It's grown in the northern and central part of the island.

- Student A doesn't have the map of Mindanao. Answer Student A's questions about Mindanao.

  EXAMPLE: **A:** Is tobacco grown in Mindanao?
  B: No, it isn't.

		MINDANAO	LUZON
G R O W	🍃 tobacco	N	Y
	🌽 corn		
	🍌 bananas		
	coffee		
	🍍 pineapples		
	sugar		
R A I S E	🐄 cattle		
	🐖 pigs		
M I N E	gold		
	manganese		
P R O D U C E	cotton		
	🌿 rubber		
	lumber		

Mindanao

B When you are finished, compare charts. Are they the same?

Index

This index is for the full and split editions. All entries are in the full book. Entries for Volume A of the split edition are in black. Entries for Volume B are in blue.